Maya Angelou

Maya Angelou has been waitress, singer, actress, dancer, activist, editor, filmmaker, writer, mother, and inaugural poet. She first thrilled the world with her autobiography *I Know Why the Caged Bird Sings*. This was followed by *Gather Together in My Name*, *Singin' and Swingin' and Gettin' Merry Like Christmas*, *The Heart of a Woman*, *All God's Children Need Travelling Shoes* and the final volume, *A Song Flung Up to Heaven* (2002). Virago also publish two works of prose: *Wouldn't Take Nothing for my Journey Now* and *Even the Stars Look Lonesome* (1998). She has also written several collections of poetry: *And Still I Rise*, *Just Give Me a Cool Drink of Water 'Fore I Diiie* and *I Shall Not Be Moved*. In 1993, Maya Angelou wrote her historic poem *On the Pulse of Morning*, for the Inauguration of President Clinton. All are included in *The Complete Collected Poems* (1995). Maya Angelou now has a life-time appointment as Reynolds Professor of American Studies at Wake Forest University of North Carolina.

MAYA ANGELOU

The Heart of a Woman

Virago

A *Virago* Book

Published by Virago Press 1986

Reprinted 1988, 1991, 1993, 1994, 1996, 1997 (three times),
1998 (twice), 2001, 2002

First published in USA by Random House 1981

A CIP catalogue record for this book
is available from the British Library

ISBN 0 86068 678 7

Printed and bound in Great Britain by Clays Ltd, St Ives plc

Virago
An imprint of
Time Warner Books UK
Brettenham House
Lancaster Place
London WC2E 7EN

www.virago.co.uk

I dedicate this book to my grandson,
Colin Ashanti Murphy-Johnson

Special thanks to a few of the many sister/friends whose love
encourages me to spell my name :
W O M A N

Doris Bullard
Rosa Guy
M. J. Hewitt
Ruth Love
Paule Marshall
Louise Merriwether
Dolly McPherson
Emalyn Rogers
Efuah Sutherland
Decca Treuhaft
Frances Williams
A. B. Williamson

The Heart of a Woman

"The ole ark's a-moverin', a-moverin', a-moverin',
the ole ark's a-moverin' along"

That ancient spiritual could have been the theme song of the
United States in 1957. We were a-moverin' to, fro, up, down and
often in concentric circles.

We created a maze of contradictions. Black and white Americans danced a fancy and often dangerous do-si-do. In our steps
forward, abrupt turns, sharp spins and reverses, we became our
own befuddlement. The country hailed Althea Gibson, the rangy
tennis player who was the first black female to win the U.S.
Women's Singles. President Dwight Eisenhower sent U.S. para-
troopers to protect black school children in Little Rock, Arkansas,
and South Carolina's Senator Strom Thurmond harangued for
24 hours and 18 minutes to prevent the passage in Congress of
the Civil Rights Commission's Voting Rights Bill.

Sugar Ray Robinson, everybody's dandy, lost his middleweight
title, won it back, then lost it again, all in a matter of months. The
year's popular book was Jack Kerouac's *On the Road,* and its title
was an apt description of our national psyche. We were indeed
traveling, but no one knew our destination nor our arrival date.

I had returned to California from a year-long European tour as
premier dancer with *Porgy and Bess.* I worked months singing in
West Coast and Hawaiian night clubs and saved my money. I
took my young son, Guy, and joined the beatnik brigade. To my
mother's dismay, and Guy's great pleasure, we moved across the
Golden Gate Bridge and into a houseboat commune in Sausalito

where I went barefoot, wore jeans, and both of us wore rough-dried clothes. Although I took Guy to a San Francisco barber, I allowed my own hair to grow into a wide unstraightened hedge, which made me look, at a distance, like a tall brown tree whose branches had been clipped. My commune mates, an icthyologist, a musician, a wife, and an inventor, were white, and had they been political, (which they were not), would have occupied a place between the far left and revolution.

Strangely, the houseboat offered me respite from racial tensions, and gave my son an opportunity to be around whites who did not think of him as too exotic to need correction, nor so common as to be ignored.

During our stay in Sausalito, my mother struggled with her maternal instincts. On her monthly visits, dressed in stone marten furs, diamonds and spike heels, which constantly caught between loose floorboards, she forced smiles and held her tongue. Her eyes, however, were frightened for her baby, and her baby's baby. She left wads of money under my pillow or gave me checks as she kissed me goodbye. She could have relaxed had she remembered the Biblical assurance "Fruit does not fall far from the tree."

In less than a year, I began to yearn for privacy, wall-to-wall carpets and manicures. Guy was becoming rambunctious and young-animal wild. He was taking fewer baths than I thought healthy, and because my friends treated him like a young adult, he was forgetting his place in the scheme of our mother-son relationship.

I had to move on. I could go back to singing and make enough money to support myself and my son.

I had to trust life, since I was young enough to believe that life loved the person who dared to live it.

I packed our bags, said goodbye and got on the road.

Laurel Canyon was the official residential area of Hollywood, just ten minutes from Schwab's drugstore and fifteen minutes from the Sunset Strip.

Its most notable feature was its sensuality. Red-roofed, Moorish-style houses nestled seductively among madrone trees. The odor of eucalyptus was layered in the moist air. Flowers bloomed in a riot of crimsons, carnelian, pinks, fuchsia and sunburst gold. Jays and whippoorwills, swallows and bluebirds, squeaked, whistled and sang on branches which faded from ominous dark green to a brackish yellow. Movie stars, movie starlets, producers and directors who lived in the neighborhood were as voluptuous as their natural and unnatural environment.

The few black people who lived in Laurel Canyon, including Billy Eckstein, Billy Daniels and Herb Jeffries, were rich, famous and light-skinned enough to pass, at least for Portuguese. I, on the other hand, was a little-known night-club singer, who was said to have more determination than talent. I wanted desperately to live in the glamorous surroundings. I accepted as fictitious the tales of amateurs being discovered at lunch counters, yet I did believe it was important to be in the right place at the right time, and no place seemed so right to me in 1958 as Laurel Canyon.

When I answered a "For Rent" ad, the landlord told me the house had been taken that very morning. I asked Atara and Joe Morheim, a sympathetic white couple, to try to rent the house for me. They succeeded in doing so.

On moving day, the Morheims, Frederick "Wilkie" Wilkerson, my friend and voice coach, Guy, and I appeared on the steps of a modest, overpriced two-bedroom bungalow.

The landlord shook hands with Joe, welcomed him, then looked over Joe's shoulder and recognized me. Shock and revulsion made him recoil. He snatched his hand away from Joe. "You bastard. I know what you're doing. I ought to sue you."

Joe, who always seemed casual to the point of being totally disinterested, surprised me with his emotional response. "You fascist, you'd better not mention suing anybody. This lady here should sue you. If she wants to, I'll testify in court for her. Now, get the hell out of the way so we can move in."

The landlord brushed past us, throwing his anger into the perfumed air. "I should have known. You dirty Jew. You bastard, you."

We laughed nervously and carried my furniture into the house.

Weeks later I had painted the small house a sparkling white, enrolled Guy into the local school, received only a few threatening telephone calls, and bought myself a handsome dated automobile. The car, a sea-green, ten-year-old Chrysler, had a parquet dashboard, and splintery wooden doors. It could not compete with the new chrome of my neighbors' Cadillacs and Buicks, but it had an elderly elegance, and driving in it with the top down, I felt more like an eccentric artist than a poor black woman who was living above her means, out of her element, and removed from her people.

One June morning, Wilkie walked into my house and asked, "Do you want to meet Billie Holiday?"

"Of course. Who wouldn't? Is she working in town?"

"No, just passing through from Honolulu. I'm going down to her hotel. I'll bring her back here if you think you can handle it."

"What's to handle? She's a woman. I'm a woman."

Wilkie laughed, the chuckle rolling inside his chest and out of his mouth in billows of sound. "Pooh, you're sassy. Billie may like you. In that case, it'll be all right. She might not, and then that's your ass."

"That could work the other way around. I might not like her either."

Wilkie laughed again. "I said you're sassy. Have you got some gin?"

There was one bottle, which had been gathering dust for months.

Wilkie stood, "Give me the keys. She'll like riding in a convertible."

I didn't become nervous until he left. Then the reality of Lady Day coming to my house slammed into me and started my body to quaking. It was pretty well known that she used heavy drugs, and I hardly smoked grass anymore. How could I tell her she couldn't shoot up or sniff up in my house? It was also rumored that she had lesbian affairs. If she propositioned me, how could

6

I reject her without making her think I was rejecting her? Her temper was legendary in show business, and I didn't want to arouse it. I vacuumed, emptied ashtrays and dusted, knowing that a clean house would in no way influence Billie Holiday.

I saw her through the screen door, and my nervousness turned quickly to shock. The bloated face held only a shadow of its familiar prettiness. When she walked into the house, her eyes were a flat black, and when Wilkie introduced us, her hand lay in mine like a child's rubber toy.

"How you do, Maya? You got a nice house." She hadn't even looked around. It was the same slow, lean, whining voice which had frequently been my sole companion on lonely nights.

I brought gin and sat listening as Wilkie and Billie talked about the old days, the old friends, in Washington, D.C. The names they mentioned and the escapades over which they gloated meant nothing to me, but I was caught into the net of their conversation by the complexity of Billie's language. Experience with street people, hustlers, gamblers and petty criminals had exposed me to cursing. Years in night-club dressing rooms, in cabarets and juke joints had taught me every combination of profanity, or so I thought. Billie Holiday's language was a mixture of mockery and vulgarity that caught me without warning. Although she used the old common words, they were in new arrangements, and spoken in that casual tone which seemed to drag itself, rasping, across the ears. When she finally turned to include me in her conversation, I knew that nothing I could think of would hold her attention.

"Wilkie tells me you're a singer. You a jazz singer too? You any good?"

"No, not really. I don't have good pitch."

"Do you want to be a great singer? You want to compete with me?"

"No. I don't want to compete with anybody. I'm an entertainer, making a living."

"As an entertainer? You mean showing some tittie and shaking your bootie?"

7

"I don't have to do all that. I wouldn't do that to keep a job. No matter what."

"You better say Joe, 'cause you sure don't know."

Wilkie came to my defense just as I was wondering how to get the woman and her hostility out of my house.

"Billie, you ought to see her before you talk. She sings folk songs, calypso and blues. Now, you know me. If I say she's good, I mean it. She's good, and she's nice enough to invite us to lunch, so get up off her. Or you can walk your ass right down this hill. And you know I'm not playing about that shit."

She started laughing. "Wilkie, you haven't changed a damn thing but last year's drawers. I knew you'd put my ass out on the street sooner or later." She turned to me and gave me a fragile smile.

"What we going to eat, baby?" I hadn't thought about food, but I had a raw chicken in the refrigerator. "I'm going to fry a chicken. Fried chicken, rice and an Arkansas gravy."

"Chicken and rice is always good. But fry that sucker. Fry him till he's ready. I can't stand no goddam rare chicken."

"Billie, I don't claim to be a great singer, but I know how to mix groceries. I have never served raw chicken." I had to defend myself even if it meant she was going to curse me out.

"O.K., baby. O.K. Just telling you, I can't stand to see blood on the bone of a chicken. I take your word you know what you're doing. I didn't mean to hurt your feelings."

I retreated to the kitchen. Wilkie's and Billie's laughter floated over the clangs of pots and the sputtering oil.

I couldn't imagine how the afternoon was going to end. Maybe I'd be lucky; they would drink all the gin and Wilkie would take her to a bar on Sunset.

She sat at the table, gingerly. Each move of her body seemed to be considered before she attempted execution.

"You set a pretty table and you ain't got a husband?"

I told her I lived alone with my son. She turned with the first sharp action I had seen since she came into my house. "I can't

8

stand children. The little crumb-crushers eat you out of house and home and never say, 'Dog, kiss my foot.' "

"My son is not like that. He's intelligent and polite."

"Yeah. Well, I can't stand to be around any of the little bastards. This is good chicken."

I looked at Wilkie, who nodded to me.

Wilkie said, "Billie, I'm going to take you to a joint on Western, where you can get anything you want."

She didn't allow the full mouth of chicken to prevent her from speaking. "Hell, nigger, if I wanted to go to a joint don't you think I could have found one without you? I know every place in every town in this country that sells anything that crosses your mind. I wanted to come to a nice lady's house. She's a good cook, too. So I'm happy as a sissy in a CCC camp. Let me have that drumstick."

While I put away the remaining chicken, she talked about Hawaii.

"People love 'the islands, the islands.' Hell, all that shit is a bunch of water and a bunch of sand. So the sun shines all the time. What the hell else is the sun supposed to do?"

"But didn't you find it beautiful? The soft air, the flowers, the palm trees and the people? The Hawaiians are so pretty."

"They just a bunch of niggers. Niggers running around with no clothes on. And that music shit they play. Uhn, uhn." She imitated the sound of a ukulele.

"Naw. I'd rather be in New York. Everybody in New York City is a son of a bitch, but at least they don't pretend they're something else."

Back in the living room, Wilkie looked at me, then at his watch. "I have a student coming in a half-hour. Come on, Billie, I'll take you back to your hotel. Thanks, Maya. We have to go."

Billie looked up from her drink and said, "Speak for yourself. All I got to do is stay black and die."

"Well, I brought you here, so I'll take you back. Anyway, Maya's probably got something to do."

9

They both stared at me. I thought for a moment and decided not to lie.

"No. I'm free. I'll take her back to the hotel when she wants to go."

Wilkie shook his head. "O.K., Pooh." His face was saying, "I hope you know what you're doing. Of course I didn't, but I was more curious than afraid.

Billie tossed her head. "So I'll see you when I see you, Wilkie. Hope it won't be another twenty years."

Wilkie bent and kissed her, gave me a very strange look and walked down to his car.

We spent the first few moments in silence. Billie was examining me, and I was wondering what subject I could introduce that would interest her.

Finally, she asked, "You a square, ain't you?"

I knew what she meant. "Yes."

"Then how come you invited me to your house?"

Wilkie really invited her, but I had welcomed his invitation.

"Because you are a great artist and I respect you."

"Bullshit. You just wanted to see what I looked like, up close." She interrupted my denial. "That's all right. That don't hurt my feelings. You see me now, though, you ain't seeing nothing. I used to be a bitch on wheels. Lot of folks thought I was pretty. Anyway, that's what they said. 'Course, you know how folks talk. They'll tell you anything to get what they want. 'Course, there are them that'll just strong-arm you and take it. I know a lot of them, too." Suddenly she withdrew into her thoughts and I sat quiet, not wanting to break into her reverie.

She raised her head and turned half away from me, toward the window. When she spoke it was in a conspiratorial whisper. "Men. Men can really do it to you. Women would too, if they had the nerve. They are just as greedy; they're just scared to let on."

I had heard stories of Billie being beaten by men, cheated by

10

drug pushers and hounded by narcotics agents, still I thought she was the most paranoid person I had ever met.

"Don't you have any friends? People you can trust?"

She jerked her body toward me. "Of course I have friends. Good friends. A person who don't have friends might as well be dead." She had relaxed, but my question put her abruptly on the defense again. I was wondering how to put her at ease. I heard Guy's footsteps on the stairs.

"My son is coming home."

"Oh. Shit. How old you say he is?"

"He's twelve and a very nice person."

Guy bounded into the room, radiating energy.

"Hey, Momhowareya? Whatwereyoudoing? What'sfordinner? CanIgoovertoTony's? CanIgoovertoTony'saftermyhomework?"

"Guy, I have a guest. This is Miss Billie Holiday." He turned and saw Billie, but was accelerating too fast to read the distaste on her face.

"Billie Holiday? Oh. Yes. I know about you. Good afternoon, Miss Holiday." He walked over and stuck out his hand. "I'm happy to know you. I read about you in a magazine. They said the police had been giving you a hard time. And that you've had a very hard life. Is that true? What did they do to you? Is there anything you can do back? I mean, sue them or anything?"

Billie was too stunned at the barrage of words to speak.

Guy reached down and took her hand and shook it. The words never stopped tumbling out of his mouth.

"Maybe they expect too much from you. I know something about that. When I come from school the first thing I have to do, after I change school clothes, of course, is go out and water the lawn. Have you not noticed we live on the side of a mountain, and when I water, if there is any wind, the water gets blown back in your face. But if I come in wet, my mother thinks I was playing with the hose. I can't control the wind, you know. Will you come out and talk to me, when I've changed? I'd really like to know

11

everything about you." He dropped her hand and ran out of the room, shouting, "I'll be back in a minute."

Billie's face was a map of astonishment. After a moment, she looked at me. "Damn. He's something, ain't he? Smart. What's he want to be?"

"Sometimes a doctor, and sometimes a fireman. It depends on the day you ask him."

"Good. Don't let him go into show business. Black men in show business is bad news. When they can't get as far as they deserve, they start taking it out on their women. What you say his name is?

"Guy, Guy Johnson."

"Your name is Angelou. His name is Johnson? You don't look old enough to have married twice."

Guy was born to me when I was an unmarried teenager, so I had given him my father's name. I didn't want Billie to know that much about our history.

I said, "Well, that's life, isn't it?"

She nodded and mumbled, "Yeah, life's a bitch, a bitch on wheels."

Guy burst into the room again, wearing old jeans and a torn T-shirt. "Ready, Miss Holiday? You want to do anything? Come on. I won't let you get wet."

Billie rose slowly, with obvious effort.

I decided it was time for me to step in. "Guy, Miss Holiday is here to talk to me. Go out and do your chores and later you can talk with her."

Billie was erect. "Naw, I'm going out with him. But how the hell can you let him wear raggedy clothes like that? You living in a white district. Everybody be having their eyes on him. Guy, tomorrow, if you mamma will take me, I'm going to the store and buy you some nice things. You don't have to look like you going to pick cotton just 'cause you doing a little work. Come on, let's go."

Guy held the door for her as she picked her way across the room and to the steps. A minute later, I watched from the window as my son directed the hose toward the rose garden and Billie maintained her balance, although the heels of her baby-doll pumps were sinking into the soft earth.

She stayed for dinner, saying that I could drop her off on my way to work. She talked to Guy while I cooked. Surprisingly, he sat quiet, listening as she spoke of Southern towns, police, agents, good musicians and mean men she had known. She carefully avoided profanity and each time she slipped, she'd excuse herself to Guy, saying, "It's just another bad habit I got." After dinner, when the baby-sitter arrived, Billie told Guy that she was going to sing him a good-night song.

They went to his room, and I followed. Guy sat on the side of his bed and Billie began, a cappella, "You're My Thrill," an old song heavy with sensuous meaning. She sang as if she was starved for sex and only the boy, looking at her out of bored young eyes, could give her satisfaction.

I watched and listened from the door, recording every sound, firmly setting in my mind the rusty voice, the angle of her body, and Guy's look of tolerance (he'd rather be reading or playing a word game).

When I dropped her off at the Sunset Colonial Hotel, she told me to pick her up the next morning, early. I was amazed to hear her say that she was having trouble sleeping, so she might as well bring her Chihuahua along and spend the time with me.

For the next four days, Billie came to my house in the early mornings, talked all day long and sang a bedtime song to Guy, and stayed until I went to work. She said I was restful to be around because I was so goddam square. Although she continued to curse in Guy's absence, when he walked into the house her language not only changed, she made considerable effort to form her words with distinction.

On the night before she was leaving for New York, she told Guy she was going to sing "Strange Fruit" as her last song. We sat at the dining room table while Guy stood in the doorway.

Billie talked and sang in a hoarse, dry tone the well-known protest song. Her rasping voice and phrasing literally enchanted me. I saw the black bodies hanging from Southern trees. I saw the lynch victims' blood glide from the leaves down the trunks and onto the roots.

Guy interrupted, "How can there be blood at the root?" I made a hard face and warned him, "Shut up, Guy, just listen." Billie had continued under the interruption, her voice vibrating over harsh edges.

She painted a picture of a lovely land, pastoral and bucolic, then added eyes bulged and mouths twisted, onto the Southern landscape.

Guy broke into her song. "What's a pastoral scene, Miss Holiday?" Billie looked up slowly and studied Guy for a second. Her face became cruel, and when she spoke her voice was scornful. "It means when the crackers are killing the niggers. It means when they take a little nigger like you and snatch off his nuts and shove them down his goddam throat. That's what it means."

The thrust of rage repelled Guy and stunned me.

Billie continued, "That's what they do. That's a goddam pastoral scene."

Guy gave us both a frozen look and said, "Excuse me, I'm going to bed." He turned and walked away.

I lied and said it was time for me to go to work. Billie didn't hear either statement.

I went to Guy's room and apologized to him for Billie's behavior. He smiled sarcastically as if I had been the one who had shouted at him, and he offered a cool cheek for my good night kiss.

In the car I tried to explain to Billie why she had been wrong but she refused to understand. She said, "I didn't lie, did I? Did I lie on the crackers? What's wrong with telling the truth?"

She decided that she didn't want to be taken to the hotel. She wanted to accompany me to the night club and catch my act. Efforts to dissuade her were unsuccessful.

14

I took her into the club and found her a front-row seat and went to my dressing room.

Jimmy Truitt of the Lester Horton Dance Troupe was in costume for their first number.

"Hey"—Jimmy was grinning like a child—"Billie Holiday is out front. And you can't believe what's happening."

The other dancers gathered around.

"The great Billie Holiday is sitting in the front row, and a little dog is drinking out of her glass." I had gotten so used to Pepe I had forgotten that Billie hardly made a move without him.

The dancers took over the stage, sliding, burning brightly in a Latin routine. When they finished, I was introduced.

After my first song, I spoke directly to the audience.

"Ladies and gentlemen. It is against the policy of the club to mention any celebrity who might be in the audience, for fear that an unseen person might be missed. But tonight I am violating that custom. I think every one will be excited to know that Miss Billie Holiday is present."

The crowd responded to my announcement with an approving roar. People stood cheering, looking around the room for Billie. She looked straight at me, then, picking up Pepe, stood up, turned to the audience and bowed her head two or three times as if she was agreeing with them. She sat down without smiling.

My next song was an old blues, which I began singing with only a bass accompaniment. The music was a dirge and the lyrics tragic. I had my eyes closed when suddenly, like a large glass shattering, Billie's voice penetrated the song.

"Stop that bitch. Stop her, goddamit. Stop that bitch. She sounds just like my goddam mamma."

I stopped and opened my eyes and saw Billie pick up Pepe and head through the crowd toward the women's toilet. I thanked the audience, asked the orchestra leader to continue playing, and headed for the women's lavatory. Twice in one night the woman had upset me. Well, she wasn't going to get away with it. She was going to learn that a "goddam square" could defend herself.

15

I had my hand on the knob when the door burst open and a very pale middle-aged white woman tore past me.

I entered and found Billie examining herself in the mirror. I began, "Billie, let me tell you something . . ."

She was still looking at her reflection but she said, "Aw, that's all right about the song. You can't help how you sound. Most colored women sound alike. Less they trying to sound white." She started laughing. "Did you see that old bitch hit it out of here?"

"I bumped into a woman just now."

"That was her. She was sitting on the toilet and when I opened the door, she screamed at me, 'Shut that door.' I screamed right back, 'Bitch, if you wanted it shut, you should have locked the goddam thing.' Then she comes out of there and asked me, 'Ain't you Billie Holiday?' I told her, 'Bitch, I didn't ask you your name.' You should have seen her fly." She laughed again, grinning into the mirror.

I said, "Billie, you know that woman might have been an old-time fan of yours."

She turned, holding on to Pepe and her purse and her jacket. "You know when you introduced me, you know how all those crackers stood up? You know why they were standing up?"

I said they were honoring her.

She said, "Shit. You don't know a damn thing. They were all standing up, looking around. They wanted to see a nigger who had been in jail for dope. I'm going to tell you one more thing. You want to be famous, don't you?"

I admitted I did.

"You're going to be famous. But it won't be for singing. Now, wait, you already know you can't sing all that good. But you're going to be real famous. Well, you better start asking yourself right now, 'When I get famous, who can I trust?' All crackers is bad and niggers ain't much better. Just take care of your son. Keep him with you and keep on telling him he's the smartest thing God made. Maybe he'll grow up without hating you. Remember Billie Holiday told you, 'You can't get too high for somebody to bring you down.' "

Outside, I found a taxi for her. A few months later, she died in a New York hospital. All the jazz and rhythm-and-blues stations had oily-voiced commentators extolling the virtues of the great artist whose like would not be seen or heard again. Jazz buffs with glorious vocabularies wrote long and often boring tributes to the pulchritudinous Lady Day, her phrasing and incredibly intricate harmonics. I would remember forever the advice of a lonely sick woman, with a waterfront mouth, who sang pretty songs to a twelve-year-old boy.

For weeks after Billie's visit, Guy treated me coolly. Neither of us mentioned the shouting scene, but he acted as if I had betrayed him. I had allowed a stranger to shout and curse at him and had not come to his defense. School semester was drawing to a close, and when I asked him whether he wanted to go to summer school or camp, or just stay home and hike the canyons, he answered, from the distance of indifference, that he had not made up his mind.

It was obvious that our home life was not going to return to normal until he aired his grievance.

"Guy, what did you think of Billie Holiday?"

"She was O.K., I guess."

"That's all you thought?"

"Well, she sure cursed a lot. If she curses that way all the time, it's no wonder people don't like her."

"So you didn't like her?"

"Anybody who curses all the time is stupid."

I had heard him use a few unacceptable words when talking in the backyard with his friend Tony. "Guy, don't you use some bad words yourself?"

"But I'm a boy, and boys say certain things. When we go hiking or in the gym. We say things you're not supposed to say in front of girls, but that's different."

I didn't think that this was a time to explain the unfairness of a double standard. He walked to his room, and standing in the doorway without turning back to face me, he said, "Oh yeah. And when I grow up, I'm not going to let anybody—no matter how famous she is—I'm not going to let anybody curse at my children."

He slammed the door.

The Billie Holiday incident had hurt him more deeply than I had imagined. I planned a recovery scheme which would return my son to normal. First I apologized to him, then for the next few days I talked softly, prepared his favorite foods, took him out to the movies and played cutthroat Scrabble with him until I had to leave for work. He was recuperating well when I received a telephone call from his school.

"Miss Angelou, I am a counselor at Marvelland School and we don't think Guy should ride the school bus next semester."

"You don't think . . . What 'we' and why not?"

"The principal, a few teachers and I. We've discussed his actions . . . and we agree—"

"What action? What did he do?"

"Well, he used profanity on the school bus."

"I'll be right there."

"Oh, there's no need—"

I hung up the telephone.

When I walked into the principal's office and saw the welcoming committee, I felt twenty feet tall and as black as midnight. Two white women and a tiny balding white man rose from their seats as I entered.

I said good morning and introduced myself.

"Really, Miss Angelou, the situation did not warrant your making a trip to the school."

The puny-looking man extended his hand. "I'm Mr. Baker, Guy's counselor, and I know he is not a bad boy. Not really."

I looked at the woman who had not spoken. It would be better to let them all have their say.

One woman said, "I teach English, and one of my students reported the incident to me this morning."

"I'd like to know what happened."

The English teacher spoke with deliberation, as if she were testing the taste of the words.

18

"As I understand it, a conversation had been going on, on a particular topic. When the bus stopped at your corner, Guy boarded it and joined the conversation. He then gave explicit details on that particular subject. When the bus arrived at school, a couple of the girls were crying and they came to me and reported Guy's behavior."

"And what did Guy say? What was his excuse?"

The second woman broke her silence. "We have not spoken to Guy. We thought there was no reason to embarrass him."

"You mean to say you have simply assumed that to be accused is to be guilty. And so you are ready to deny him the right of using the school bus, which is paid for with my taxes, without hearing his side? I want to see Guy. And I want to see him now. I don't know why I thought white teachers would be fair to a Negro child. I want to hear what Guy has to say. And now."

The moment of confrontation brought about an unexpected metamorphosis. The three teachers who had seemed individually small and weak, shifted and swam together coalescing into one unit, three bodies with one brain. Their faces hardened, their eyes hardened.

"We do not interrupt students during class, for anyone. And we do not make a student a special case, just because he happens to be Negro. And we do not allow Negro boys to use foul language in front of our girls."

The two women stood silent and approving.

Mr. Baker spoke for them, as well as for white people everywhere.

The impossibility of the situation filled my mouth with bitter saliva. How could I explain a young black boy to a grown man who had been born white? How could the two women understand a black mother who had nothing to give her son except a contrived arrogance? If I had an eternity and the poetry of old spirituals, I could not make them live with me the painful moments when I tried to prove to Guy that his color was not a cruel joke, but a healthful design. If they knew that I described God to my son as looking very much like John Henry, wouldn't they think me blasphemous? If he was headstrong, I had made him so. If, in his adolescent opinion, he was the best representative of the human race, it was my doing and I had no apology to make. The radio and posters, newspapers and teachers, bus drivers and salespersons told him every day in thousands of ways that he had come from nothing and was going nowhere.

"Mr. Baker, I understand you. Now, I'd like to see Guy." I kept my voice low and under control.

"If we take him out of class, you'll have to take him home. We do not interrupt classes. That is our policy."

"Yes. I'll take him home."

"He'll be marked absent for the day. But I guess that doesn't matter."

"Mr. Baker, I'll take my son home." I had to see Guy, to hear him speak. Nothing would be gained by further conversation. He would have to return to the school, but for the moment, I wanted to know that he was not broken or even bruised.

"I'll wait for him outside. Thank you."

Guy jumped into the car, his face active with concern. "What's the matter, Mom?"

I told him about the meeting with the teachers.

He relaxed. "Aw, gee, Mom, and you came to school for that? It was nothing. Some of those kids are so stupid. They were talking about where babies come from. They said some of the funniest things and they should know better. So I told them about the penis, and the vagina and the womb. You know, all that stuff in my book on the beginnings of life? Well, some of the crazy girls started crying when I said their fathers had done it to their mothers." He began to laugh, enjoying the memory of the girls' tears. "That's all I said. I was right, wasn't I?"

"Sometimes it's wiser to be right in silence, you know?"

He looked at me with the suspicion of youth. "But you always say, 'Speak up. Tell the truth, no matter what the situation.' I just told the truth."

"Yes, honey. You just told the truth."

Two days later, Guy brought home a message which infuriated me. My son was reasonably bright, but he had never been more than a competent student. The letter he brought home, however, stated that due to his wonderful grades, he had been advanced and would be attending another school at the end of the term.

The obvious lie insulted both my son and me, but I thought it wise to remove Guy from the school as soon as possible. I didn't want an already prejudiced faculty and administration to use him as their whipping boy.

I began searching for another school and another house. We needed an area where black skin was not regarded as one of nature's more unsightly mistakes.

The Westlake district was ideal. Mexican, black American, Asian and white families lived side by side in old rambling houses. Neighbors spoke to each other as they mowed their lawns or shopped in the long-established local grocery stores.

I rented the second floor of a two-story Victorian, and when Guy saw the black children playing on our new street, he was giddy with excitement. His reaction made me see how much he had missed the close contact with black people.

"Boy!" He jumped and wriggled. "Boy! Now, I'm going to make some friends!"

1

For the next year and a half, save for my short out-of-town singing engagements, we lived in the area. Guy became a part of a group of teenagers whose antics were rambunctious enough to satisfy their need to rebel, yet were acceptable to the tolerant neighborhood.

I began to write. At first I limited myself to short sketches, then to song lyrics, then I dared short stories. When I met John Killens he had just come to Hollywood to write the screenplay for his

21

novel *Youngblood,* and he agreed to read some of what he called my "work in progress." I had written and recorded six songs for Liberty Records, but I didn't seriously think of writing until John gave me his critique. After that I thought of little else. John was the first published black author I had really talked with. (I'd met James Baldwin in Paris in the early fifties, but I didn't really know him.) John said, "Most of your work needs polishing. In fact, most of everybody's work could stand rewriting. But you have undeniable talent." He added, "You ought to come to New York. You need to be in the Harlem Writers Guild." The invitation was oblique but definitely alluring.

I had met the singer Abbey Lincoln. We met years earlier and we became friends during the time I stayed in the Westlake district. But she had moved to New York City. Whenever I spoke to her on the telephone, after she stopped praising Max Roach, her love and romantic ideal, she lauded New York City. It was the hub, the absolute middle of the world. The only place for an intelligent person to be, and to grow.

Just possibly if I went to New York, I thought, I could find my own niche, settle down in it and become a success.

There was another reason for wanting to leave Los Angeles. Guy, once so amusing, was growing into a tall aloof stranger. Our warm evenings of Scrabble and charades were, for him, a part of the long ago. He said the childhood games simply did not hold his attention. When he obeyed my house rules, he did so with the attitude that he was just too bored to contest them.

I didn't understand, at the time, that adolescence had invaded him and deposited its usual hefty burden of insecurity and apprehension. My wispy sometimes-lover, who lived nearby, was too tediously pious to help me comprehend what was happening to my son. Indeed, his reverence for Eastern religions, a vegetarian diet and sexual abstinence rendered him almost, but not quite, incapable of everything except deep conversations on the meaning of life.

I called my mother and she answered after the first ring.

22

"Hello?"

"Lady?"

"Oh hello, baby." She spoke as crisply as a white woman.

I said, "I'd like to see you. I'm going to move to New York and I don't know when I'll come back to California. Maybe we could meet somewhere and spend a couple of days together. I could drive north, part of the way—"

She didn't pause. "Of course, we can meet, of course, I want to see you, baby." Six feet tall, with a fourteen-year-old son, and I was still called baby. "How about Fresno? That's halfway. We could stay at that hotel. I know you read about it."

"Yes. But not if there's going to be trouble. I just want to be with you."

"Trouble? Trouble?" The familiar knife edge had slipped into her voice. "But, baby, you know that's my middle name. Anyway, the law says that hotel has to accept Negro guests. I'll swear before God and five other responsible men that my daughter and I are Negroes. After that, if they refuse us, well . . ."—she laughed hopefully and high-pitched—"well, we'll have a board to fit their butts."

That part of the conversation was finished. Vivian Baxter sensed the possibility of confrontation and there would be no chance of talking her out of it. I realized too late that I should simply have taken the Southern Pacific train from Los Angeles to San Francisco and spent the two days in her Fulton Street house, then returned to pack for my continental move.

Her voice softened again as she relayed family gossip and set a date for our meeting in the middle of the state.

In 1959, Fresno was a middling town with palm trees and a decidedly Southern accent. Most of its white inhabitants seemed to be descendants of Steinbeck's Joads, and its black citizens were farm hands who had simply exchanged the dirt roads of Arkansas and Mississippi for the dusty streets of central California.

I parked my old Chrysler on a side street, and taking my

23

overnight case, walked around the corner to the Desert Hotel. My mother had suggested that we meet at three, which meant that she planned to arrive at two.

The hotel lobby had been decorated with welcome banners for a visiting sales convention. Large florid men mingled and laughed with portly women under low-hanging chandeliers.

My entrance stopped all action. Every head turned to see, every eye blazed, first with doubt, then fury. I wanted to run back to my car, race to Los Angeles, back to the postered walls of my house. I straightened my back and forced my face into indifference and walked to the registration desk. The clock above said two forty-five. "Good afternoon. Where is the bar?" A round-faced young man dropped his eyes and pointed behind me.

"Thank you."

The crowd made an aisle and I walked through the silence, knowing that before I reached the lounge door, a knife could be slipped in my back or a rope lassoed around my neck.

My mother sat at the bar wearing her Dobbs hat and tan suede suit. I set my case down inside the door and joined her.

"Hi, baby," her smile was a crescent of white. "You're a little early." She knew I would be. "Jim?" And I knew she'd already have the bartender's name and his attention. The man grinned for her.

"Jim, this is my baby. She's pretty, isn't she?"

Jim nodded, never taking his eyes away from Mother. She leaned over and kissed me on the lips.

"Give her a Scotch and water and another little taste for yourself."

She caught him as he started to hesitate. "Don't refuse, Jim. No man can walk on one leg." She smiled, and he turned to prepare the drinks.

"Baby, you're looking good. How was the drive? Still got that old Chrysler? Did you see those people in the lobby? They're so ugly they make you stop and think. How's Guy? Why are you going to New York? Is he happy about the move?

24

Jim set my drink down and lifted his in a toast.

Mother picked up her drink. "Here's looking at you, Jim." And to me. "Here's a go, baby." She smiled and I saw again that she was the most beautiful woman I had ever seen.

"Thanks, Mother."

She took my hands, put them together and rubbed them.

"You are cold. Hot as it is, your hands are freezing. Are you all right?"

Nothing frightened my mother except thunder and lightning. I couldn't tell her that at thirty-one years old, the whites in the lobby had scared me silly.

"Just fine, Mother. I guess it's the air conditioning."

She accepted the lie.

"Well, let's drink up and go to our room. I've got some talk for you."

She picked up the bills from the bar, counted them and pulled out two singles.

"What time do you come on, Jim?"

The bartender turned and grinned. "I open up. At eleven every morning."

"Then, I'll break your luck for you. Scotch and water, remember. At eleven. This is for you."

"Oh, you don't have to do that."

Mother was off the stool. "I know. That's why it's easy. See you in the morning."

I picked up my suitcase, followed her out of the dark bar into the noisy lobby. Again, the buzz of conversation diminished, but Mother never noticed. She switched through the crowd, up to the desk.

"Mrs. Vivian Baxter Jackson and daughter. You have our reservation." My mother had married a few times, but she loved her maiden name. Married or not, she often identified herself as Vivian Baxter.

It was a statement. "And please call the bellboy. My bag is in my car. Here are the keys. Set your bag down here, baby." Back to the registration clerk. "And tell him to bring my daughter's case to our room." The clerk slowly pushed a form across the counter. Mother opened her purse, took out her gold Sheaffer and signed us in.

"The key, please." Again using slow motion, the clerk slid the key to Mother.

"Two ten. Second floor. Thank you. Come on, baby." The hotel's color bar had been lifted only a month earlier, yet she acted as if she had been a guest there for years. There was a winding staircase to the right of the desk and a small group of open-mouthed conventioneers standing by the elevator.

I said, "Let's take the stairs, Mother."

She said, "We're taking the elevator," and pushed the "up" button. The waiting people looked at us as if our very presence had stripped everything of value from their lives.

When we got out of the elevator, mother took a moment, then turned and walked left to 210. She unlocked the door and when we entered, she threw her purse on the bed and walked to the window.

"Sit down, baby. I'm going to tell you something you must never forget."

I sat on the first chair as she opened the drapes. The sunlight framed her figure, and her face was indistinct.

"Animals can sense fear. They feel it. Well, you know that human beings are animals, too. Never, never let a person know you're frightened. And a group of them . . . absolutely never. Fear brings out the worst thing in everybody. Now, in that lobby you were as scared as a rabbit. I knew it and all those white folks knew it. If I hadn't been there, they might have turned into a mob. But something about me told them, if they mess with either of us, they'd better start looking for some new asses, 'cause I'd blow away what their mammas gave them."

She laughed like a young girl. "Look in my purse." I opened her purse.

"The Desert Hotel better be ready for integration, 'cause if it's not, I'm ready for the Desert Hotel."

Under her wallet, half hidden by her cosmetic case, lay a dark-blue German Luger.

"Room service? This is two ten. I'd like a pitcher of ice, two glasses, and a bottle of Teachers Scotch. Thank you."

The bellboy had brought our bags, and we had showered and changed.

"We'll have a cocktail and go down for dinner. But now, let's talk. Why New York? You were there in '52 and had to be sent home. What makes you think it has changed?"

"I met a writer, John Killens. I told him I wanted to write and he invited me to New York."

"He's colored, isn't he?" Since my first marriage to a Greek had dissolved, Mother had been hoping for a black son-in-law.

"He's married, Mother. It's not like that."

"That's terrible. First ninety-nine married men out of a hundred never divorce their wives for their girl friends, and the one that does will probably divorce the new wife for a newer girl friend."

"But really, it's not that way. I've met his wife and children. I'll go to New York, stay with them for a couple of weeks, get an apartment and send for Guy."

"And where will he stay for two weeks? Not alone in that big house. He's only fourteen."

She would explode if I told her I planned for him to stay with the man I was leaving. Vivian Baxter had survived by being healthily suspicious. She would never trust a rejected lover to treat her grandson fairly.

"I've made arrangements with a friend. And after all, it's only two weeks."

We both knew that she had left me and my brother for ten years to be raised by our paternal grandmother. We looked at each other and she spoke first.

"You're right. It is only two weeks. Well, let me tell you about me. I'm going to sea."

"To see. See what?"

"I'm going to become a merchant marine."

I had never heard of a female merchant seaman.

"A member of the Marine Cooks and Stewards Union."

"Why?" Disbelief raised my voice. "Why?" She was a surgical nurse, a realtor, had a barber's license and owned a hotel. Why did she want to go to sea and live the rough unglamorous life of a seaman?"

"Because they told me Negro women couldn't get in the union. You know what I told them?"

I shook my head, although I nearly knew.

"I told them, 'You want to bet?' I'll put my foot in that door up to my hip until women of every color can walk over my foot, get in that union, get aboard a ship and go to sea." There was a knock at the door. "Come in."

A uniformed black man opened the door and halted in surprise at seeing us.

"Good evening. Just put the tray over there. Thank you."

The bellboy deposited the tray and turned.

"Good evening, you all surprised me. Sure did. Didn't expect to see you. Sure didn't."

Mother walked toward him holding money in her hand.

"Who did you expect? Queen Victoria?"

"No. No, ma'am. I mean . . . Our people . . . in here . . . It's kinda new seeing us . . . and everything."

"This is for you." She gave him the tip. "We are just ordinary guests in the hotel. Thank you and good night." She opened the door and waited. When he walked out mumbling good night, she closed the door with finality.

"Mom, you were almost rude."

"Well, baby, I figure like this. He's colored and I'm colored, but we are not cousins. Let's have a drink." She smiled.

During the next two days, Mother showed me off to some old card-playing friends she had known twenty years earlier.

"This is my baby. She's been to Egypt, all around Milan, Italy, and Spain and Yugoslavia. She's a singer and dancer, you know."

28

When her friends were satisfactorily impressed with my accomplishments, Mother made certain of their wonder by adding, "Of course, I'll be shipping out myself in a few days."

We hugged in the empty lobby of the Desert Hotel; the convention had ended the day before our departure.

"Take care of yourself. Take care of your son, and remember New York City is just like Fresno. Just more of the same people in bigger buildings. Black folks can't change because white folks won't change. Ask for what you want and be prepared to pay for what you get." She kissed me and her voice softened to a whisper. "Let me leave first, baby. I hate to see the back of someone I love."

We embraced again and I watched her walk, hips swaying, into the bright street.

Back at home I collected myself and called Guy, who responded by coming into the living room and then walking back to lean against the doorjamb.

"Guy, I want to talk to you. Please sit down." At this stage, he never sat if he could stand, towering above the boredom of life. He sat, obviously to pacify me.

"Guy, we're going to move." Aha, a flicker of interest in his eyes, which he quickly controlled.

"Again? Okay. I can pack in twenty minutes. I've timed myself." I held on to the natural wince that struggled to surface.

In his nine years of schooling, we had lived in five areas of San Francisco, three townships in Los Angeles, New York City, Hawaii and Cleveland, Ohio. I followed the jobs, and against the advice of a pompous school psychologist, I had taken Guy along. The psychologist had been white, obviously educated and with those assets I knew he was also well-to-do. How could he know what a young Negro boy needed in a racist world?

When the money was plentiful, we lived in swank hotels and called room service. At other times we stayed in boardinghouses. I strung sheets as room dividers, and cooked our favorite food

29

illegally on a two-burner hot plate. Because we moved so often, Guy had little chance to make or keep friends, but we were together and generally we had laughed a lot. Now that post-puberty had laid claim to him, our friendly badinage was gone and I was menacing him with one more move.

"This is the last time. Last time, I think."

His face said he didn't believe me.

"We're going to New York City." His eyes lit up again and just as quickly dulled.

"I want to leave Saturday. John and Grace Killens are looking for an apartment for us. I'll stay with them and in two weeks you'll join me. Is that all right?" Parent power becomes so natural, only children notice it. I wasn't really asking his permission. He knew it and didn't answer.

"I thought I'd ask Ray if he'd like to stay in the house with you for two weeks. Just to be company for you. That O.K. with you?"

"That's perfectly all right, Mother." He stood up. He was so long, his legs seemed to start just at his arm sockets. "If you'll excuse me."

Thus he ended our unsatisfactory family chat. I still had to speak to my gentleman friend.

As we sat close in the morning's sunshine, Ray's handsome yellow face was as usual in benign repose.

"I'm leaving Saturday for New York."

"Oh? Got a contract?"

"No. Not yet."

"I don't think that I'd like to face New York without a contract . . ."

Here it was.

"Just Guy and I are going. We're going to stay."

His whole body jumped, the muscles began to skitter around his face. For the first time I thought that maybe he cared for me. I watched him command his body. After long minutes his fists fell open, the long fingers relaxed and his lips lost their hardened ridges.

30

"Is there anything I can do to help you?"

He consented to stay in the house and send Guy to me in two weeks. After, he might take the house himself, otherwise he would close it. Of course, we would remain friends.

2

John and Grace Killens lived with their two children and his mother in a roomy brownstone in Brooklyn. They accepted me as if I were a friend returning from a long journey. John met me at the door. "Girl, you finally got out of the country. Kick the mud off your shoes, come inside and make yourself at home."

Grace was quieter. "Welcome to New York. I'm glad you came."

Their hospitality was casual, without the large gestures that often discomfort a guest. The first days of my stay were filled with learning the house and studying the personalities of its inhabitants. John genuinely enjoyed being passionate. He was good-looking, and his dark-brown eyes in a light-brown face could alternately smolder or pierce. He talked animatedly, waving his hands as if offering them as gifts to his listeners.

Grace was pretty and petite, but she never allowed John's success or the fact that she was his great love interfere with independent thought.

John's mother, Mom Willie, who wore her Southern background like a magnolia corsage, eternally fresh, was robust and in her sixties. She was one of the group of black women who had raised their children, worked hard, fought for her principles and still retained some humor. She often entranced the family with graphic stories set in a sullen, racist South. The tales changed, the plots varied; her villains were always white and her heroes upstanding, courageous, clever blacks.

Barbara, the younger of the Killens children, was a bright tomboy who spoke fast and darted around the house like a cinnamon-colored wind. Her brother, Jon, larger and more gentle, moved slowly, spoke seldom and seemed to have been burdened with the responsibility of pondering the world's imponderables.

Everyone except Jon, whose nickname was Chuck, talked incessantly, and although I enjoyed the exchange, I found the theme inexplicably irritating. They excoriated white men, white women, white children and white history, particularly as it applied to black people.

I had spent my life on city front steps, in country backyards, kitchens, living rooms and bedrooms, joining in and listening to the conversations of black people, but I had never heard so much attention given to the subject of whites.

Of course, in Arkansas, when I was young, black children knowing that whites owned the cotton gin, the lumber mill, the fine houses and paved streets, had to find something which they thought whites did not possess. This need to have something all one's own coincided with the burgeoning interest in sex. The children sang, beyond the ears of adults and wistfully:

"Whites folks ain't got the hole . . .
And they ain't got the pole . . .
And they ain't got the soul . . .
To do it right . . . real right . . . All night."

In the ensuing years in California the jokes came scarcer and the jobs grew meaner. Anger was always present whenever the subject of whites entered our conversations. We discussed the treatment of Rev. Martin Luther King, Jr., the murder of Emmett Till in Mississippi, the large humiliations and the petty snubs we all knew were meant to maim our spirits. I had heard white folks ridiculed, cursed and envied, but I had never heard them dominate the entire intimate conversation of a black family.

In the Killens' home, if entertainment was mentioned, someone would point out that Harry Belafonte, a close family friend, was working with a South African singer, Miriam Makeba, and South Africa was really no different from South Philly. If the West Indies or religion or fashion entered the conversation, in minutes we were persistently examining the nature of racial oppression, racial progress and racial integration.

I fretted at the unrelenting diatribe, not because I disagreed but because I didn't think whites interesting enough to consume all my thoughts, nor powerful enough to control all my movements.

I found an apartment in the Killens' neighborhood. I spent the days painting the two bedrooms and sprucing up the furniture I bought in secondhand stores, and returned each night to sleep at the Killens' house.

One evening after the rest of the family had gone to bed, I sat up having a nightcap with John. I asked why he was so angry all the time. I told him that while I agreed with Alabama blacks who boycotted bus companies and protested against segregation, California blacks were thousands of miles, literally and figuratively, from those Southern plagues.

"Girl, don't you believe it. Georgia is Down South. California is Up South. If you're black in this country, you're on a plantation. You have to deal with masters. There might be some argument over whether they are vicious masters, but be assured that they all think they are masters . . . And if they think that, then you'd better believe they think you are the slave. Maybe a smart slave, a pretty slave, a good slave, but a slave just the same."

I reminded John that I had spent a year in New York, but he countered, "You were a dancer. Dancers don't see anything except other dancers. They don't see; they exist to be seen. This time you should look at New York with a writer's eyes, ears and nose. Then you'll really see New York."

John was right. Seven years earlier, when I studied in New York, my attention was unequally distributed between the dance studio where I was studying on scholarship, my son and my first, disintegrating marriage. Truly I had had neither the time nor mind to learn New York.

John's eyes were blazing, and although I was his only audience, he was as intense as if he were speaking to a filled room.

"I tell you what to do. Go to Manhattan tomorrow. Go first to Times Square. You'll see the same people you used to see in Arkansas. Their accents might be different, their dress might be different, but if they are American whites, they're all Southern crackers. Then go to Harlem. Harlem is the largest plantation in this country. You'll see lawyers in three-piece suits, real estate brokers in mink coats, pimps in white Cadillacs, but they're all sharecropping. Sharecropping on a mean plantation."

I intended to see Harlem with John's advice in mind, but Guy arrived before I had the opportunity. I picked him up at the airport, and when he walked into the house I saw that he was already too large for the living room. We had been separated a month and he seemed to have grown two inches taller and years away from me. He looked at the hastily painted white walls and the Van Gogh prints I had chosen and matted.

"It's O.K.. It looks like every other house we've lived in."

I wanted to slap him. "Well, it's a little better than the street."

"Oh, Mother, come now. That wasn't necessary." The superiority in his voice was an indication of how he had been hurt by our separation.

I grinned. "O.K. Sorry. How about the desk? You always said you wanted a big office desk. Do you like it?"

"Oh sure, but you know I wanted a desk when I was a little kid. Now . . ."

The air between us was burdened with his aloof scorn. I understood him too well.

When I was three my parents divorced in Long Beach, California, and sent me and my four-year-old brother, unescorted, to our paternal grandmother. We wore wrist tags which informed anyone concerned that we were Marguerite and Bailey Johnson, en route to Mrs. Annie Henderson in Stamps, Arkansas.

34

Except for disastrous and mercifully brief encounters with each of them when I was seven, we didn't see our parents again until I was thirteen.

Our reunion with Mother in California was a joyous festival, studded with tears, hugs and lipsticked kisses. Under and after the high spirits was my aching knowledge that she had spent years not needing us.

Now my angry son was wrestling with the same knowledge. We had been apart less than a month—he had stayed an unwelcome guest in his own home, while I had gloried in every day of our separation.

He covered the hurt with a look of unconcern, but I knew his face better than my own. Each fold, every plane, the light or shadow in his eyes had been objects of my close scrutiny. He had been born to me when I was an unmarried adventurous seven-teen-year-old; we had grown up together. Since he was fatherless most of his fourteen years, the flash of panic in his eyes was exchanged for scorn whenever I brought a new man into our lives. I knew the relief when he discovered the newcomer cared for me and respected him. I recognized the confusion that changed his features each time the man packed to leave. I understood the unformed question. "She made him leave. What will she do if I displease her too?" He remained standing, hands in his pockets, waiting for me to convince him of the stability of my love. Words were useless.

"Your school is three blocks away, and there's a large park almost as nice as the one on Fulton Street."

At the mention of the San Francisco park where we picnicked and he learned to ride a bike, a tiny smile tried to cross his face, but he quickly took control and sent the smile away.

". . . and you liked the Killens children. Well, they live around the corner."

He nodded and spoke like an old man. "Lots of people are different when they're visiting than when they're at home. I'll see if they're the same in New York as they were in California."

Youthful cynicism is sad to observe, because it indicates not so much knowledge learned from bitter experiences as insufficient trust even to attempt the future.

"Guy, you know I love you, and I try to be a good mother. I try to do the right thing, but I'm not perfect"—his silence agreed —"I hope you'll remember whenever I've done something that hurts you that I do love you and it's not my intention . . ."

He was studying my face, listening to the tone of my voice. "Mom . . ." I relaxed a little. "Mother" was formal, cold, disapproving. "Mom" meant closeness, forgiveness.

"Mom, I know. I know you do the best you can. And I'm not really angry. It's just that Los Angeles . . ."

"Did Ray do anything . . . mistreat you?"

"Oh no, Mom. He moved about a week after you left."

"You mean you lived alone?"

Shock set my body into furious action. Every normal function accelerated. Tears surfaced and clouded my vision. Guy lost half his age and suddenly he again was a little boy of seven who slept with a butcher's knife under his pillow one summer at camp. What did he slip under his pillow in Los Angeles while I partied safely in New York?

"My baby. Oh honey, why didn't you tell me when I phoned? I would have come back."

Now his was the soothing voice. "You were trying to find a job and a house. I wasn't afraid."

"But Guy, you're only fourteen. Suppose something had happened to you?"

He stood silent and looked at me, evaluating my distress. Suddenly, he crossed the room and stopped beside my chair. "Mom, I'm a man. I can look after myself. Don't worry. I'm young, but I'm a man." He stood, bent and kissed me on the forehead. "I'm going to change the furniture around. I want my desk facing the window." He walked down the hall.

The black mother perceives destruction at every door, ruination at each window, and even she herself is not beyond her own

36

suspicion. She questions whether she loves her children enough —or more terribly, does she love them too much? Do her looks cause embarrassment—or even more terrifying, is she so attractive her sons begin to desire her and her daughters begin to hate her. If she is unmarried, the challenges are increased. Her singleness indicates she has rejected, or has been rejected by her mate. Yet she is raising children who will become mates. Beyond her door, all authority is in the hands of people who do not look or think or act like her and her children. Teachers, doctors, sales clerks, librarians, policemen, welfare workers are white and exert control over her family's moods, conditions and personality; yet within the home, she must display a right to rule which at any moment, by a knock at the door, or a ring of the telephone can be exposed as false. In the face of these contradictions, she must provide a blanket of stability, which warms but does not suffocate, and she must tell her children the truth about the power of white power without suggesting that it cannot be challenged.

"Hey, Mom, come and see."

Every piece of furniture was in a new place, and the room looked exactly the same.

"Like it? After dinner, I'll play you a game of Scrabble. Where is the dictionary? What are we having for dinner? Does the television work? Gee, I'm famished."

My son was home and we were a family again.

The Harlem Writers Guild was meeting at John's house, and my palms were sweating and my tongue was thick. The loosely formed organization, without dues or membership cards, had one strict rule: any invited guest could sit in for three meetings, but thereafter, the visitor had to read from his or her work in progress. My time had come.

Sarah Wright and Sylvester Leeks stood in a corner talking softly. John Clarke was staring at titles in the bookcase. Mary Delany and Millie Jordan were giving their coats to Grace and exchanging greetings. The other writers were already seated around the living room in a semicircle.

John Killens walked past me, touching my shoulder, took his seat and called the meeting to order.

"O.K., everybody. Let's start." Chairs scraped the floor and the sounds reverberated in my armpits. "As you know, our newest member, our California singer, is going to read from her new play. What's the title, Maya?"

"One Love. One Life." My usually deep voice leaked out high-pitched and weak.

A writer asked how many acts the play had. I answered again in the piping voice, "So far only one."

Everyone laughed; they thought I was making a joke.

"If everyone is ready, we can begin." John picked up his note pad. There was a loud rustling as the writers prepared to take notes.

I read the character and set description despite the sudden perversity of my body. The blood pounded in my ears but not enough to drown the skinny sound of my voice. My hands shook so that I had to lay the pages in my lap, but that was not a good solution due to the tricks my knees were playing. They lifted voluntarily, pulling my heels off the floor and then trembled like disturbed Jello. Before I launched into the play's action, I looked around at the writers expecting but hoping not to see their amusement at my predicament. Their faces were studiously blank. Within a year, I was to learn that each had a horror story about a first reading at the Harlem Writers Guild.

Time wrapped itself around every word, slowing me. I couldn't force myself to read faster. The pages seemed to be multiplying even as I was trying to reduce them. The play was dull, the characters, unreal, and the dialogue was taken entirely off the back of a Campbell's soup can. I knew this was my first and last time at the Guild. Even if I hadn't the grace to withdraw voluntarily, I was certain the members had a method of separating the wheat from the chaff.

"The End." At last.

The members laid their notes down beside their chairs and a few got up to use the toilets. No one spoke. Even as I read I knew the drama was bad, but maybe someone would have lied a little.

The room filled. Only the whispering of papers shifting told me that the jury was ready.

John Henrik Clarke, a taut little man from the South, cleared his throat. If he was to be the first critic, I knew I would receive the worst sentence. John Clarke was famous in the group for his keen intelligence and bitter wit. He had supposedly once told the FBI that they were wrong to think that he would sell out his home state of Georgia; he added that he would give it away, and if he found no takers he would even pay someone to take it.

"*One Life. One Love?*" His voice was a rasp of disbelief. "I found no life and very little love in the play from the opening of the act to its unfortunate end."

Using superhuman power, I kept my mouth closed and my eyes on my yellow pad.

He continued, his voice lifting. "In 1879, on a March evening, Alexander Graham Bell successfully completed his attempts to send the human voice through a little wire. The following morning some frustrated playwright, unwilling to build the necessary construction plot, began his play with a phone call."

A general deprecating murmur floated in the air.

"Aw, John" and "Don't be so mean" and "Ooo Johnnn, you ought to be ashamed." Their moans were facetious, mere accompaniment to their relish.

Grace invited everyone to drinks, and the crowd rose and started milling around, while I stayed in my chair.

Grace called to me. "Come on, Maya. Have a drink. You need it." I grinned and knew movement was out of the question.

Killens came over. "Good thing you stayed. You got some very important criticism." He, too, could slide to hell straddling a knotted greasy rope. "Don't just sit there. If they think you're too sensitive, you won't get such valuable criticism the next time you read."

The next time? He wasn't as bright as he looked. I would never see those snooty bastards as long as I stayed black and their asses pointed toward the ground. I put a nasty-sweet smile on my face and nodded.

"That's right, Maya Angelou, show them you can take anything they can dish out. Let me tell you something." He started to sit down beside me, but mercifully another writer called him away.

I measured the steps from my chair to the door. I could make it in ten strides.

"Maya, you've got a story to tell."

I looked up into John Clarke's solemn face.

"I think I can speak for the Harlem Writers Guild. We're glad to have you. John Killens came back from California talking about your talent. Well, in this group we remind each other that talent is not enough. You've got to work. Write each sentence over and over again, until it seems you've used every combination possible, then write it again. Publishers don't care much for white writers." He coughed or laughed. "You can imagine what they think about black ones. Come on. Let's get a drink."

I got up and followed him without a first thought.

Ten different conversations were being held in the kitchen.

The writers were partying. Gone were the sober faces and serious eyes. As John Clarke and I entered, another writer spoke to me. "So, Maya, you lived through your baptism. Now you're a member of the flock." Sarah, a pretty little woman with fastidious manners, put her hand on my arm. "They were easy on you this evening, dear. Soft, you might say. Because it was your first reading. But you'll see, next week you watch how they treat Sylvester."

Paule Marshall, whose book *Brown Girl, Brown Stones* was going to be made into a television movie, smiled conspiratorially. "See, I told you, it wasn't too bad, was it?" They had stripped me, flayed me, utterly and completely undone me, and now they were as cheery as Christmas cards.

I sipped the cool wine and thought about the evening's instruction. Because I had a fairly large vocabulary and had been reading constantly since childhood, I had taken words and the art of arranging them too lightly. The writers assaulted my casual approach and made me confront my intention. If I wanted to write, I had to be willing to develop a kind of concentration found mostly in people awaiting execution. I had to learn technique and surrender my ignorance.

John Killens interrupted my thoughts. "Maya, how long will it take you to rewrite that play?"

I hadn't decided on a rewrite, or even whether I would attend another Guild meeting.

"I need to know so I can schedule your next reading."

"I'm not sure. Let me think about it."

"There are a lot of people ready to read. You'd better decide, otherwise you'll have to get in line."

"I'll call you tomorrow."

John nodded and turned away. He lifted his voice. "O.K., everybody. What about Cuba? What about Castro? Are we going to sit back and watch the United States kick Castro's ass, like its been kicking our ass, and say nothing?"

In the second following John's question, the air held quiet, free of chatter. Then voices rose.

"All black people ought to support Castro."

"Cuba is all right. Castro is all right."

"Castro acts like he grew up in Harlem."

"He speaks Spanish, but it could be niggerese."

John waited until the voices fell.

"There's no time like right now. You know about the slave who decided to buy his freedom?" Small smiles began to grow on the black, brown and yellow faces. Grace chuckled and bit into her cigarette holder.

"Well, this negero was a slave, but his owner allowed him to take jobs off the plantation at night, on weekends and holidays. He worked. Now, mind you, I mean, he would work on the plantation and then walk fifteen miles to town and work there, then walk back, get two hours' sleep and get up at daybreak and work again. He saved every penny. Wouldn't marry, wouldn't even take advantage of the ladies around him. Afraid he'd have to spend some of his hard-earned money. Finally, he saved up a thousand dollars. Lot of money. He went to his master and asked how much he was worth. The white man asked why the question. The negero said he just wanted to know how much slaves cost. The white man said he usually paid eight hundred to twelve hundred dollars for a good slave, but in the case of Tom, because he was getting old and couldn't father any children, if he wanted to buy himself, the master would let him go for six hundred dollars.

"Tom thanked the slave owner and went back to his cabin. He dug up his money and counted it. He fondled and caressed the coins and then put them back in their hiding place. He returned to the white man and said, 'Boss, freedom is a little too high right now. I'm going to wait till the price come down.' "

We all laughed, but the laughter was acrid with embarrassment. Most of us had been Toms at different times of our lives. There had been occasions when the price of freedom was more than I wanted to pay. Around the room faces showed others also were remembering.

"There is a Fair Play for Cuba organization. An ad is going to be taken out in the daily newspapers. The ad will cost money. Anyone who wants to sign it can find the form in the living room. Put your name down and if you can afford to, leave some money in the bowl on the cocktail table."

A few people began to move hurriedly toward the front room, but John stopped them.

"Just a minute. I just want to remind you all that if your name appears in the ad this afternoon, you can bet ten thousand dollars and a sucker that by nightfall it'll be in the FBI files. You'll be suspect. Just remember that."

John Clarke coughed his laugh again. "Hell, if you're born black in the United States, you're suspect of being everything,

42

except white, of course." We laughed, relieved at the truth told in our own bitter wit. I thought of lines in Sterling Brown's poem "Strong Men":

> We followed away, and laughed as usual.
> They heard the laugh and wondered.

Just before I left the house, I signed the already-filled application form.

Paule Marshall stopped me at the door. "I really want to hear your rewrite. You know, lots of people have more talent than you or I. Hard work makes the difference. Hard, hard unrelenting work."

The meeting was over. Members were embraced, kissed lips or cheeks and patted each other. John Killens offered to drive me home.

Grace hugged me and whispered. "Ya did good, kid, and I know you were scared witless."

When John parked in front of my house, I gathered my papers and asked, "What's the hardest literary form, John?"

"Each one is the hardest. Fiction is impossible. Ask me. Poetry is impossible. Ask Langston or Countee. Baldwin will say essays are impossible. But everyone agrees, short stories are so impossible, they almost can't be written at all."

I opened the car door, "John, put me down for a reading in two months. I'll be reading a new short story. Good night."

I thought about my statement as I walked up the stairs. I had gathered from the evening's meeting that making a decision to write was a lot like deciding to jump into a frozen lake. I knew I was going in, so I decided I might as well try what John Killens suggested as the deepest end: the short story. If I survived at all, it would be a triumph. If I swam, it would be a miracle. As I unlocked my door, I thought of my mother putting her age back fifteen years and going into the merchant marines. I had to try. If I ended in defeat, at least I would be trying. Trying to overcome was black people's honorable tradition.

3

There is an awesome reality to Rent Day. It comes trumpeting, forcing the days before it into a wild scramble. My rent day seemed to come due every other day, and Guy always needed just one more pair of jeans. The clothes I had to have were eternally in the cleaners, and staples disappeared from my kitchen with an alarming regularity.

I could get a job singing, but I didn't have an agent. Harlem theatrical representatives sought light-skinned Cotton Club–type beauties for their traveling revues. Midtown white agents would only book unknown black entertainers for out-of-town or night gigs, stag parties or smokers. I knew one white New York club owner who had been a loyal friend to me, but with my recently acquired new level of black dignity I refused to go pleading to him for work.

I found a job on my own. The little club on the Lower East Side was a joint where people came when they didn't have any other place to go. There was a long bar, diluted drinks, dinner-plate-sized tables and no dressing rooms (I changed in the women's toilet) and the work itself embarrassed me.

I sang in the club for two miserable months. People I admired were doing important things. Abbey and Max Roach were performing jazz concerts on liberation themes. Lorraine Hansberry had a play on Broadway which told some old truths about the black American Negro family to a new white audience. James Baldwin had the country in his balled fist with *The Fire Next Time*. Killens' *And Then We Heard the Thunder* told the uncomfortable facts about black soldiers in a white army. Belafonte included the South African singer Miriam Makeba in his concerts, enlarging his art and increasing his protest against racial abuse. And I was still singing clever little songs only moderately well. I made the decision to quit show business. Give up the skintight dresses and manicured smiles. The false concern over

44

sentimental lyrics. I would never again work to make people smile inanely and would take on the responsibility of making them think. Now was the time to demonstrate my own seriousness.

Two weeks after my firm decision, I received an offer to appear at the Apollo Theatre, and the idea of rejecting the invitation never occurred to me. The Apollo, in Harlem, was to black entertainers the Met, La Scala and a Royal Command Performance combined. Pearl Bailey, Dizzy Gillespie, Count Basie, Duke Ellington had played on that stage.

Frank Schiffman, the manager, sat in the darkened theater listening to rehearsal. Tito Puente's big band with Willie Bobo and Mongo Santamaria dropped dancing notes in the air like dust particles in a windstorm.

Schiffman sat rigid in the first row. I rehearsed my songs with the band, spurred on by the timbales of Willie Bobo and Mongo Santamaria's conga. I enlarged on my initial interpretation of the music, singing better than I was usually capable of. Schiffman didn't move or speak until I started to rehearse "Uhuru," an audience-participation song which I used as an encore.

"No audience participation in the Apollo." His voice was as rusty as an old iron bar.

"I beg your pardon?" Always get siditty when you're scared, was my policy. "Were you speaking to me?"

"Yeah, no audience participation in the Apollo."

"But that's my act. I always use 'Uhuru' as an encore. The word means freedom in Swahili. Babatunda Olatunje, the great Nigerian drummer, taught it to me—"

"No audience participation—."

"Is that your policy, Mr. Schiffman? If so . . ."

A few musicians rustled sheet music; others talked in Spanish.

"It's not a policy. The only policy in the Apollo is 'Be Good.' I'm telling you no audience participation because Apollo audiences won't go along with it. You'll die. Die on the stage if you try to get this audience to sing with you." He gave a little laugh and continued, "Most of them can sing better than you anyway."

A few musicians who understood English laughed. Many people could sing better than I, so Schiffman had told me nothing I didn't already know.

"Thanks for your advice. I'm going to sing it anyway."

"It'll be a miracle if they don't laugh you off the stage." He laughed again.

"Thank you." I turned back to the orchestra. "I don't have sheet music, but the song goes like this . . ."

I didn't expect Schiffman to know that my life, like the lives of other black Americans, could be credited to miraculous experiences. But there was one other thing I was sure he didn't know. Black people in Harlem were changing, and the Apollo audience was black. The echo of African drums was less distant in 1959 than it had been for over a century.

One Hundred and Twenty-fifth Street was to Harlem what the Mississippi was to the South, a long traveling river always going somewhere, carrying something. A furniture store offering gaudy sofas and fake leopard-skin chairs shouldered Mr. Micheaux's book shop, which prided itself on having or being able to get a copy of any book written by a black person since 1900. It was true that sportily dressed fops stood on 125th and Seventh Avenue saying, "Got horse for the course and coke for your hope," but across the street, conservatively dressed men told concerned crowds of the satanic nature of whites and the divinity of Elijah Muhammad. Black women and men had begun to wear multicolored African prints. They moved through the Harlem streets like bright sails on a dark sea.

I also knew that fewer people giggled or poked the sides of their neighbors when they noticed my natural hair style.

Clever appliance-store owners left their TV sets on the channels broadcasting U.N. affairs. I had seen black people standing in front of the stores watching the faces of international diplomats. Although no sound escaped into the streets, the attentive crowds appeared. I had waited with a group of strangers one night near St. Nicholas Avenue. The mood was hopeful, as if a promise was soon to be kept. The crowd tightened, pulled itself closer together and toward the window, as a small dark figure appeared on all the screens at once. The figure was that of an African wearing a patterned toga, striding with theatrical dignity toward the camera. The sidewalk audience was quiet but tense. When the man's face was discernible and the part in his hair distinct, the crowd began to talk.

"Hey, Alex. Hey, brother."

"He's a good-looking thing."

"That African walk like God himself."

"Humph. Ain't that something."

The man's mouth moved and the crowd quieted, as if lip reading. Although it was impossible to understand his message, his air of disdain was not lost on the viewers.

One fat woman grinned and giggled, "I sure wish I knew what that pretty nigger was saying."

A man near the back of the crowd grunted. "Hell. He's just telling all the crackers in the world to kiss his black ass."

Laughter burst loudly in the street. Laughter immediate and self-congratulatory.

Schiffman had been in Harlem since the beginning of the Apollo. He had given first contracts to a number of black performers who went on to become internationally famous. Some people in the area said he was all right, and he had black friends. He understood who was running numbers, who was running games and who was square and respectable. But he wasn't black. And he was too mired in the Harlem he had helped to fashion to believe that the area was moving out of his control and even beyond his understanding.

"Uhuru" was definitely going to be my encore.

Fortunately my first show was at one o'clock on a Monday afternoon. About forty people sat staggered in an auditorium which could hold seven hundred. Tito Puente's big band echoed in the room with the volume of an enlarged symphony orchestra. The comedian delivered his jokes for his own amusement, and the small audience responded as if he were a favorite nephew entertaining in the family living room. The tap dancer sent a private message in heel-and-toe code, and the audience sent back its answer in applause. The male singer sang a Billy Eckstein–like arrangement and he was well received.

I walked onto the stage wearing my sky-blue chiffon gown and the blue high heels, dyed to match.

The first few calypso songs elicited only polite responses, but when I sang a Southern blues, long on moaning and deep in content, the audience shouted back to me, "Tell the truth, baby." And "Sing, tall skinny mamma. Sing your song." I was theirs and they were mine. I sang the race memory, and we were united in centuries of belonging. My last song was "Baba Fururu," a Cuban religious song, taught to me by Mongo Santamaria a year earlier when I had joined Puente on a tour of six Eastern theaters. Speaking only a few words of English, Mongo taught me the song syllable by syllable. Although he couldn't translate the lyrics, he said the song was used in black Cuban religious ritual.

That first Apollo audience consisted of grandparents, raising the children of their own absent children, and young women on welfare, too good to steal and too timid to whore, and young men, made unnecessary.

The Afro-Cuban song ignored hope and laid itself down in despair. The blue notes humped themselves and became the middle passage. They flattened and moaned about poverty and how it felt to be hated. The Apollo audience shouted. They had understood. When I returned and announced that my encore was another African song, called, in Swahili, "Freedom," they applauded, ready to go with me to that wished-for land.

I explained, "If you believe you deserve freedom, if you really want it, if you believe it should be yours, you must sing:

"*U hu uhuru* oh yea freedom
U hu uhuru oh yea freedom
Uh huh Uh hum"

48

Willie Bobo, Mongo and Juliano set four-four, five-four and six-four times on conga, timbales and caracas, and I started singing. I leaned back on the rhythms and began

"O sawaba huru
O sawaba huru
O sawaba huru"

I joined the audience on the refrain:

"Oh yea, oh yea freedom
uh huh
uh hum
uh hum
uh hum."

The audience sang passionately. They were under my voice, before my voice. Understanding beyond my own understanding. I was the singer, the entertainer, and they were the people who were enduring. They accepted me because I was singing the anthem and carrying the flag.

By evening of the first day, I saw the power of the black grapevine. During the six o'clock show someone screamed from the audience, "Sing Freedom, Sing Freedom." It was my encore, so I had to sing the routine of planned songs. The audience clapped until I returned. I began, "If you believe you deserve freedom. If you . . ."

"Uh huh *uhuru* yea freedom
uh huh *uhuru* yea freedom
uh huh *uhuru* yea freedom
uh huh, oh yea free-dom."

The audience had it and gone.

"Just a minute. Some of you all know the song, but let me explain it to the folks who don't know."

A voice from the audience screamed. "All right, but don't wait for slowpokes. We ready to sing."

I continued with my explanation and the drums began. The audience pounded out the rhythm, moving it, controlling and possessing the music, the orchestra and me.

> "Uh, uh, oh huh.
> O yea, freedom,
> Uh huh. Uh huh"

As the song ended the small crowd thundered a hot appreciation. Even as I bowed, I knew the applause was only in a small part for me. I had been merely the ignition which set off their fire. It was our history, our painful passage and uneven present that burned luminously in the dark theater.

For six days and three shows per day, the tumultuous response was repeated. On the last day of the run, John and Grace brought Guy, Barbara and Chuck Killens. I watched the three teen-agers from a curtain peephole. The comedian's routines were beyond their understanding, the singer's laments about unrequited love didn't catch their concern. The tap dancer made his complicated routine seem too easy. When I went on stage the exoticism of seeing a familiar person in an unfamiliar setting did not hold their attention past the first few minutes. Before I finished my first song, I looked down and saw the three mumbling among themselves. When I finished, however, the children joined energetically with the audience on "Uhuru," not so much singing the music as screaming the words. Guy's cracking lopsided voice pierced high above the ensemble sound. Schiffman had been right and wrong. Some people sang better than I, but no one laughed me off the stage.

After the Killens and Guy left my dressing room, I prepared for the last show. I knew I would never again make an appearance as a singer. There was only one Apollo Theater, and no other place had the allure to melt my resolve. While the run had given me stature among my New York acquaintances, its real value was in the confidence it gave me. I had not won world-wide fame, or gained stunning wealth, but I was leaving show business at the right time: stepping down from the pinnacle of the Apollo stage. And an I-told-you-so imp had grinned behind my eyes all week long. Apollo audiences had been filling Frank Schiffman's ears with "Oh yea, oh yea, freedom," so he hadn't spoken to me since opening night. It was going to be an hallelujah time when he gave me my check. I finished the set and waited in the wings while the audience yelled for my return. I went back to the microphone and began, "Thank you, ladies and gentlemen. This last piece needs audience participation. It is a song from Africa. It's called 'Uhuru,' which means freedom. I'd like the people of this side of the theater to sing, *uh uhuru,* oh yea freedom"—the drums began to roll in a quick promise—"and this side . . ."

"Damn, why don't you do your act, girl? If you can't sing, come back on Wednesday. That's amateur night."

The man's voice came from the balcony, strident and piercing the dark theater like an unexpected light. My heart thumped, and I couldn't think of a thing to say. A few giggles from around the room encouraged him.

"Anyway"—his voice was meaner and louder—"anyway, if you like Africa so much, why don't you go back there?"

The only thing I knew was I would never get off the stage. Hell's eternity would find me rooted in front of the mute microphone, my feet glued to the floor. The baby-blue spotlight blinding me and holding me forever in that place. A grumble began in the balcony and was joined by sounds of displeasure on the main floor. I still couldn't move. Suddenly a lemon-sour voice from the front rows shouted, "Shut up, up there, you bastid. I paid money to come in here."

Some "yeahs" and "that's rights" popped up in the theater.

They angered my detractor. He shouted, "Go to hell, you old bitch. I paid for this shit too."

"Aw, cool it, goddammit. Let the woman sing," a man's bass

voice ordered from the rear. "Yeah." Another man spoke from the balcony and sounded dangerously near to the heckler. "Yeah, you don't like it. Get your ass down on the stage and do what you can do."

That was it. Either there would be a bloody fight with cutting and shooting or the heckler was going to come on the stage, take the microphone and make me look even more foolish than I thought I was. I was surprised to realize that the drummers were still playing.

The woman, my first defender, lifted her voice . . .

"Freedom, freedom, freedom."

She was in tempo but the melody was wrong.

More voices joined, "Freedom, Freedom." The drums rolled on like an irate river. "Freedom, Freedom." The singers in the audience increased. "Freedom." The entire main floor seemed to have joined the drums. They had taken my side and taken the song away from me.

The bass voice cut through the music, "Sing girl, goddammit, sing the goddam song."

I sang *"O sawaba huru, O sawaba huru.* Oh yea. Oh yea, freedom." We didn't sing the song Olatunji had taught me, but we sang loudly and gloriously, as if the thing we sang about was already in our hands. My closing show reminded me of Mother's advice: "Since you're black, you have to hope for the best. Be prepared for the worst and always know that anything can happen."

When Schiffman gave me my check, we both grinned.

4

I thought Godfrey Cambridge was one of the prettiest men I had ever seen. His features had the immutability of a Benin mask, and his white teeth were like flags of truce. His skin was the color of rich black dirt along the Arkansas River. He was tall and big and

52

spoke English with the staccato accent of a New York–born descendant of West Indian parents. He was definitely the one.

He was introduced to me at a Greenwich Village party. He said that he was an unemployed actor, and because I mistook his curiosity for romantic interest, I pursued. We exchanged phone numbers and when I called and invited him to dinner, he accepted. Guy and Godfrey became a team in the first ten minutes. Guy enjoyed Godfrey's funny stories about his job as a taxi driver and his adventures auditioning for white musicals. We ate a four-course meal (I always used my cooking to enhance my sex appeal) and laughed a lot. After Guy went to bed, Godfrey and I sat in the living room listening to records and drinking cognac-laced coffee. To my disappointment, the jokes continued. Godfrey talked about crazy passengers, egotistic actors and tyrannical directors, and each story led to a punch line which begged for laughter. The stories became more forced and time moved haltingly. Despite my availability, my cooking and my willingness, together we ignited no passionate fires.

When I let him out of the house, he gave me a brother's kiss and I scratched him off my list as a possibility.

The Harlem church was full, with standees in the rear. A few white people sat in the middle rows, stiffly, not moving, not turning to look at the black people, who buzzed like hived bees. Godfrey and I had come to hear Rev. Martin Luther King, Jr. He had just been released from jail, and was in New York to raise money for the Southern Christian Leadership Conference and to make Northerners aware of the fight being waged in Southern states.

Five black men marched in single-file onto the rostrum, their solemnity a perfect foil for the raucous welcome of the audience.

The host minister introduced Wyatt Walker, a Baptist preacher whom I thought too handsome for virtue and too young for wisdom.

He spoke, in a purely Baptist voice, of Alabama and the right-eous struggle for justice. Fred Shuttlesworth, another attractive minister, was introduced. I wondered if the SCLC had a policy of keeping the ugly preachers at home and sending only the good-looking ones to the North. Shuttlesworth leaned his thin body over the podium, jutting a black hawklike face at the audi-ence. His words were sharp and his voice accusatory. He became a hatchet of a man. Chopping away at our geographic security. What were we doing in New York City, while black children were being set upon by dogs, black women were raped and black men maimed and killed? Did we think New York City could escape the righteous wrath of God? This was our chance to join the holy crusade, pick up the gauntlet flung down in hate, carry it through the bloody battleground to the region of peace and justice and equality for all. The audience stood up and the Reverend Shuttles-worth sat down.

Ralph Abernathy was introduced next. He moved slowly and quietly toward the podium. He stood a few seconds, looking down at his hands, which rested on top of the desk. His speaking voice was a surprise and his delivery a shock. He didn't have the fire of Walker or the anger of Shuttlesworth. His message was clear and quick, and in an unnerving way, the most powerful. The South was in a phase of change, and everyone must pay for change because everyone will benefit from change. As Christians, we all should be ready for change because if we think about it, Jesus was the greatest changer in history. He changed the idea of an eye for an eye, and a tooth for a tooth. He ran the moneylenders from the temple because they were cheating the people and taught forgiveness even of one's enemies. Rev. Abernathy reminded the audience that only with God could we develop the courage to change the unchangeable. When he moved, ponderously, slowly to his seat, there was a long moment when the audience sat still. Because his words had not been coated with passion or fashioned in eloquent prose, they took longer to swallow. The host minister rose again, and all rustling stopped. The room held its breath.

The preacher told us what we already knew about Martin Luther King, the dangers he had experienced and the triumphs he had won. The listeners didn't move. There was a yawping expectancy under the stillness. He was here, our own man, black, intelligent and fearless. He was going to be born to us in a moment. He would stand up behind the pulpit, full grown, and justify the years of sacrifice and the days of humiliation. He was the best we had, the brightest and most beautiful. Maybe today would be the day we would find ourselves free.

The introduction was over and Martin Luther King, Jr., rose. The audience, collectively, lost its composure, pews scraped against the floor as people stood, rearing back, pushing, leaning forward, shouting.

"Yes, Lord. Come on, Dr. King. Just come on."

A stout short woman in red, standing next to me, grabbed me around the waist and squeezed. She looked at me as if we were old friends, and whispered, "If I never drew another breath, I could die happy."

She released me and caught the arm of a man on her right, pulling the arm to her breast, cradling it and whispering, "It's all right, now. He's right here and its all right."

Martin Luther King, Jr., stood on the dais, away from the podium, allowing the audience full view of his body. He looked at the audience, smiling, accepting the adulation but strangely apart from it. After a minute, he walked to a position behind the podium and raised both hands. It was at once a surrendering and a quelling gesture. The church became quiet, but the people remained standing. They were trying to fill their eyes with the sight of the man.

He smiled warmly and lowered his arms. The audience sat immediately, as if they had been attached by invisible strings to the ends of his fingers.

He began to speak in a rich sonorous voice. He brought greetings from our brothers and sisters in Atlanta and in Montgomery, in Charlotte and Raleigh, Jackson and Jacksonville. A lot of you, he reminded us, are from the South and still have ties to the land. Somewhere there was an old grandmother holding on, a few uncles, some cousins and friends. He said the South we might remember is gone. There was a new South. A more violent and ugly South, a country where our white brothers and sisters were terrified of change, inevitable change. They would rather scratch up the land with bloody fingers and take their most precious document, the Declaration of Independence, and throw it in the deepest ocean, bury it under the highest mountain, or burn it in the most flagrant blaze, than admit justice into a seat at the welcome table, and fair-play room in a vacant inn.

Godfrey and I slid close, until our shoulders and thighs were touching. I glanced at him and saw tears glistening on his dark face.

Rev. King continued, chanting, singing his prophetic litany. We were one people, indivisible in the sight of God, responsible to each other and for each other.

We, the black people, the most displaced, the poorest, the most maligned and scourged, we had the glorious task of reclaiming the soul and saving the honor of the country. We, the most hated, must take hate into our hands and by the miracle of love, turn loathing into love. We, the most feared and apprehensive, must take fear and by love, change it into hope. We, who die daily in large and small ways, must take the demon death and turn it into Life.

His head was thrown back and his words rolled out with the rumbling of thunder. We had to pray without ceasing and work without tiring. We had to know evil will not forever stay on the throne. That right, dashed to the ground, will rise, rise again and again.

When he finished washing us with his words, caressing our scarred bodies with his optimism, he led us in singing "Oh, Freedom."

Strangers embraced tightly; some men and women wept

openly, choking on sobs; others laughed at the waves of spirit and the delicious tide of emotion.

Godfrey and I walked from Harlem to the Hudson River in near-silence. From time to time, he would throw his arm around my shoulder, or I would take his hand and squeeze it. We were confirming. We sat on a bench overlooking the sluggish water.

"So what's next? What are we going to do about it?" Godfrey beat me to the question and I had no answer. "We got to do something. Reverend King needs money. You know damn well we're not going down to Hang 'em High and let some cracker sheriff sap up on our heads. And we're not going to no Southern jail; so what are we going to do?"

He was asking the wind, the dark river and himself. I answered, "We could get some actors and singers and dancers together." Years before, Hollywood musicals had shown how young talented unknowns put on gloriously successful shows with no money, and although I over was thirty years old, I still believed in the youthful fantasy.

Godfrey said, "We can put on a show, maybe run it through the summer." When he grinned at our future success, he showed that he was as youthful and fanciful as I.

Godfrey had a friend, Hugh Hurd, an actor who knew everybody and had fabulous organizational skills. He would talk to Hugh. There were a lot of singers from *Porgy and Bess* who hadn't worked since the opera folded, and I agreed to talk to them.

It occurred to us that we should get permission from the people at the SCLC in order to raise money in their name. Godfrey said since I was the Christian, I ought to be the one to make the contact.

Within one hour our plans were laid. I would write a show, Godfrey would do a funny skit, and he and I would produce it. Hugh Hurd, if he agreed, would direct it. We would pay the performers and ourselves union scale, and all other monies would go to the SCLC. We had no idea where the show would be held, who would perform, how much we would charge or even whether the religious organization would welcome our intentions. There was a lot to do and we had to get started.

The SCLC offices were on 125th Street and Eighth Avenue in the center of Harlem. I had telephoned and made an appointment to speak to Bayard Rustin. When I walked up the dusty stairs to the second floor, I rehearsed the speech I had tried out on John Killens. "Mr. Rustin, I want to say first that not only do I and my colleague, Godfrey Cambridge, appreciate and laud the activities of Reverend Martin Luther King and the SCLC, we admire your own work in the field of race relations and human rights." John had told me that Bayard Rustin had led protest. marches in the United States during the forties, worked to better the condition of the untouchables in India, and was a member of the War Resisters' League. "We want to show our appreciation and support by putting on a show here in New York. A show which will highlight the meaning of the struggle and, at the same time, raise money for the Southern Christian Leadership Conference." He couldn't possibly refuse the offer.

At the head of the stairs, a receptionist, sitting behind a warped wooden desk, told me that Mr. Rustin had been called away on an emergency mission, but Stanley Levison would see me. I was stopped. Could I still use my speech? Levison sounded Jewish, but then John Levy and Billy Eckstein were black men with Jewish names.

The woman spoke on the telephone and then pointed to a door. "Mr. Levison will see you now."

He was short, stockily built, well dressed and white. I had come to talk to a black man about how I and Godfrey, also black, could help ourselves and other black people. What was there to say to a white man?

Stan Levison waited. His square face blank, his eyes direct, unapologetic.

I began. "I am a singer. That is, I was a singer, now I'm a writer. I want to be a writer . . ." My poise was gone and I hated myself.

How could I dream of confronting an entire country of bigots, when facing a lone white man threw me into confusion.

"Yes, and how can the SCLC help you?" He saw my indecision. In desperation, I leaped into my prepared speech. "I want to say first, that not only do I and my colleague, Godfrey Cambridge . . ."

"Oh the comedian, Cambridge. Yes, I've heard him." Levison leaned back in his chair.

". . . appreciate and support . . ." I cut out the part about Bayard Rustin and finished with "and raise money for the SCLC."

Levison moved forward. "Where will the play be shown?"

"Uh." Dammit, caught again. If only Bayard Rustin had been in the office, I could have counted on a few minutes during which he would thank me for realizing who he was, and appreciating what he had done.

"We don't have a theater yet, but we will have one. You can bet your life we will get one." Insecurity was making me angry.

"Let me call in someone. He's a writer and might be able to help you." He picked up the telephone. "Ask Jack Murray to step into the office, please." He hung up the phone and asked, with only a little interest, "And what do you know about the SCLC?"

"I was at church yesterday. I heard Dr. King."

"Oh yes. That was a great meeting. Unfortunately, we didn't take in the money we expected."

The door opened, and a little man wearing brown slacks and an open shirt and sports jacket walked in, in a hurry. "Jack Murray" had sounded black, but he was as white as Stanley Levison.

"Yeah, Stanley. What is it?"

Levison stood, and waving his arm in my direction, said, "This is Miss Angelou. Maya Angelou. She had an appointment with Bayard, but he was called away. She's got an idea. Maya, this is Jack. He also works with the SCLC."

I stood and offered my hand to Murray, and watched a little-boy's smile cross his middle-aged face.

"Glad to know you, Miss Angelou. What's your idea?"

I explained that we wanted to stage a play, a kind of revue, using whatever good talent available, and that we planned to develop the show on the theme of liberation.

Stanley Levison laughed for the first time. "I was right to call in Jack. Do you know anything about *Pins and Needles*?" I didn't, so he told me that Jack Murray had been involved with *Pins and Needles* in the thirties and it became a Broadway show, but based on the problems of the working class.

"Do you have a theater?" Again, I had to confess that we, my colleague and I, hadn't got that far.

"How large is the cast? How long do you need for rehearsal?" His tone was friendly, but if I admitted that so far our plans had only gone as far as an emotional conversation on the banks of the Hudson, the two white men would think me childish.

I said, "We have a number of actors and on-call singers. My friend is out making contacts." I blathered on about the need to keep the cast good, but small, so that there would be a substantial amount of money left over for the Southern Christian Leadership Conference.

When Jack Murray got a chance to speak, he repeated, "How long will you need for rehearsal?" I spoke the first thought that offered itself to me. "Two weeks."

Stanley coughed. "That's a very short rehearsal period, isn't it?"

I looked at him and he seemed as solid as a bank building. Maybe he was right. Two weeks might not be enough time, but my ego was at stake.

"We're going to use black entertainers. Professional people." It was my intention to stop the irritating interrogation and put the two white men back in the white race where they belonged.

Stanley cleared his throat and chuckled, "Oh, Miss Angelou, you're surely not trying to tell us that Negro entertainers don't need the same time as white entertainers because they are just naturally endowed with talent?"

That was exactly what I had said, and exactly what I meant. But it sounded wrong coming out of the mouth of a white man. Arrogance prevented me from retraction and was about to lead me into a corner from which there was no escape.

"Black entertainers have had to be ten times better than anyone else, historically . . ."

Jack Murray's voice floated softly into my tirade, "Miss Angelou, I assure you, you don't have to convert the converted. Historically, the exploited, the enslaved, the minority, has had to strive harder and be more qualified just in order to be considered in the running. Stanley and I understand that. That's why we are full-time volunteers at SCLC. Because we understand."

I was grateful that his words were apt and his voice soothing; in the next eighteen months I was to find myself frequently in debt to Jack Murray for throwing life lines to me as I floundered in seas of confusion or frustration.

"Do you know the Village Gate?" Every performer in the United States had heard of the Greenwich Village night club where Lenny Bruce, Nina Simone and Odetta might be found playing on the same night.

Murray said, "Art D'Lugoff owns it and he's an okay guy. He usually has a few unbooked days during the summer. After your plans are a little further along, maybe we could have a little meeting with Art. How soon do you expect to be ready?"

"All we needed was permission from your organization. We'll be ready in a few days. When can I see Mr. Rustin?"

There was something wrong with asking white men for permission to work for my own cause.

Levison looked at me and without answering, picked up the telephone. "Has Mr. Rustin come in? Good. Let me speak to him."

I waited while he continued. "Bayard, I've got a young woman in here who is going to put on a play to raise money for the organization . . . Right. She had an appointment. She's coming in to see you now."

I shook hands with both men and walked out of the office. Stanley Levison didn't say "wants to put on a play" but "is going to put on a play." An oblique permission, admittedly, but it was what I came for.

Bayard Rustin stood, shook my hand and welcomed me.

"Miss Angelou? Ah hum, sorry I wasn't here when you arrived. Stanley says you have a play. Have a seat. Care for coffee? Have you got money for your production? Cash? A theater? What is the play's message? While we at SCLC are grateful for all efforts, understandably what the play says or doesn't say can be of more importance than the money it raises. You understand that?" Words stepped out of his mouth sharply, fast, clipped in the accent of a British Army sergeant. He was tall, lean, dark brown and good-looking.

I explained again, revealing a little more to Bayard than I had to Stanley or Jack. Neither Godfrey nor I had any experience at producing a show, but we knew people and if the SCLC gave us the go-ahead, that's exactly what we would do. I added that Jack Murray had offered to intercede with Art D'Lugoff, and if that worked, we would use the Village Gate as a theater.

Bayard nodded and told me he'd have to see the script first and, if it was acceptable, the SCLC would approve and even lend us its mailing list.

The telephone rang before I could express my excited thanks. After speaking briefly into the receiver, he stood and offered his hand to me.

"Miss Angelou, an important call from Atlanta. Please excuse me. Get the script in to me as soon as possible. Thank you and good luck."

He was sitting back down even as we shook hands, his attention directed to the telephone.

I was out on the street. Burning to talk to Godfrey. We had permission, maybe we had a theater, we had the desire and the talent. Now all we needed was a cast, musicians and a script. I stopped on the corner of 125th Street. Hell, how did one write a script?

Godfrey brought Hugh to a diner on Broadway where we had scheduled our meeting. Hugh substantiated Godfrey's confidence; he acted efficient. His skin was the color of an unbroken coconut, and he looked just about as hard to crack.

His attitude was in contradiction to his youth, but Godfrey later explained to me that Hugh's parents, West Indians, also owned liquor stores, and Hugh had grown up coping with stock, greedy salesmen, shifty employees and drunken customers.

"Naturally," he "supported Martin Luther King. Any black man who didn't deserved to be thrown in an open ditch and covered with shit." Of course he would direct the show, but he needed absolute autonomy. Certainly he would work for scale and if things went well, he might contribute his salary to the SCLC, and where the hell was the script?

After a week, our plans were gelling. Godfrey had lined up actors. I telephoned singers and dancers, Hugh arranged with musicians, but we still had no script. I had sat late into the night trying to pick plots out of the air. We needed a story which had the complexity of *Hamlet* and the pertinence of *A Raisin in the Sun*. Facile ideas came swiftly and had to be discarded without regret. My characters had the predictability of a B cowboy movie and the naïveté of a Sunday School play.

Godfrey, Hugh and I met Jack Murray down at the Village Gate. Art D'Lugoff, reminding me of a tamed California bear, said we could use the theater on Sundays, Monday and Tuesday nights. We had to pay the lighting technician unless we furnished our own, but D'Lugoff would contribute the room free. By the way, what was the play about and could he see the script?

Guy had found a part-time job in a bakery near by, and dawns found him showering and dressing, and me sitting at a typewriter, constructing plot after unacceptable plot and characters so unreal they bored even me.

One morning, Guy stood looking over my shoulder at the blank page in the typewriter.

"Mom, you know, you might be trying too hard."

I turned quickly and blurted, "This is important. It's for Martin

L. King, for the SCLC, for black people everywhere. I can't possibly try too hard."

He stepped back, hurt by my brusqueness. "Well, I'm just reminding you of something you said all the time. 'If it don't fit, don't force it.' Bye, I'm going to work."

I hadn't spanked him since he was seven years old. Now that he was a tall fifteen-year-old the temptation to slap the water out of him was almost irresistible.

John Killens was expectedly sympathetic and, unfortunately, unhelpful. "You've got a theater and no cash, a cause and no play. Yep. Your work is cut out for you. Good luck. Keep trying."

Time and need had me in their clutches. Entertainers who had been contacted were calling Hugh or Godfrey every day; they in turn, telephoned me, asking when we could start auditions. I wasn't working, so at fifteen Guy was the only breadwinner. His money provided food, and John and Grace lent me money for rent so that I didn't have to touch my small savings account. I needed the American Guild of Variety Artists scale I would receive once the play was on.

Desperation had triumphed the day Godfrey stopped by my house. He had dropped off a fare in the next block and decided to ring my bell and see if I was in.

When I opened the door and saw his face, I started crying. He stepped into the foyer and took me in his arms.

"I've had women scream when they saw me, and some broads laugh when I come up on them all of a sudden, but I never had anybody break down and start crying." He was patting my shoulder. "You're a first, baby. I appreciate what you're doing. You're a first. Cry on. Cry your heart out. I'm enjoying this."

I had to laugh.

"No, keep on crying. I'll write you down in my diary. I've heard of women who cry when a man leaves, but you cry when . . ."

Laughter defeated my tears. I led him into the living room and went to the kitchen for coffee. I washed my face and composed myself. The tears had been as much a surprise to me as they were to Godfrey.

"Godfrey, I can't write the play. I don't even know where to start."

"Well, hell, you start with Act I, Scene I, same way Shakespeare started."

My throat hurt and tears began to well up behind my eyes.

"I can't write the damn thing. I've agreed to do something I can't do."

"Well, don't do it, then. Nobody's going to die if you don't write the damn play. Fact is, it might be better if you didn't write a word. There's a lot of people who would be grateful not to have to sit through one more bad play. Personally, I wish a lot of playwrights would have said just what you said. 'I can't write the damn thing.' " He laughed at himself.

"But what can we do? The SCLC is waiting. Art D'Lugoff is waiting. Hugh and the entertainers are ready. And I'm the bottleneck."

He drank the coffee and thought for a minute. "We'll let the entertainers do their acts. Most of them have been out of work so long, they'll jump quicker than a country girl at a hoedown. You don't have to write a play. If you've got a skit or two, you can give it to them. We'll do a cabaret kind of thing. That's all."

When I realized that Godfrey's idea was workable, the burden of tension left my body and for the first time in weeks I relaxed and my brain started to function.

"We could ask them for songs and dances and turns particularly black."

"The old Apollo routines. Something like Redd Foxx and Slappy White. You know: 'I'm Fox' and the other one says, 'I'm White,' then Foxx answers, 'You're either a fool or you're color blind.' "

The ideas were springing. There was no reason to worry. We would have a show. We would raise money. The reputation I didn't even have was not going to be ruined.

Godfrey looked at his watch. "Gotta go. Some fool without a dime in his pocket is waiting to get me to take him to the Bronx."

He got up. "This stop was okay. I helped a damsel in distress. Maybe my next fare will pay me in Canadian dimes."

We stood at the door and I looked at the rusted and dented taxi, illegally parked in front of my house.

"You could have got a ticket."

He said, "That would have been the only thing given to me today. You're okay now. We've got a show. A cabaret." He had the taxi door open.

I shouted, "We'll call it 'Cabaret for Freedom.' O.K.?"

"Yeah, that sounds serious. Entertaining and serious. Just what we ought to be. See you."

Straight out of the movies. We were the talented unknowns, who with only our good hearts, and those of our friends, would create a show which professional producers would envy. Our success would change the hearts of the narrow-minded and make us famous. We would liberate the race from bondage or maybe we would just go on and save the entire world.

At dress rehearsal, Guy and Chuck sat with me in the shadows of the Village Gate. Singers and dancers moved across the stage, making themselves familiar with the boards, and the microphone. Godfrey stood under the lights near the stage, and Hugh Hurd sat in the rear, clothed in the importance of being the director.

Jay "Flash" Riley started his comedy routine. His face and body jumped and skittered and his eyes opened and shut in rhythm; his lines were funny and unexpected, so the boys beside me howled in appreciation. Later a female singer, Leontyne Watts, sang a sultry, moaning song for a man loved and lost, and I identified with her song.

Although I had not really loved and lost, I was lonely and even missed the pedestrian love affair I left in Los Angeles. Godfrey and I were being molded into a friendship which had no room for romance. John Killens was concretely married; John Clarke had another interest and was, in any case, too hard for my liking. Sylvester Leeks had hugged me often, but never asked for my phone number. If I had the chance, I could moan some salty songs. I had been living with empty arms and rocks in my bed. I was only saved from utter abstinence by accidentally running into a musician who remembered me from my touring days. He lived on the Upper West Side and, once a week, I would visit his studio apartment. Because of the late hours of his job, he slept until after two. He told me he preferred me to catch him as he was waking. It kept him from having to make up the sofa twice and take two showers in the same day. I always left satisfied, so I was glad to oblige. We were not only not in love and just slightly in like, our weekly ferocious rendezvous stopped just short of doing each other bodily harm.

5

On opening night, customers took every seat in the cavernous Village Gate. The Harlem Writers Guild members, their families and friends had arrived, and after wishing me luck, took seats near the stage. I imagined them, after the house lights dimmed, taking copious and critical notes in the dark. John and Grace Killens filled tables with their famous friends. Sidney and Juanita Poitier and Danny Barajanos, Lorraine Hansberry, Bob Nemiroff, Ossie Davis and Ruby Dee, an editor from the *Amsterdam News,* New York's black newspaper, a Brooklyn lawyer and a few politicians from Harlem.

Backstage the cast assembled, nervous over the presence of celebrities and excited with the expected opening night jitters. Bayard Rustin spoke to the performers in his tight, clipped voice, explaining the importance of the project and thanking them for their art and generosity. Godfrey made jokes about the opportunity to work, to be paid, and to do some good, all at the same time. I quoted Martin Luther King, "Truth dashed to earth shall rise again," and then Hugh Hurd asked us to leave so that he could give his cast a last-minute pep talk.

The show began and the performers, illuminated with the spirit, hit the stage and blazed. Comfortable with the material of their own routines, comedians made the audience howl with pleasure and singers delighted the listeners with familiar romantic songs. The revue, which is what the show had become, moved quickly until a scene from Langston Hughes's *The Emperor of Haiti* brought the first note of seriousness. Hugh Hurd, playing the title role, reminded us all that although as black people we had a dignity and a love of life, those qualities had to be defended constantly.

Orson Bean, the only white actor in the cast, shuffled up to the microphone and began what at first seemed a rambling remembrance. In minutes, the audience caught his point and laughed in appreciation. Leontyne Watts sang a cappella, "Sometimes I Feel Like a Motherless Child," and everyone knew that the words meant that oppression had made orphans of black Americans and forced us to live as misfits in the very land we had helped to build.

The entire cast stood in a straight line and sang "Lift every voice and sing . . ."

The audience stood in support and respect. Those who knew the lyrics joined in, building and filling the air with the song often called "The Negro National Anthem."

After the third bow, Godfrey hugged me and whispered, "We've got a hit. A hit, damn, a hit."

Hugh Hurd said, "He's standing up out there."

Godfrey said, "Hell, man, everybody who's got feet is standing up."

Hugh said, "Aw, man. I know that. I mean Sidney. Sidney Poitier is standing up on the table." A few of us rushed to the sidelines, but were unable to see through the crush of people still crowding toward the stage.

The next afternoon, Levison, Godfrey, Hugh, Jack Murray and I met in Art D'Lugoff's office. We sat tall on the dilapidated chairs, proud of the success of Cabaret for Freedom.

Art said that not only could we use his night club without

charge for five weeks, he would make his mailing list available. Stanley accepted the offer but said unfortunately there was no one in the SCLC office to take advantage of it. The small paid staff was swamped with organizational work, sending out direct-mail appeals, and promoting appearances of visiting Southern ministers. That was unfortunate because the mailing list included people out in Long Island and up in New Rochelle. People who wouldn't ordinarily hear of our revue, but who would support it and maybe even make contributions to SCLC if they could be contacted. Godfrey, Hugh and I looked at each other. Three white men were willing to lay themselves out for our cause and all I was ready to do was sing and dance, or at best, encourage others to sing and dance. The situation was too historic for my taste. My people had used music to soothe slavery's torment or to propitiate God, or to describe the sweetness of love and the distress of lovelessness, but I knew no race could sing and dance its way to freedom.

"I'll take care of it." I spoke with authority.

Stanley allowed a little surprise into his voice. "Are you volunteering? We can't afford to pay a salary, you know."

Hugh said, "I'll help any way I can." He understood that we just couldn't let the white men be the only contributors.

Godfrey smiled. "And, you know, me too."

Jack said, "You'll have to draft a release and you can type it on stencils. We've got a mimeograph machine in the office."

Stanley continued, "We can provide paper and envelopes, but you'll have to address the envelopes by hand. Some of the money you've already made can be used for postage. We can't use the franking machine for your project, I'm sorry, but we'll be glad to help you."

I had no idea of how to work a mimeograph machine, nor did I know what a stencil or franker was. The only thing I had understood, and which I knew I could do was address envelopes by hand. Again, and as damn usual, I had opened my mouth a little too wide.

69

Art shook hands and told me to pick up the mailing list the next day at a midtown address.

Outside in the afternoon sunshine, Stanley and Jack thanked us all again, and said they'd see me the next day. They hailed a taxi.

Godfrey, Hugh and I went to a bar across the street. Hugh said, "You were right, girl. I was proud of you and you know I meant what I said. I'll be up there to help whenever I can."

"Yeah." Godfrey paid for the drinks. "But you got to understand. I'm not going to address no envelopes. If I did, my handwriting is so bad, the post office would send the mail to the Library of Congress for framing and posterity. I'll drive you anywhere you want to go. I'll help you stuff the envelopes and I'll come over to your house and have dinner."

I told them I had never worked a mimeograph machine. Hugh asked if I could type a stencil. When I admitted that my two-finger typing had been limited to an occasional letter, they looked at me with wry alarm.

"You've got a hell of a lot of nerve. You volunteered to 'take care of it' and you don't know shit." Hugh spoke more with admiration than anger.

"She knows she's got to do it. Come hell or the Great Wall of China. She's got to do it. I'm betting on you, kid." Godfrey called out to the bartender, "Play it again, Sam. For my buddies and me."

I wrote a simple announcement of Cabaret for Freedom listing the actors, the producers and the director. The mimeograph machine was much simpler than I expected. I took Guy to the office with me the first day, and he explained how the machine worked. The stencils were a little more complicated, but after a while, I realized that all I had to do was take my time, admittedly a lot of time, typing the script. Soon Godfrey was taking hundreds of envelopes to the morning and afternoon post.

The Village Gate filled to capacity to see our revue. The actors were happy and after they were paid, some took bills from their pockets, offering the money to the SCLC.

"Did a gig last week. King needs this five dollars more than I do."

"I put my money where my mouth is. It's not much but . . ."

Time, opportunity and devotion were in joint. Black actors, bent under the burden of unemployment and a dreary image of cinematic and stage Uncle Tom characterizations, had the chance to refute the reflection and at the same time, work toward the end of discrimination.

After Cabaret for Freedom, they would all be employed by suddenly aware and respectful producers. After Martin Luther King won freedom for us all, they would be paid honorable salaries and would gain the media coverage that their talents deserved.

"Give me that check. I'm going to sign it over to the SCLC. I'm sticking this week."

It was the awakening summer of 1960 and the entire country was in labor. Something wonderful was about to be born, and we were all going to be good parents to the welcome child. Its name was Freedom.

Then, too soon, summer and the revue closed. The performers went back to the elevator-operating or waiting-on-tables jobs they had interrupted. A few returned to unemployment or welfare lines. No one was hired as a leading actor in a major dramatic company nor as a supporting actor in a small ensemble, or even as a chorus member in an Off-Off-Broadway show. Godfrey was still driving his beat-up cab, Hugh continued to work split shifts in his family's liquor stores, and I was broke again. I had learned how to work office machines, and how to hold a group of fractious talented people together, but a whole summer was gone; I was out of work and Guy needed school clothes.

During the revue's run, Guy had been free to spend his part-time salary on summer entertainment. He and Chuck Killens spent fortunes at Coney Island. They pursued the mysteries of pinball machines and employed the absence of adults to indulge in every hot-dog and spun-sugar fantasy of childhood.

Although Godfrey collected me when he could and took me to

Harlem or delivered me back to Brooklyn, the money used for other transportation and the lunches at Franks on 125th ate away at my bankroll. Rent was due again.

Grossman, a night-club owner from Chicago, phoned. Would I be interested in singing in his new club, the Gate of Horn? I kept the relief out of my voice with great effort. Two weeks at a salary which would pay two months' rent and pay for Guy's back-to-school clothes.

After I accepted the offer, with secret but abject gratitude, I began to wonder what to do with Guy.

Grace and John offered to let him stay at their house, but Guy wouldn't hear of that. He had a home. He was a man. Well, nearly, and he could look after himself. I was not to worry about him. Just go and work and return safely.

I called a phone number advertised in the Brooklyn black newspaper. Mrs. Tolman answered. I explained that I wanted someone who would come for three hours a day in the afternoon. Just cook dinner for my fifteen-year-old, clean the kitchen and make up his room.

I diminished her reluctance by saying that I was a woman alone, raising a boy, and that I had to go away for two weeks to work. I asked her over to the house to see how respectful my son was. I implied that he was well raised but didn't say that outright. If I was lucky, when I returned from Chicago, she'd use those words herself.

Despite the harshness of their lives, I have always found that older black women are paragons of generosity. The right plea, arranged the right way, the apt implication, persuade the hungriest black woman into sharing her last biscuit.

When I told Mrs. Tolman that if I didn't take the job in Chicago, I wouldn't be able to pay my rent or buy shoes for my son, she said, "I'll take the job, chile. And I'm going to take your word that you've got a good boy."

Convincing Guy that we needed a housekeeper demanded at least as much finesse. After I told him about Mrs. Tolman, I waited quietly for the minutes he needed to explain how well he could look after himself and how she was going to get in the way and how well he could cook and that he wouldn't eat a bite of her food and after all, what did I think he was? A little baby? And "Oh please, Mother, this is really boring."

"Guy, Mrs. Tolman is coming because of the neighborhood. I've been looking at it very carefully."

Against his will, he was interested.

"I'm convinced that a few professional burglars live down the street. Too much new furniture going in and out of the house. If those people don't see an adult around here, they may take advantage of the hours when you're away and clean us out."

He got caught in the excitement of the possibility of crime.

"You think so? Which people? Which house?"

"I'd rather not point the finger without knowing for sure. But I've been watching closely. Mrs. Tolman will come around three, she'll be gone by six. Since she's going to be here, she'll cook dinner for you and wash your clothes. But that's a front. She's really here to make the burglars think our house is always occupied."

He accepted the contrived story.

John understood Guy's display of independence, and told me it was natural. He urged me to go to Chicago, sing, make the money and come home to New York where I belonged. He would keep an eye on my son.

The modest Gate of Horn on Chicago's Near North Side was located only a few blocks from the plush Mr. Kelly's. The Gate had in warmth what Mr. Kelly's had in elegance. I arrived in the middle of the Clancy Brothers' rehearsal. Mike was at the microphone checking the sound system.

"Is this loud enough" Too loud? Can you hear us or are we blowing the ass back out of the room?"

The Irish accent was as palpable as mashed potatoes and rich as lace.

73

After the sound was adjusted, the brothers and Tommy Makem sang for their own enjoyment. Their passion matched the revolutionary lyrics of their songs.

> ". . . The shamrock is forbid by law
> to grow on Irish ground."

If the words Negro and America were exchanged for shamrock and Irish, the song could be used to describe the situation in the United States.

The Clancy Brothers already had my admiration when we met backstage.

Amanda Ambrose, Oscar Brown, Jr., and Odetta came to opening night. We sat together and made joyful noises as the Irish singers told their stories.

The two weeks sped by, punctuated by telephone calls to Guy, who was understandably "doing just fine," and to John Killens, who said everything was smooth. Oscar Brown and I spent long afternoons volleying stories. He was writing a play, *Kicks & Co.*, for Broadway and I bragged that I had just come from a successful run of Cabaret for Freedom, which I partly wrote and co-produced.

We set each other afire with anger and complimented ourselves on our talent. We were meant for great things. The size and power of our adversaries were not greater than our capabilities. If we admitted that slavery and its child, legal discrimination, were declarations of war, then Oscar and I and all our friends were generals in the army and we would be among the officers who accepted the white flag of surrender when the battle was done. Amanda's husband, Buzz, inspired by the fever of protest, made clothes for me based on African designs. Odetta, newly married, and radiant with love, was off to Canada. Before she left she gave me an afternoon of advice. "Keep on telling the truth, Maya. Stay on the stage. I don't mean the night-club stage, or the theatrical stage. I mean on the stage of life." And my Lord she was beautiful.

74

"And remember this, hon, don't you let nobody turn you 'round. No body. Not a living ass."

Closing night had been a hilarious celebration. The Clancy Brothers' fans had found room to accept my songs, and the black people who had come to hear me had been surprised to find that not only did they enjoy the Irish singers' anger, they understood it. We had drunk to each other's resistance.

The next morning Oscar stood with me in the hotel lobby as I waited to pay my bill.

A uniformed black man came up to me.

"Miss Angelou? There's a phone call for you from New York."

Oscar said he'd keep my place in the line and I went to the phone.

"Maya?" John Killens' voice was a spike, pinning me in place. "There's been some trouble."

"Trouble?" Somewhere behind my kneecaps there was a place that waited for trouble. "Is Guy all right?" The dread, closer than a seer's familiar, which lived sucking off my life, was that something would happen to my only son. He would be stolen, kidnapped by a lonely person who, seeing his perfection, would be unable to resist. He would be struck by an errant bus, hit by a car out of control. He would walk a high balustrade, showing his beauty and coordination to a girl who was pretending disinterest. His foot would slip, his body would fold and crumple, he would fall fifty feet and someone would find my telephone number. I would be minding my own business and a stranger would call me to the phone.

"Hello?"

A voice would say, "There's been trouble."

My nightmare never went further. I never knew how serious the accident was, or my response. And now real life pushed itself through the telephone.

"Guy is okay." John Killens' voice sounded as if it came from farther than New York City. "He's here with us. I'm just calling to tell you not to go to your house. Come straight here." Oh, the house burned down. "Was there a fire? Is anything left?" I had no insurance.

"There wasn't a fire. Don't worry. Just come to my house when your plane arrives. I'll tell you when you get here. It's nothing serious." He hung up.

Oscar Brown was at my side. His green eyes stern. He put his hand on my shoulder.

"You O.K.?"

"That was John Killens. Something's happened."

"Is Guy O.K.? What was it?"

"Guy's O.K., but John wouldn't say."

"Well, hell, that's a bitch, ain't it? Calling up saying something's wrong and not saying . . ." He went over and picked up my bags.

"You pay your bill, I'll bring the car to the front door."

The drive to the airport was an adventure in motoring and a lesson in conversational dissembling. Oscar made erratic small talk, driving with one hand, leaning his car around corners, passing motorists with such speed that our car threatened to leave the road entirely. His chatter was constantly interrupted with "Guy's O.K. Now, remember that." He would turn to look at me. Fixing a stare so intense it seemed hypnotic. Noticing that he was conducting a car, he would swivel his head occasionally and give a moment's attention to the road.

At the airport, he held me close and whispered. "Everything's going to be O.K., little mother. Call me. I'll be at home waiting."

I dreaded the flight. Afraid that I would begin to cry and lose control. Afraid that the plane would crash and I would not be around to look after Guy and take care of the unknown problem.

"Well, and isn't it the wonder of Maya?" The accent was unmistakable. I raised up and looked in the seat behind me. Mike Clancy was grinning over a glass of whiskey with Pat next to him. Liam and Tommy were seated across the aisle.

"You thought you could lose us, did you? Never, little darling. We have sworn to follow you to the ends of the earth. How's about a tipple to cinch the agreement."

I said I'd order something when the stewardess came around.

There was no need to wait. Mike had prepared against the eventuality of a stingy attendant or a plane run by teetotalers. He reached under the seat and when he straightened up, he was holding a bottle of whiskey. Pat pulled a glass from the pocket of the seat in front of him.

Mike said, "If you insist on frivolities such as ice and water, you'll wait until the serving lady comes. If not, I'll start pouring now and you tell me when to stop."

I didn't wait.

The trip was riotous. Many passengers were incensed that four white men and a black woman were laughing and drinking together, and their displeasure pushed us toward silliness. I asked Liam to translate a Gaelic song that I had heard him sing a cappella. He said he'd sing it first.

His clear tenor floated up over the heads of the already-irate passengers. The haunting beauty of the melody must have quelled some of the irritation, because no one asked Liam to shut up.

Mike tried in vain to start conversations with two stone-grey men who sat behind him, but they retained their granite aloofness.

As the plane landed in New York, we sang a rousing chorus of "The Wearing of the Green."

The Clancys offered to share a taxi into the city, but I said I was going to Brooklyn.

Brooklyn and Guy. My heart dropped and I sobered. The company and the drink had erased Guy and the problem from my mind.

I thanked them and got into a taxi with my bags and a load of new guilt.

What a poor kind of mother I was. Drinking and laughing it up with a group of strangers, white men at that, while my son was in some kind of trouble.

When the taxi arrived at John's house, I was abject as well as apprehensive.

Grace hugged me and smiled. "Welcome home, Maya." Her

smile told me things couldn't be too bad. Mom Willie called from the dining room, "That her?" I answered and she walked into the foyer. She was looking serious and shaking her head. Her look and gesture said, "Well, boys will be boys, and that's life." That was a relief. I asked where Guy was. Grace said he was upstairs in Chuck's room but John wanted to speak to me first.

Mom Willie gave me coffee as John explained what happened. A group of boys had threatened Guy and John heard about it and decided Guy would be safer at his house until I returned.

I nearly laughed aloud. Only a disagreement among kids.

John continued, "The boys are a gang called the Savages. They killed a boy last month, and as he lay in the funeral home, the Savages went in and stabbed the body thirty-five times."

Oh my God.

"They terrorize everybody. Even the cops are scared of that bunch. When I heard that Guy had offered to fight them, I drove over to your house and got him. He didn't want to go. He had stuck all your butcher knives in the curtain at your door and told me he was waiting for them to come back. I said, 'Boy you'd better get your butt in this car.' I told the woman downstairs to tell the gang, when they came back, that his uncle came to get him."

Mom Willie spoke first. "Well, honey, raising boys in this world is more than a notion. Ask me about it. While they're young, you pray you can feed them and keep them in school. They get up some size and you pray some crazy white woman don't scream rape around them and get them lynched. They come of age and white men call them up to go fight, and you pray they don't get killed over there fighting some white folks' war. Naw. Raising a black boy makes you sit down and think."

John had respectfully waited for his mother to finish her remembrances. "I'll get Guy now." He went to the stairs and called, "Guy, come down. Your mother's here."

I heard the heavy steps rushing down the stairs and I wanted to stand, but my body wouldn't obey. Guy bounded into the kitchen and the sight of him brought tears to my eyes.

"Hi, Mom. How was the trip?" He bent down and kissed my cheek. "Gee, it's great to have you home." He read my face and stopped smiling. "Oh, I guess Mr. Killens told you about the little incident. Well, it wasn't really serious, you know." He patted my shoulder as if he were the reassuring parent, and I the upset child.

"What happened, Guy? How did you get involved with a gang like that? What—"

"I'll discuss that with you. Privately, please." He was back on his dignity, and I couldn't deflate him. Whatever the story, I had to wait until we were alone.

John understood and said he'd drop us off at home. Guy shook his head. "Thanks, Mr. Killens. We'll walk." He turned to me. "Where are your bags, Mom?"

I nodded toward the entry and he walked away.

Grace said, "He wants to be a man so much, my God. It would be funny if it wasn't so serious."

John said, "Everything in this society is geared to keeping a black boy from growing to manhood. You've got to let him try for himself."

I joined Guy at the door and we said good night to the Killens.

We walked through the dark streets, and as Guy asked about Oscar Brown and other Chicago friends, I saw phantoms of knife-wielding boys jumping from behind trees, hiding behind cars, waiting in gloomy doorways.

I asked Guy to tell me about the incident, adding that Brooklyn was more dangerous than New York City. He said, "Let's wait till we get home. But I'll tell you this, Mother." A pronouncement was on its way. "I don't want you to think about moving. I'm living here and I have to walk these streets. If we moved, the same thing could happen and then we'd move again. I'm not going to run. 'Cause once you do, you have to keep on running."

We walked the rest of the way in silence.

He made a pot of coffee for me and I sat waiting until he was ready to talk.

We sat opposite each other in the living room and I tried to keep serenity on my face and my hand on the coffee cup.

It had all begun with the housekeeper. One day, the week before, Mrs. Tolman had brought her granddaughter to our house. Susie was fifteen, cute and eager. She and Guy talked while Mrs. Tolman cooked and cleaned. The next day Susie came back with her grandmother. Again the teenagers talked and this time they played records. On the third morning, Susie came alone. They played records and, this time, they danced together in the living room. Susie said she liked Guy, really liked him. Guy told her that he was already dating a girl but that he appreciated Susie's honesty. She became angry and Guy explained that he and his girl friend didn't cheat on each other. Susie said Guy was stuck-up and thought he was cute. They had an argument and Guy put her out of the house.

I wondered if he meant he had asked her to go. He said no. He walked to the door and opened it and *told* her to get out.

He continued explaining that today when the bell rang, he opened the door and a fellow about eighteen was standing there. He said his name was Jerry and he was Susie's boyfriend. He said he was the chief of the Savages and he had just heard that Guy had hit Susie. Guy told him that was a lie. He balled up his fist and said, "If I ever hit anybody with this, no one has to ask if I hit them." He went on to explain to Jerry that Susie was angry because of a little run-in they had. He told Jerry to remember the old line about a woman scorned. Jerry had never heard the phrase and told Guy that he and his friends would be back in the afternoon and Guy could explain it then.

As soon as Jerry left the doorstep, Guy called Chuck Killens and told him about his visitors and asked him to come over and bring his baseball bat. He then went to the kitchen and gathered all my knives and placed them strategically in the lace curtain at the front door. He figured that with Chuck swinging the bat, and him parrying with a large knife and a cleaver, they could hold off at least eight of the Savages.

When I asked if he had heard of the gang before, he answered, "Everybody knows the Savages; a few of them even go to my school."

"How large is the gang?"

"Only fifteen active members. But when they have a rumble, they can get about thirty together."

And this crazy young army was threatening my son. He saw my concern.

"I'll handle it, Mom. We're going to live here and I'm going to walk the streets whenever I want to. Nobody's going to make me run. I am a man."

He kissed me good night and picked up the coffee cup. I heard him moving in the kitchen. In a few seconds, his bedroom door closed, and I remained, glued to my chair in the living room. After an hour or so, the bloody pictures of my son's mutilated body began to disappear. I went to the kitchen and filled the ice bucket, got a pitcher of water and the Scotch bottle. I brought my collection to the living room and sat down.

First I had to understand the thinking of the Savages. They were young black men, preying on other young black men. They had been informed, successfully, that they were worthless, and everyone who looked like them was equally without worth. Each sunrise brought a day without hope and each evening the sun set on a day lacking in achievement. Whites, who ruled the world, owned the air and food and jobs and schools and fair play, had refused to share with them any of life's necessities—and somewhere, deeper than their consciousness, they believed the whites were correct. They, the black youth, young lords of nothing, were born without value and would creep, like blinded moles, their lives long in the darkness, under the earth, chewing on roots, driven far from the light.

I understood the Savages. I understood and hated the system which molded them, but understanding in no wise licensed them to vent their frustration and anger on my son. Guy would not countenance a move to safer ground. And if I insisted, without his agreement, I could lose his friendship and thereby his love. I wouldn't risk that; yet something had to be done to contain the lawless brood of alienated teenagers.

As the sun's first soft light penetrated the curtains, I telephoned my musician lover in Manhattan. I told him quickly what had happened and what I needed. I had awakened him, but he heard my need and said he'd get up and be at my house in an hour or less.

He stood in the doorway, refusing my invitation to come in for coffee. He handed me a small box, a big grin, and wished me luck. Guy arose, showered, dressed, had a glass of milk, refusing breakfast. He ran out of the house, to warm up before a morning basketball game. He seemed to have forgotten that the Savages were out to get him. I calmed my fears by telling myself that fellows like the Savages were mostly night creatures, and that in the early mornings the streets were at their safest.

At nine o'clock, I telephoned Mrs. Tolman and told her I'd like to come over and pay her. She said she'd be waiting.

I took the pistol out of its fitted box and slipped it in my purse. The three blocks between our houses were peopled with workers en route to jobs, men washing cars and children running and screaming in such normal ways. I felt I had gone mad and was living in another dimension, removed totally from the textured world around me. I was invisible.

Mrs. Tolman introduced me to her buxom daughter, who was breast-nursing a baby. The woman said yes when I asked if she was also Susie's mother.

I gave Mrs. Tolman cash, counting out the bills carefully, using the time to pacify my throat so that my voice would be natural.

"Mrs. Tolman, is Susie here?"

"Why, yes. They just got up. I heard them laughing in her room."

Mrs. Tolman was happy to oblige.

Susie stood in the doorway leading to the kitchen. Her face was still sultry from sleep and she was pretty. If I had been lucky enough to have a second child, she could have been my daughter.

"Susie, I've heard about you, and I'm happy to meet you."

"Yeah," she mumbled, not too interested. "Nice to meet you too." I caught her as she was turning to go.

"Susie, your boyfriend is Jerry?" She perked up a little. "Yeah, Jerry's my boyfriend."

Mrs. Tolman giggled. "I'll tell the world."

"Where does he live? Jerry."

"He lives down the street. In the next block." She was pouting again, uninterested.

I spoke again, fast, collecting her thoughts.

"I have something for him. Can we go together to his house?" She smiled for the first time. "He's not there. He's in my room."

Her mother chuckled. "Seem like that's where he lives."

"Could he come out? I'd like to have a few words with him."

"O.K." She was a sweet play pretty, in her baby-doll shortie nightgown and her hair brushed out around her face.

I sat with only a silly smile, looking at the nursing mother and the old woman who was pressing out the money in her lap.

"Here he is. This is Jerry." A young man stood with Susie in the doorway. A too-small T-shirt strained its straps against his brown shoulders. His pants were unbuttoned and he was barefoot. I took in his total look in a second, but the details of his face stopped and held me beyond my mission. His eyes were too young for hate. They glinted with promise. When he smiled, a mouthful of teeth gleamed. I jerked myself away from enchantment.

"Jerry. I'm Miss Angelou. I'm Guy's mother." He closed his lips and the smile died.

"I understand that you are the head of the Savages and you have an arrangement with my son. I also understand that the police are afraid of you. Well, I came 'round to make you aware of something. If my son comes home with a black eye or a torn shirt, I won't call the police."

His attention followed my hand to my purse. "I will come over here and shoot Susie's grandmother first, then her mother, then I'll blow away that sweet little baby. You understand what I'm saying? If the Savages so much as touch my son, I will then find your house and kill everything that moves, including the rats and cockroaches."

I showed the borrowed pistol, then slid it back into my purse.

For a second, none of the family moved and my plans had not gone beyond the speech, so I just kept my hand in the purse, fondling my security.

Jerry spoke, "O.K., I understand. But for a mother, I must say you're a mean motherfucker. Come on, Susie." They turned and, huddling together, walked toward the rear of the house.

I spent a few more minutes talking to Mrs. Tolman about the trip and the weather.

We parted without mentioning my son, her granddaughter or my trim Baretta, which lay docile at the bottom of my purse.

Guy brought afternoon heat into the house along with gym clothes for the laundry. He was grinning.

"We won the game. I made ten shots." I acted interested. "I'm getting pretty good. Coach says I'm among his best athletes." He feinted and jumped.

"Good, dear. Oh, by the way, did you see any of the Savages at school?"

He stopped dribbling an imaginary ball and looked at me, surprised, as if I had asked if he had seen an extraterrestrial.

"Yeah. Sure I saw the guys this morning. I walked to school with some of the members. We talked." He started toward his room, protecting his masculine secrecy.

"Excuse me, but please tell me what you talked about. I'd really like to know."

"Aw, Mom." He was embarrassed. "Aw, I just made up something. I said my gang in California always fought to the death, but never on hearsay. And I said I'd meet him and one other person on neutral ground. With knives or fire or anything. I said I wasn't about to run. I told you, Mom, that I'd handle it." He grinned. "What's for dinner?"

I had to laugh. He was definitely my son, and following my footsteps, bluffing all the way.

I had only threatened the young vultures hovering over my son; Guy had offered to literally fight fire with fire. Fortunately we were believed—because maybe neither of us was bluffing.

Revolución had accepted my short story. That it would appear only in Cuba, and probably in Spanish, did not dilute the fact that I was joining the elite group of published writers. The Harlem Writers Guild celebrated. Rosa Guy, a founding member, who had been in Trinidad when I joined the group, had returned and offered her house for the week's reading and a party in my honor.

Rosa was tall, beautiful, dark-brown and fiery. She danced, argued, shouted, laughed with an exciting singleness of mind. We were alike in boldness and fell quickly into a close friendship. She had been born in Trinidad, and although she had lived in New York City since she was seven years old, her speech retained a soft Caribbean slur.

6

I made my way through the busy streets of Harlem, dressed in my best and wearing just enough make-up. Along the way, I received approval from lounging men or passers-by.

"Hey, baby. Let me go with you."

"Oowee, sugar. You look good to me."

"Let me be your little dog, till your big dog come."

I smiled and kept walking. The compliments helped to straighten my back and put a little swing to my hips, and I needed the approval.

I was en route to the SCLC to meet Bayard Rustin. I had seen him a few times at fund-raising parties since the closing of Cabaret for Freedom, but we had not had a private meeting since the first time in the organizational offices, and I imagined a thousand reasons why I had been asked to return.

The receptionist told me Mr. Rustin was waiting. He stood up and leaned over the crowded desk, offering me his hand.

"Maya, thank you for coming. Have a seat. I'll call Stan and Jack."

I sat and ran through my mind all the possibilities. There was a discrepancy in the figures from Cabaret for Freedom. They wanted me to produce another revue. They wanted me to write a play about Martin Luther King and the struggle. They didn't know I couldn't type, so they were going to offer me a job as secretary. They needed volunteers and . . .

Stan and Jack came in smiling (that could mean that the receipts had been O.K., but I wasn't sure).

We all shook hands, exchanged the expected small greetings and sat down.

Bayard said, "You speak first, Stanley."

Stan Levison cleared nonexistent phlegm from his throat. "Uh, Maya, you know we're proud and pleased at the way you handled Cabaret for Freedom."

Jack interrupted. "The content was brilliant. Just brilliant. The performers . . ."

Stanley harrumphed and continued, "We think you've got administrative talent." He looked at Bayard.

Just as I thought. I was going to be offered a typing job.

Bayard spoke. "We are going to have a shift in the organization and we're going to need someone, a trustworthy person, reliable, and someone who knows how to get along with people." He looked over at Jack.

It was Jack's turn. "We watched how you dealt with that cast. You kept order; and if anybody knows, I know the egos of actors. You never raised your voice, but when you did speak everyone respected what you had to say."

He nodded to Stanley, who began to speak immediately.

"You understand what the struggle is about. You did say you grew up in the South, didn't you?"

I nodded. Stamps, Arkansas, with its dust and hate and narrow-ness was as South as it was possible to get.

"We are sorry to say that Bayard is going to be leaving the SCLC."

I looked at Bayard. His long, handsome face was lined, and his eyes appeared troubled.

Oh, he was sick. He had to be sick to leave an organization he loved so dearly and had worked for so diligently. I was so saddened by my speculation that I did not connect Bayard's leaving and my invitation to the office.

"I'm going for a short rest." Distance was already in Bayard's voice, confirming my assessment. "And I'll be joining A. Phillip Randolph and the Brotherhood of Sleeping Car Porters." His face said he was already there.

I said, "I'm sorry to hear that, Bayard. Is there anything I can do?"

"Yes." Bayard was back with us, connected again to the office conversation. "We're looking around for someone to take my place. I suggested that you were capable."

Only shock, which held me viselike, prevented me from jump-ing and running out of the office and down the street. Take Bayard Rustin's place. He had worked for the Quakers, led march-es in Washington, D.C., during the forties, had been to India and worked with the Untouchables. He was educated, famous, and he was a man.

I didn't say anything because I couldn't speak.

Stanley said, "When Bayard came up with your name, we were quite surprised. But we've thought about it and come to an agreement. You're the person we would all like to run the office."

Jack nodded a slight happy smile to me.

Bayard said, "The position that's being offered to you, Maya, is coordinator for the SCLC. Of course, that's a little like an umbrella. Many chores fall under its spread."

I blurted out stupidly, "I can't type."

The men laughed, and I could have kicked myself for giving them the chance to patronize me.

Jack said, "You'll have a secretary to do your typing." He laughed again. "And answer your telephone."

Stanley said, "Now, let's talk salary. You know the SCLC is in need of money and always will be, so we are able to pay only a living wage."

I was torn. I could think of nothing more gratifying than to work for Martin Luther King, and the Lord knew I needed a living wage. But maybe bodaciousness was leading me to a dangerous height where I'd find breathing difficult. And another nagging uneasiness intruded upon my excitement: Suppose I was being used to force Bayard out of his position.

I gathered myself and stood. "Gentlemen, thank you. I am honored by your invitation. I'd like to think about it. I'll telephone you tomorrow." And I was out the door, down the stairs and back to the safety of Harlem streets.

John Killens agreed to meet me at a downtown hotel where he had taken a room to do a rewrite. We sat in the hotel dining room.

"If you feel that way, call Bayard. Ask him directly. He's a man. Personally, I don't believe he'd have suggested you if he didn't want you to take the job."

"All right, but what is a coordinator? Can I do it? I'd rather not try than try and fail."

"That's stupid talk, Maya. Every try will not succeed. But if you're going to live, live at all, your business is trying. And if you fail once, so what? Old folks say, Every shuteye ain't sleep and every goodbye ain't gone. You fail, you get up and try again."

He could talk, he was already a success. I wasn't convinced.

"Anyway, coordinator is a nice way of saying fund-raiser. You'll be putting on affairs and sending out mailing lists and speaking and arranging speaking engagements to raise money. There's no mystery to that. And if you're not going to sing again 'ever in life', then this sounds like your best bet."

Bayard met me between appointments. "If you take the position or if you refuse it, I'm leaving. Understand now, I will always support Martin. Even with my life. But it's time for a move."

He stood beside my barstool at Frank's Restaurant on 125th Street. "I've worked with Randolph for many years and he wants to build a new organization for union workers. I'm not leaving the war, just joining another battle. Take it. You'll do a good job." He patted my shoulder and walked out, taking his mystery and leaving me still not quite decided.

I heard on the morning radio that some black youngsters had sat down at a dining-room counter in North Carolina and that Martin was in jail again. The telephones rang constantly and the office swirled with activity. Hazel Grey, who had come to work as my assistant, was allotting chores to volunteers as I walked in. She looked up from her desk.

"Maya, the printing returned and a bunch of kids from Long Island are coming over this morning to stuff envelopes."

"Good." I walked into my office. Hazel followed. "They're coming from an all-white school."

"Why? Who invited them and how old are they?"

"High school students. Boys and girls. Their counselor called; he's coming with them." That white youngsters were going to brave Harlem was in itself startling, but that a white adult, in a responsible position, not only agreed, but was willing to officiate in the unusual situation was befuddling. It looked as if the world that would never change was changing.

I had a brief meeting with the black volunteers.

"You're going to have some help in an hour or two with jobs you've been unable to complete."

A grandmother from a local church said, "Bless the Lord."

I went on, "Thirty young people are on their way, and we have to decide on how they can help us. We may not have this opportunity again. Now, you tell me what needs to be done."

"The mimeograph machine needs to be moved away from the window. The sunshine is melting the ink."

89

"I wish somebody would take all that junk out of the back office."

"Somebody ought to file that stack of papers in the hall."

"We need the steps cleaned. Don't look right to come to Martin Luther King's office and have to walk up dirty steps."

The counselor looked like an old Burgess Meredith. He was dressed in grey and looked as grey as a winter sky. His casualness was studied and his contrived shamble attractive. He was shorter than most of his charges.

"Miss Angelou, these students have been excused from their classes. In support of the students sitting in in North Carolina, they chose to give the day to the Martin Luther King organization. We are ready to do whatever job you assign us."

He stood in the middle of the youthful energy like a dull drake among a brood of white ducklings.

I called in the volunteer captains and introduced them. Hazel and I sat through lunch in my office. We chuckled over the white youngsters who were scrubbing the steps and sweeping the floor and doing the jobs for us which were being done in their homes and in their streets by black women and men. We knew that what we were seeing was a one-time phenomenon, so were determined to enjoy it.

The children and their counselor filed in to say goodbye. They accepted my thanks and the thanks of the SCLC. I made a little speech about the oneness of life and the responsibility we all had to make the world livable for everyone. They left and we turned up the volume on the news station. Martin was still in jail. The police had dragged the blacks out of the diner. The North Carolina black community was angry, but nothing had happened yet. The office was drifting back to normal when Hazel buzzed my phone.

"Hey, Maya. Got something else for you. Are you ready?"

"Yes."

"Two groups of whites are coming tomorrow and a high school class from an integrated school. Have we got work for them?"

I listened, speechless.

Hazel laughed, "I asked you if you were ready."

The weeks ran together, the days raced. White and black people were changing as Martin Luther King traveled to and from jail and across the United States, his route covered by the national media. Malcolm X could be seen stripping white television reporters of their noise on the evening news. In Harlem, the Universal Negro Improvement Association formed in the twenties by Marcus Garvey was being revived, and the Ethiopian Association was coming back to life.

White movie stars attracted by Harry Belafonte and Sidney Poitier were lending their names to the struggle, and their sincerity stood up against the most suspicious scrutiny. One evening at Belafonte's house, Shelley Winters explained why she was glad to contribute her money and her time to the SCLC.

"It's not that I love Reverend King or all black people or even Harry Belafonte. I have a daughter. She's white and she's young now, but when she grows up and finds that most of the people in the world are black or brown or yellow, and have been oppressed for centuries by people who look like her, she's going to ask me what I did about it. I want to be able to say, 'The best I could.' " I was still suspicious of most white liberals, but Shelley Winters sounded practical and I trusted her immediately. After all, she was a mother just like me, looking after her child.

At home Guy talked about the movement. I was pleased that he and Chuck had joined a youth group of the Society Against Nuclear Energy, and I gave him permission to participate in a march protesting nuclear war.

Avoiding the evening subway rush, I always stopped in a bar near the 125th Street stop of the A train. The place was rough because its bartender and regulars were living lives of little gentleness.

The ice would slide away in my glass while street-wise men and world-wise women marveled over the nation's excitement.

"You see them Negroes in North Carolina. They mean business."

"Charlie better straighten up. We're tired of this shit."

"Man, that Martin Luther King. He's not a man made of blood."

"He's a fool. Love your enemies? Jesus Christ did that and you saw what happened to him."

"Yeah, they lynched him."

"Black people ought to be listening to Malcolm X. He's got it right. Crackers are blue-eyed devils."

"I don't go for that hate talk. Negroes ain't got time to be hating anybody. We got to get together."

I returned from lunch. In the outer office Millie Jordan was working over a table of papers. Hazel was busy on the telephone. I walked into my office and a man sitting at my desk, with his back turned, spun around, stood up and smiled. Martin King said, "Good afternoon, Miss Angelou. You are right on time."

The surprise was so total that it took me a moment to react to his outstretched hand.

I had worked two months for the SCLC, sent out tens of thousands of letters and invitations signed by Rev. King, made hundreds of statements in his name, but I had never seen him up close. He was shorter than I expected and so young. He had an easy friendliness, which was unsettling. Looking at him in my office, alone, was like seeing a lion sitting down at my dining-room table eating a plate of mustard greens.

"We're so grateful for the job you all are doing up here. It's a confirmation for us down on the firing line."

I was finally able to say how glad I was to meet him.

"Come on, take your seat back and tell me about yourself."

I settled gratefully into the chair and he sat on the arm of the old sofa across the room.

"Stanley says you're a Southern girl. Where are you from?" His voice had lost the church way of talking and he had become just

92

a young man asking a question of a young woman. I looked at him and thought about the good-looking sexy school athlete, who was invariably the boyfriend of the high-yellow cheerleader.

I said, "Stamps, Arkansas. Twenty-five miles from Texarkana."

He knew Texarkanà and Pine Bluff, and, of course, Little Rock. He asked me the size and population of Stamps and if my people were farmers. I said no and started to explain about Mamma and my crippled uncle who raised me. As I talked he nodded as if he knew them personally. When I described the dirt roads and shanties and the little schoolhouse on top of the hill, he smiled in recognition. When I mentioned my brother Bailey, he asked what he was doing now.

The question stopped me. He was friendly and understanding, but if I told him my brother was in prison, I couldn't be sure how long his understanding would last. I could lose my job. Even more important, I might lose his respect. Birds of a feather and all that, but I took a chance and told him Bailey was in Sing Sing.

He dropped his head and looked at his hands.

"It wasn't a crime against a human being." I had to explain. I loved my brother and although he was in jail, I wanted Martin Luther King to think he was an uncommon criminal. "He was a fence. Selling stolen goods. That's all."

He looked up. "How old is he?"

"Thirty-three and very bright. Bailey is not a bad person. Really."

"I understand. Disappointment drives our young men to some desperate lengths." Sympathy and sadness kept his voice low. "That's why we must fight and win. We must save the Baileys of the world. And Maya, never stop loving him. Never give up on him. Never deny him. And remember, he is freer than those who hold him behind bars."

Redemptive suffering had always been the part of Martin's argument which I found difficult to accept. I had seen distress fester souls and bend peoples' bodies out of shape, but I had yet to see anyone redeemed from pain, by pain.

There was a knock at the door and Stanley Levison entered. "Good afternoon, Maya. Hello, Martin. We're about ready."

Martin stood and the personal tenderness disappeared. He became the fighting preacher, armed and ready for the public fray.

He came over to my desk. "Please accept my thanks. And remember, we are not alone. There are a lot of good people in this nation. White people who love right and are willing to stand up and be counted." His voice had changed back to the mellifluous Baptist cadence raised for the common good.

We shook hands and I wondered if his statement on the existence of good whites had been made for Stanley's benefit.

At the door, he turned. "But we cannot relax, because for every fair-minded white American, there is a Bull Connor waiting with his shotgun and attack dogs."

I was sitting, mulling over the experience, when Hazel and Millie walked in smiling.

"Caught you that time, didn't we?"

I asked her if she had set up the surprise. She had not. She said when Martin came in he asked to meet me. He was told that I was due back from lunch and that I was fanatically punctual. He offered to play a joke by waiting alone in my office.

Millie chuckled. "He's got a sense of humor. You never hear about that, do you?"

Hazel said, "It makes him more human somehow. I like a serious man to be able to laugh. Rounds out the personality."

Martin King had been a hero and a leader to me since the time when Godfrey and I heard him speak and had been carried to glory on his wings of hope. However, the personal sadness he showed when I spoke of my brother put my heart in his keeping forever, and made me thrust away the small constant worry which my mother had given me as a part of an early parting gift: Black folks can't change because white folks won't change.

During the next months, Mother's warning dwindled further from my thoughts. The spirit in Harlem was new and old and dynamic. Black children and white children thronged the streets, en route to protest marches or to liberation offices, where they did small but important chores. Black Nationalists spoke on street corners, demanding freedom now. Black Muslims charged the white community with genocide and insisted on immediate and total segregation from the murdering blue-eyed devils. Wells Restaurant and the Red Rooster served the best soul food and offered great music at evening sessions to parties of blacks and whites and visiting African diplomats. The Baby Grand, where Nipsy Russell had played for years, had closed, but the Palm Café was a haven for hard drinkers and serious players. The *Amsterdam News* was vigilant in its weekly attack against the "forces of evil," and G. Norwood, one of its social and political columnists, kept the community informed on who was doing what, to whom and with how much success.

The national mood was one of action, and the older groups, such as the NAACP and the Urban League, were losing ground to progressive organizations. Young blacks had begun calling Roy Wilkins a sellout Uncle Tom and Whitney Young, a dangerous spy. Only Martin and Malcolm commanded respect, and they were not without detractors.

The Harlem Writers Guild meeting at Sarah Wright's house was ending. As we were saying goodbye, Sarah's phone rang. She motioned us to wait and answered it. When she hung up, she said excitedly that the Cuban delegation to the United Nations, led by President Castro, had been turned out of a midtown hotel. The group was accused of having brought live chickens to their rooms, where they were to use them in voodoo rites. The entire delegation had been invited to the Teresa Hotel in Harlem.

We all shouted. Those few writers and would-be writers who were not members of Fair Play for Cuba nonetheless took delight in Fidel Castro's plucky resistance to the United States.

In moments, we were on the street in the rain, finding cabs or private cars or heading for subways. We were going to welcome the Cubans to Harlem.

To our amazement, at eleven o'clock on a Monday evening, we

were unable to get close to the hotel. Thousands of people filled the sidewalks and intersections, and police had cordoned off the main and side streets.

I hovered with my friends on the edges of the crowd, enjoying the Spanish songs, the screams of *"Viva* Castro," and the sounds of conga drums being played nearby in the damp night air.

It was an *olé* and hallelujah time for the people of Harlem.

Two days later, Khrushchev came to visit Castro at the Teresa. The police, white and nervous, still guarded the intersection of 125th Street and Seventh Avenue, which even in normal times was accepted as the most popular and possibly most dangerous crossroad in black America.

Hazel, Millie and I walked down a block from the office, pushing through the jubilant crowd. We watched as Castro and Khrushchev embraced on 125th Street, as the Cubans applauded and the Russians smiled broadly, showing metal teeth. Black people joined the applause. Some white folks weren't bad at all. The Russians were O.K. Of course, Castro never had called himself white, so he was O.K. from the git. Anyhow, America hated Russians, and as black people often said, "Wasn't no Communist country that put my grandpappa in slavery. Wasn't no Communist lynched my poppa or raped my mamma."

"Hey, Khrushchev. Go on, with your bad self."

Guy left school, without permission, to come to Harlem with a passel of his schoolmates.

They trooped into the SCLC office after the Russian and Cuban delegations had left the neighborhood for the United Nations building.

Millie called and told me my son was in the back, stamping envelopes.

Surprise and a lack of sensitivity made me confront him before his friends.

"What are you doing here? You're supposed to be in school."

He dropped the papers and said in a voice cold and despising, "Do you want to speak to me privately, Mother?"

Why couldn't I know the moment before I had spoken what I knew as soon as my question hit the air. I turned without apology and he followed.

We stopped and faced each other in the hallway.

"Mother, I guess you'll never understand. To me, a black man, the meeting of Cuba and the Soviet Union in Harlem is the most important thing that could happen. It means that, in my time, I am seeing powerful forces get together to oppose capitalism. I don't know how it was in your time, the olden days, but in modern America this was something I had to see. It will influence my future."

I looked at him and found nothing to say. He had an uncanny sense of himself. When I was young I often wondered how I appeared to people around me, but I never thought to see myself in relation to the entire world. I nodded and walked past him back to my office.

Abbey, Rosa and I decided what was needed was one more organization. A group of talented black women who would make themselves available to all the other groups. We would be on call to perform, give fashion shows, read poetry, sing, write for any organization from the SCLC to the Urban League that wanted to put on a fund-raising affair.

7

For six months I had been coordinator of the SCLC. I knew how to contact reliable philanthropists, the first names of their secretaries, and which restaurants the donors used for lunches. I carried a brief case, and sat on subways, sternly studying legal papers. I was called Miss Angelou in my office and took copious notes in business conferences with Stan Levison and Jack Murray. Martin Luther King was sacred and fund-raising was my calling. Days were crammed with phone calls, taxi rides and serious letters reminding the mailing list that freedom was costly and that a donation of any amount was a direct blow against the citadel of oppression which held a helpless people enthralled.

After a day of such heart-stirring acts, I would travel back to my apartment. Somewhere after sunset and before I reached Brooklyn, the glorious magic disappeared. When I stepped off the subway at Park, I was no longer the bright young woman executive dedicated to Justice, Fair Play for Cuba and a member of the Harlem Writers Guild. I was an unmarried woman with the rent to pay and a fifteen-year-old son, who had decided that anything was better than another dull evening at home with Mother. Secretly, I agreed with him.

Tony's Restaurant and Bar on nearby Sterling Place became a sanctuary. It was not so dull that it attracted churchgoing families exclusively, nor so boisterous as to promise company combined with danger to unescorted women.

The first time I went into Tony's, I chose a barstool and ordered a drink, offering my largest bill, and invited the bartender to take out enough for one for himself. (Vivian Baxter told me when I was seventeen and on my own that a strange woman alone in a bar could always count on protection if she had treated the bartender right.)

He poured out my second drink loosely, allowing the gin to spill over the measuring jigger, then he told me his name.

Teddy was a small, neat man, his light toast-colored skin pulled tight across his face. He had large, slow eyes, which raked the bar while his little hands snapped at bottles, glasses and ice, and he talked with everyone along the counter, stepping into and out of conversations without losing a name or mixing up a drink.

"New in the neighborhood?" He carried drinks to the end of the bar, collected money, rang the register and asked, "Where're you from?"

"Are you a working girl or do you have a job?"

The softness of his voice belied the fact that he was asking if I was a prostitute. I knew better than to act either ignorant or offended. I said my name was Maya. I was from California and I had a job in Manhattan, lived alone with my teenage son three blocks away.

He returned from the other end of the bar carrying a drink.

"This one's on me, Maya. I want you to feel at home. Come in anytime."

I left a good tip, thanked him and decided to return the next evening.

Within a month, Teddy and I had a sly joking relationship, and the regulars nodded to me coolly but without hostility.

Appearances to the contrary, there is a code of social behavior among Southern blacks (and almost all of us fall into that category, willingly or not) which is as severe and distinct as a seventeenth-century minuet or an African initiation ritual. There is a moment to speak, a tone of voice to be used, words to be carefully chosen, a time to drop one's eyes, and a split-second when a stranger can be touched on the shoulder or arm or even knee without conveying anything more than respectful friendliness. A lone woman in a new situation knows it is correct to smile slightly at the other women, never grin (a grin is proper only between friends or people making friendship), and nod to unknown men. This behavior tells the company that the new woman is ready to be friendly but is not thirsting after another woman's mate. She should be sensual, caring for her appearance, but taking special care to minimize her sexuality.

The big man and I had noticed each other several times, but, although he was always alone, he had never spoken to me. One evening I walked into the bar and settled myself on a corner stool. Teddy served me my first drink and called me the Harlem Girl Friday. Then the man called from his stool at the bar's extreme end.

"Hey, Bar, that one's on me."

Teddy looked at the man, then at me. I shook my head. Teddy didn't move, but his eyes swung back to the man, who nodded, accepting my refusal.

Accepting the first drink from a strange man is very much like a nice girl having sex on a first date. I sat waiting for the second offer.

"My name is Tom, Maya, why won't you have a drink with me?"

I hadn't seen him move and suddenly he was close enough for me to feel his body heat. He spoke just above a whisper.

"I didn't know you, I didn't know your name. A lady can't drink with a nameless man." I smiled, pressing my cheek muscle down to show the hint of a dimple.

He was a reddish-tan color which Southern blacks called mariney. His face was freckled and his smile a blur of white.

"Well, I'm Thomas Allen. I live on Clark off Eastern Parkway. I'm forty-three and unmarried. I work in Queens and I work hard and I make pretty good money. Now you know me." He raised his voice, "Bar, give us another one like that other one," then dropped his voice. "Tell me, why are you all alone? Have the men gone blind?"

Although I knew it was an expected move in the courting game, flirting made me uncomfortable. Each coy remark made me feel like a liar. I wiggled on the stool and giggled and said, "Oh, stop."

Thomas was smooth. He led, I followed; at the proper time he withdrew and I pulled forward; by the end of our introductory ceremony, I had given him my address and accepted an invitation to dinner.

We had two dinner dates, where I learned that he was a bail bondsman and divorced. I went to his house and received lavish satisfaction. After a few nights of pleasure I took him home to meet my son.

He was Tom to his friends, but to establish myself as a type different from the people he knew, I called him Thomas. He was kind to me, always speaking gently, and generous to Guy. We were a handsome trio at the movies, at the zoo, and at Coney Island. His family treated me with courtesy, but the looks they traded with each other spoke of deep questions and distrust.

What did I want with their brother? A grown woman, who had been in show business and the Good Lord knew what else. Her teenage son, whose sentences were threaded with big words, who talked radical politics and went on protest marches. What was Tommy going to do with them? And for goodness' sake, she wasn't even pretty, so what did he see in her?

If they had asked me, instead of each other, I could have informed them with two words: sex and food.

At first, my eagerness in the bedroom shocked him, but when he realized that I wasn't a freak, just a healthy woman with a healthy appetite, he was proud to please me. And I introduced him to Mexican and French menus, spreading glories of food on my dining-room table. We enjoyed each other's gifts and felt easy together. I had only one regret. We didn't talk. He never introduced a subject into our evenings and answered with monosyllables to any questions asked.

After the most commonplace greetings, our conversations were mostly limited to my shouting in his bedroom and his grunts at my dining-room table. He treated my work at the SCLC as just another job.

A large donation or a successful money drive would send me away from the office sparkling. Thomas would accept the news with a solemn nod, then thump the newspaper, so that I would know he was really busy reading. His replies to questions about the quality of his workday were generally given in a monotone.

"It was O.K."

Were any interesting people arrested?

"No. Just the same old whores and pimps and murderers."

Aren't some of those criminals dangerous?

"Walking down the street is dangerous."

Wasn't he ever afraid of gun-toting criminals?

"I've got a gun too, and a license to carry it."

But for my arrogance, our relationship would never have progressed beyond the reach of our carnal appetites.

The Writers Guild had met at Rosa's apartment and people

were arranging rides to a late-night party in Harlem. I declined, saying Thomas was coming to take me home.

Someone suggested I bring him to the party, but before I could respond, another writer asked if it was true that fella was a bail bondsman. He was a bail bondsman, so what? The woman said, "Humph," and hunched her shoulders. "Well, I hope you're not getting serious about him. Because he sure as hell wouldn't be welcome in my house. They're as bad as cops. Living on poor folks' misery."

I had no time to think of the consequences of what I was going to say. The woman, of course, was not my friend, but even a polite acquaintance would not have tried to embarrass or challenge me in public. She had never bought me a pound of dried lima beans and was utterly unable to make me ugly up my face between the sheets. She could blow it out of her behind.

"I'm marrying him, and I'm tearing up your invitation to the wedding."

John Killens turned. "What the hell you say?"

Rosa, who knew all my secrets, widened her eyes and asked, "Since when?"

I dealt with all the questions with a coolness I didn't feel.

It was true that Thomas had not asked me to marry him, and Guy had no special regard for him. I knew I wasn't in love with him, but I was lonely and I would make a good wife. I could cook, clean house and I had never been unfaithful, even to a boyfriend. Our lives would be quiet.

I was getting used to the idea and even liking it. We'd buy a nice house out on Long Island, where he had relatives. I would join a church and some local women's volunteer organizations. Guy wouldn't mind another move if he was assured that it was definitely the last one. I would let my hair grow out and get it straightened and wear pretty hats with flowers and gloves and look like a nice colored woman from San Francisco.

When I told Thomas that I wanted to get married, he nodded and said, "I've been thinking about that myself. I guess it's time."

102

Guy accepted the news gravely. After a few seconds of silence, he said, "I hope you'll be happy, Mother." He turned away, then back again. "We'll be moving again, won't we?"

I lied about my daydreams, reminding him that Thomas had a large apartment only blocks from our house, which meant that he wouldn't have to change schools again. I thought to myself, maybe we wouldn't buy our house on Long Island until Guy went away to college.

My announcement was cheerfully received at the office. Hazel hugged me and said, "There's nothing like having a good man." She was happily married, so I expected her response.

Abbey looked at me quizzically. "Maya Angelou, I hope you know what you're doing."

"I don't, but I'm going to pray a lot."

She laughed and promised to pray with me. She was diligently minding her new marriage, keeping her penthouse immaculate and recording complicated music with Max.

Rosa was practical. "He's not jealous, is he? If you marry a jealous man, life will be hell." I told her he wouldn't have any reason for jealousy.

Rosa was writing every day, coping with her large rambunctious family, being courted by handsome African diplomats and working in a factory to pay her rent.

My two closest friends were too busy with the times and their own lives to talk me out of my rash decision.

Thomas gave me an engagement ring and said we'd marry in three months. We would be married in Virginia, his home state, in the church where his parents were married. Then we would drive to Pensacola, Florida, because he always wanted to fish in the Gulf of Mexico. Guy would stay with his family while we were away.

Obviously he didn't require my agreement, since he didn't ask for it. The decision to marry me automatically gave him authority to plan all our lives. I ignored the twinge which tried to warn me that I should stop and do some serious thinking.

I had never seen Virginia or Florida. Travel was a lovely thing to look forward to.

Time and opportunity were remolding my life. I closed my lips and agreed, with a new demureness.

8

One Monday morning Hazel told me that over the weekend she had heard a South African freedom fighter speak. He was so thorough and so brilliant that even the biggest fool in the world had to see that Apartheid was evil and would have to be brought down. His name was Vusumzi Make (pronounced Mah-kay).

A few volunteers, standing in the outer offices, had also heard the speaker. They joined in the conversation with added compliments.

"The smartest and calmest African I've ever heard."

"A little fat, but cute as he wants to be."

"Reminded me more of Dr. King than anybody I've ever seen."

I asked his name again.

Hazel said she had written it down and that the man was in the United States to petition at the United Nations against South Africa's racial policy. He was speaking again later in the week. Maybe we could attend the lecture together. I said maybe.

A mound of cardboard boxes stood against my office wall. I opened them all. Each contained a beautiful piece of luggage and a note: "Best Wishes to My Bride." I carried pleasure to my desk.

Frank Sinatra, Peter Lawford, Joey Bishop and Sammy Davis, Jr., had agreed to give a benefit performance for the SCLC at Carnegie Hall. Jack O'Dell, a highly respected organizer, had joined the organization, and he was breaking down the hall's seating. Stanley, Jack, Jack Murray and I had to separate sections and price seats.

Hotel accommodations had to be arranged for the famous

"Rat Pack" and its entourage. Musicians' union officials had to be contacted and tickets drafted and ordered. High-paying patrons needed to be solicited and church groups contacted and asked to take blocks of seats.

We were working late on Friday afternoon when Hazel said she had to go. She reminded me that Make was speaking and she was meeting her husband across town early so they could get good seats. (She knew my being able to go along was out of the question.)

As she left, I asked her to take notes for me and tell me all about it on Monday.

Work took over my weekend. I saw Guy only during the few hours on Saturday when he came to the office to join other black and white young volunteers. Thomas was working a night shift, so I took a late-night subway to Brooklyn and walked the quiet streets home. Guy's note on the dining-room table informed me that he was at a party. "Home at 12:30 A.M." Twelve-thirty was absolutely the limit. After all, he was barely fifteen. I was strict and he was usually agreeable. I would lie across my bed with a book and stay awake to make sure that he honored his note.

Morning found me in the same position and Guy sleeping innocently in his bedroom.

Make had been more eloquent than the previous time. Hazel said a heckler had asked why sixteen million Africans allowed three million whites to control them, reminding Make that we black Americans were only a tenth of the United States population, but we had stood up and fought back ever since we were brought here as slaves.

Hazel said Make was devastating. First, he spoke of the black American struggle. He knew the history better than most black Americans. He talked about Denmark Vesey and Gabriel, and all the known leaders of slave rebellions. He quoted Frederick Douglass and Marcus Garvey. He said that Dr. DuBois was the father of Pan-Africanism, having attended the Pan-African Congress in Paris in 1919, where he stated clearly the idea of a free and united

Africa. Make then, systematically, explained how Africa was bludgeoned by slavery, having her strongest sons and daughters stolen and brought to build the country of the slaves. He spoke of colonialism, the second blow that brought the continent to abjection. He said the spirit of Africa lives, but it is most vital in its descendants who have been struggling away from the motherland. At home, in South Africa, the people needed help and encouragement from those of us who, knowing slavery firsthand, had found the oppressor to be a formidable but opposable foe.

I made a note to go to hear Make the next time he spoke. Again, my responsibilities crowded out my intention. John Killens phoned on Thursday morning.

"Maya, I heard Make last night. Kind of expected to see you there."

I explained that we were nearing the Carnegie Hall date.

"Well," he said, "if you're free tomorrow night, come over to my place. Grace and I have asked a few people over to meet him."

"I'm working late tomorrow night, too."

"Come anytime. We'll get started around eight. We'll probably be going on until one or two. Make is the representative of the Pan-African Congress. That's the radical organization, but he's coming with Oliver Tambo, the head of the African National Congress. The ANC is to the PAC what the NAACP is to the Black Muslims. The two get along, though. Try to make it."

Before leaving for work the next morning, I woke Guy and asked him to go to John's for dinner, and said I would meet him there at nine-thirty.

Chagrin at being a capricious and too-often-absent mother would get me to the Killens' house.

I left the office a little early, and after John opened the door, I walked through the milling crowd of acquaintances and strangers to find Guy, Chuck, Barbara and Mom Willie in the kitchen. Guy looked up, then back at his watch and grinned.

Mom Willie offered me food, but I declined and said I'd better go shake hands with the honored guests.

Guy said, "He's going to knock you out, Mom. We talked a little. He's more brilliger than the slighy toves." Guy was working so hard to appear grown-up, I was surprised to hear him use his favorite childhood phrase. Make had made my reserved son relax and talk like a child again.

I went to the living room and greeted Paule and John Clarke, Sarah Wright and Rosa.

The air in the room crackled like static. John Killens introduced me to a small, trim dark man.

"Maya Angelou, meet Oliver Tambo, a warrior from South Africa." Tambo shook my hand and bowed.

John continued, "And come here and meet Vusumzi Make, another South African warrior."

Make's appearance surprised me. I had imagined him very tall and older. He was three inches shorter than I and his baby face was surrounded by fat. He had broad shoulders and a wide waist, all encased in a beautifully cut pin-stripe suit, and he was in his early thirties.

"Miss Angelou. Glad to meet you. You represent the black hero Martin King, as I represent the South African black hero Robert Sobukwe. Hazel Grey has been telling me about you. If we had not met I would have known you anyway. I've met Guy."

His accent was delicious. A result of British deliberateness changed by the rhythm of an African tongue and the grace of African lips. I moved away after smiling, needing to sit apart and collect myself. I had not met such a man. He was intense and contained. His movements were economical and delicate. And he didn't seem to know that he was decidedly overweight. John's introduction was probably apt. He was a warrior, sure of his enemies and secure with his armament.

Rosa left her African diplomat to join me on the couch. "You met Make. He'd been asking to meet you. Take it easy, kid." She smiled for me alone and went back to her escort.

Paule Marshall stood in front of me. "Listen, Maya Angelou. What did you do to Make? He says he wants to know you better."

107

I told her I only said hello.

She said, "Must have been a hell of a hello. He asked me how well I knew you and if you were married." Paule laughed and flicked her eyes. "I didn't say a word. It's up to you."

John and Grace corralled their guests back to the living room, where everyone found seats. After the chairs and sofas filled, people rested on footstools or wedged themselves between couches on the floor. John introduced Oliver Tambo, who talked about South Africa, the ANC and its leader, Chief Albert Luthuli, in terse and controlled anger.

We applauded the man and the cause that brought him to the United States. Then John introduced Mr. Make, and my love no longer was in the hands of Thomas Allen.

Make started talking from a seated position, but passion lifted his voice and raised him out of the chair. He had been a defendant charged with treason in the trials after the Sharpville Massacre. The Africans, ANC and PAC members, along with people who belonged to neither organization, had met in 1958 to oppose oppression in their country. They had been inspired by Martin Luther King and the SCLC. (He looked over at me and nodded.) They had been encouraged by Malcolm X and the Muslims to set themselves apart from their oppressors.

When he finished, he asked for questions and sat down, dabbing at his face with a cloud of white handkerchief.

My first reaction was to wish I could be the white cloth in his dark hand touching his forehead, digging softly in the corners of his lips. Intelligence always had a pornographic influence on me.

He asked for questions and was immediately satisfied.

"Which organization was the most popular in South Africa?" Was he really flirting with me?

"Did Luthuli and Sobukwe get along?" Did fat men make love like thin ones?

"When would the average South African become politically aware?" Was he married?

"What could we, as black Americans, do to speed along the

struggle?" How long was he going to stay in New York?

Make and Tambo shared the questions, volleying answers back and forth with the ease of professional tennis players.

Make turned. "Doesn't Miss Angelou have a question?" Stage experience kept me from squirming. All attention shifted to me and I shoved my real questions to the back of my head and asked, "Mr. Make, would it be possible to solve the South African problem with an employment of nonviolence?"

He stood and walked to my corner. "That which works for your Reverend King cannot work in South Africa. Here, whether it is honored or not, there is a Constitution. You at least have laws which say, Liberty and justice for all. You can go to courts and exact an amount of success. Witness your Supreme Court ruling of 1954. In South Africa, we Africans are written out of all tenets dealing with justice. We are not considered in the written laws dealing with fair play. We are not only brutalized and oppressed, de facto, we are ignored de jure."

He was standing over me, and I felt lucky. Fortunate to be a black American, and in comparison to him and his people, only slightly impaired by racism. But even more so fortunate. His eyes were on me and I would have had to be thicker than raw pigskin to know that something about me hooked him.

I folded my arms and sat back as he used the time to develop his statement. He finished to standing applause, and was wrapped around in seconds by a group of excited people.

We caught sight of each other through the shifting bodies but he never returned to my corner. After another drink, I went to collect Guy; my days started early and Guy had his bakery job again.

At the door, Make stopped us.

"Miss Angelou, just a minute. Guy, I would be honored to see your mother home."

Make knew that asking Guy's permission would please us both. My son smiled, loving the Old World formality, straight out of the Three Musketeers and the Corsican brothers.

109

"Thank you, Mr. Make. I am seeing her home."

I could have pinched him until he screamed.

Make said, "Of course, thank you anyway." The big lunk almost bowed from the waist. "I hope we'll meet again, Miss Angelou. Good night. Good night, Guy."

He walked away and we went out the door.

"He doesn't know that you're engaged, or he wouldn't have asked to take you home." Guy chattered all the way. "But he's really smart. He's from the Xhosa tribe. You know, Miriam Makeba's click song; well, that's his language. He was a barrister, that's a lawyer, before he was placed in exile and escaped from South Africa."

"When did he tell you all that?"

"He came into the kitchen and talked to Chuck and Barbara and me. He just walked in, introduced himself and sat down."

Most politicians I had met, excluding Martin Luther King, thought talking to children a waste of their adult time. I was liking the African more and more. And obviously I'd never see him again, and if we did meet, Thomas and my looming marriage stood between us.

The next morning, Paule rang to say she was giving a little party that evening and I had to come. I had another late night at work and once I got to Brooklyn and changed, I really wouldn't be up to going back to Manhattan. She urged me to stop by after work, reassuring me that the party was to be very casual. I said I'd drop in.

Late that afternoon I called John to say how much I enjoyed meeting Make, adding that he was very impressive. He agreed and said I'd get to see him again that night at Paule's. The party was being given for Oliver Tambo and Make. I mulled over the possibilities for hours. If we met and he pursued, would I have the strength to resist and did I really want to? Of course, last night was over, and he might bring a woman to Paule's. If he persisted and if I surrendered, I'd have to break off with Thomas, and my dream of quiet security would evaporate. Make would leave the country and I'd be back to where I was, or even worse. I'd be lonely and broken-hearted.

I took a train directly to Brooklyn. It was Friday night. Guy gulped down his food and gave me a kiss. He was off to a party, but would be in by twelve-thirty.

After a shower, I settled in my bed with a book, a drink and a package of cigarettes. The ghost of Paule's party invaded the room. Specters of laughing black people, shouting and arguing, crowded around my bed. Make was in the middle of the throng, his pretty full-moon face intense, his accent curving words into new shapes, his logic unarguable. If I went to the party . . . I called Thomas. He didn't answer. I did have a nice, rather new outfit that I could wear, and open high-heel sandals. Actually, it wouldn't take long to dress and if I took a subway to Times Square, I could change to the AA local and get off three blocks from Paule's building. Within a half-hour, I was ringing her doorbell. Inside, the men and women crowded together in jubilation. The record player was on to a moderate volume, and jazz music weaved among the voices.

I headed toward the living room, pushing through the crowded hallway. As I passed the kitchen, off to my left, I heard Make's voice.

"Miss Angelou." He came to me, grinning a white-teeth welcome. "I had just about given you up." He took my hand. "Paule said you'd come from work. But I suppose you went home to freshen up."

I nodded and excused myself, saying I had to see Paule. In fact, I had to get away from the man's electricity. Sparks seemed to be shooting from him to my nipples and my ears. My underarms tingled and my stomach contents fell to my groin. I had never fainted in my life, but at that moment I felt I was sinking into a warm black and friendly pool.

Paule laughed when she saw me. "I know you didn't wear that to work. You're setting out to get him, aren't you, Maya Angelou?"

111

I got huffy and denied her accusation. "I'm going to be married, Paule. I'm no chickenshit floozy."

Her ready temper answered, "Well, excuse the hell out of me." She went to join other guests. I was a fool. I lied and offended my friend at the same time. Make made no further attempt to talk to me.

The music was stopped and Tambo's voice could be heard as the talking quieted. He spoke briefly, repeating the speech of the night before. Ken Marshall asked Make to say a few words, and he walked to the center of the living room. I didn't listen to his words but used the time to study his body. He had closely cut, soft crinkled hair and an even dark-brown skin. Big round black eyes, which moved slowly, taking in the details of his listeners. There were a few hairs on his chin, which he fingered with small hands as he talked. His chest bloomed above an indented waist, then his hips widened out in a nearly feminine voluptuousness. Fat thighs touched, under the sharply creased trousers, and his small feet were encased in highly polished shoes. I completed the investigation and decided Make was the ideal man.

I gave him a few sultry looks, and when his back was turned, I raced downstairs and stopped a cab. I justified the expense of a taxi ride to Brooklyn by telling myself I was paying for my honor.

The American Society for African Culture had its annual black-tie ball on Saturday night in the ballroom of a midtown hotel, and as coordinator for the SCLC, I was expected to attend. Thomas was working late, so Rosa and her escort met me in Manhattan. Her African diplomat wore embroidered pants and a matching voluminous overshirt which reached the floor. The man was blue-black and spectacular. His unquestionable dignity gave lie to the concept that black people were by nature inferior. His presence alone refuted the idea that our descendants had been naked subhumans living in trees three centuries before, when the whites raided them on the African continent. That elegance could not have been learned in three hundred years.

The dance auditorium was filled with black women made up

and coiffed and beautiful in Dior and Balenciaga gowns or in dresses run up by local seamstresses. African women floated, serene-faced in their colorful national dress, and a few whites mingled with black men in tuxedos or outfits like that worn by Rosa's friend. I left my friends to check in at the table reserved for the SCLC. The Greys were watching the dancing couples, and when I greeted them, Hazel jumped.

"Oh, there you are. So you met him after all." I knew who she meant. "He was over here a few minutes ago, asking for you."

I saw him coming across the dance floor, like an ocean liner plying through tugboats toward a pier. He asked me to dance.

He moved surprisingly well for his bulk, and his enjoyment of the dance made him seem less serious. He pulled me to him, and I felt the hardness under the layers of surrounding fat. He laughed.

"You're afraid of me, aren't you? A big girl like you, an American sophisticate, frightened by a little black man from The Dark Continent."

"Why should I be afraid of you?"

He was still laughing. "Maybe you think I'll think you are a missionary and I'll eat you."

"I don't think that. Anyway, if more Africans had eaten more missionaries, the Continent would be in better shape."

He stopped dancing and looked at me with approval. "Miss Angelou, you have every reason to be alarmed. I intend to change your life. I am going to take you to Africa."

I drew my body straight and made my face uninviting. "Mr. Make, I am going to be married in two months. So your plan is impossible."

"I have heard that, but where is the elusive groom? I've seen you three times and, except for your son, you've been without male companionship."

I defended Thomas. "My fiancé is working."

"And what does this diligent man do?"

He was smirking. He knew the answer to his question.

113

"He's a bail bondsman. And I'm going to see him after the dance tonight."

Make grabbed my hand and led me back to my table. He pulled out my chair and after I sat, he leaned to me and whispered, "I owe it to our people to save you. When you see your bloody fiancé, tell him that I'm after you and that with me every day is Saturday Night and I'm black and I'm dangerous."

He left and my heart threatened to stop.

I went home early and alone. Guy was asleep and the house was cavernous.

Thomas answered the telephone. Had I enjoyed the fancy-dress ball? No, he was too tired to come and pick me up. No, I shouldn't call a taxi. After all, we'd see each other the next day. He was taking me to the movies.

Sleep didn't come to me willingly. Thoughts raced, chasing each other like lively children in a game of tag. Marry a man I hadn't even slept with and go to Africa. Leave Martin King and my own struggle. But all the black struggles were one, with one enemy and one goal. Thomas would shoot me with his service pistol. Why did Make want me? He didn't know me or my background. But then, I didn't know him either. What about Guy? Surely Make didn't expect me to leave my son. A chance for Guy to finish growing up in Africa. Suppose the man was too fat to make love. I knew of black women who had maimed husbands who refused them sex. I wouldn't go to that extreme; on the other hand, I didn't think I would stay with a man who couldn't satisfy me. Speculation was a waste of time. I was going to marry Thomas, and we'd live a nice complacent life in Brooklyn.

The next night the movie was deadly boring. I got up on the pretext of wanting a soft drink and I sat in the lobby smoking and wondering what Make was doing. Patrice Lumumba was in New York. Rosa was going to meet him and his assistant Thomas Kanza. Abbey and Max were performing in the Village. Malcolm X was speaking at a public meeting in Harlem, and somewhere Make was showering his listeners with glittering words. Guy was

114

attending a youth rally in Washington Square Park. The world was on fire.

Thomas headed the car toward his street.

"I don't feel like going to your house," I told him.

He looked over at me, but I kept my face straight ahead.

"Are you all right? It's not that time of month, is it?"

"No. I just want to go home."

No, he hadn't offended me. No, I wasn't sick.

I told him we were living in exciting times and that because of the United Nations, Africans and oppressed people from all over the world were making New York the arena where they fought for justice.

"I haven't lost anything in Africa and they haven't lost anything in our country. They can all go back where they came from as far as I'm concerned. Anyhow, I get all the excitement I need in my job and I don't want to hear about politics at home."

It was a long speech for Thomas and a disastrous one for our relationship. I could imagine future aborted conversations when I would be silenced. Days, weeks, months would pass with neither of us going beyond small talk.

I prepared dinner at home and waited alone for Guy to return.

The next days brought bouquets of mixed flowers and vases of red roses to cover my desk and make me feel like a desirable courtesan. The accompanying cards read "From Vusumzi Make to Maya Angelou Make." Hazel looked worried and Millie grinned as if she and I were sharing a secret.

Thomas chose the same time to have more wedding presents delivered. Young, shabbily dressed men hauled boxes up the stairs and deposited them in the outer offices. "Tom to Maya." I opened the cartons to find an expensive record player covered in smooth leather and two more pieces of matching luggage. It was a flattering present, but I couldn't dispel the idea that the set was stolen property.

I refused Make's daily invitations to lunch and declined Thomas' offer to visit his apartment.

115

Confusion had me spread-eagled. I couldn't run nor could I dodge.

Office politics were further irritations. Despite the long hours and what I thought of as my diligent commitment, two more men had been brought in to help in the running of the organization. I had had nothing to say about their employment.

After a business lunch with the president of a national Negro women's club where we discussed the selling of a large block of tickets, it was suggested that I report the results to the office newcomers. When I refused to do so, insisting on my own autonomy, loyalties began to shift. Welcoming smiles faded or gleamed sunshine-bright. Small groups of workers crowded the desks of the new arrivals, while Hazel and Millie used every slight occasion to enter my office, bringing me news or coffee, fresh papers or mail.

9

Thursday morning I agreed to meet Make for lunch a few blocks from my office. I would explain to him why he had to accept my rejection.

Wells Restaurant, pride of Harlem, on 132nd Street and Seventh Avenue, had been popular since the twenties, when it was a favorite stop on the route of whites, visiting what many called "Nigger Heaven."

The food had remained good, the menus still listed white items such as steaks and lamb chops, but its main offerings, fried chicken, smothered pork chops, short ribs and biscuits catered to the local palates.

Make stood as I entered. He wore yet another well-tailored suit and custom-made shirt. I didn't need to look at his shoes to know they were shining like new money. He began talking before I sat down.

He was pleased that I had overcome my timidity. My coming

116

showed I had courage, a virtue which we both knew was a prerequisite in the struggle. He had talked to Paule Marshall, by telephone, and told her that his intention was to marry me and take me to Africa. I couldn't focus on the menu, but we ordered lunch. He continued talking and I ate food I could neither see nor taste.

He had been jailed for political action in South Africa. When the government released him, the police took him to an isolated desert area near South-West Africa and left him there, hundreds of miles from the nearest human beings. A city-bred man, with no knowledge of open country, he had scrabbled over rocky ridges and found water. He pulled caterpillars from shrubs and ate them (they taste a lot like shrimp). He encountered a group of Hottentot hunters and because he could speak a little of their language, they gave him dried meat and a small water pouch. Keeping away from large towns and following the stars, he walked out of South Africa into Bechuanaland. The Boers' control and spies had pervaded that country as well, so he kept to the forest. He made a slingshot and killed small animals and ate them raw, or cooked when it was safe enough to light a fire. Their skins padded his worn-out shoes or were laid inside his shirt for warmth. Days passed when the only things he saw moving were the vultures that lazed high in the sky above him. He walked through South and North Rhodesia, making sparse contacts with revolutionaries he had heard about, who were themselves in hiding or on the run. He took his first breath of freedom when he crossed into Ethiopia.

"I was the first Pan-African Congress member to escape. But, Miss Angelou, when I left exile without water or food, I intended to reach Ethiopia. When I knew I was coming to the yew ess, I came with the intention of finding a strong, beautiful black American woman, who would be a helpmate, who understood the struggle and who was not afraid of a fight. I heard about you and you sounded like the one. I met Guy and I was impressed with his manliness and intelligence, obviously your work, and then I saw you."

He reached across the table and took my hand. His little brown fingers tapered down to small white nails. I tried to picture those exquisite hands carrying caterpillars, wiggling to his mouth.

"You are exactly what I dreamed on my long march. Tall and clear-eyed. Needing to be loved. Ready to fight and needing protection. And not the protection of a bloody bail bondsman."

Oh Lord, that reminded me.

"Mr. Make, I agreed to have lunch with you to tell you I am going to marry the bloody bail bondsman."

He leaned his bulk back in the chair and his face darkened and clouded over with resignation.

"You are breaking my heart. I am an African with large things to do. I have left my father and mother in Jo'Burg, and given the ordinary run of time, I shall never see them again. Unless the revolution takes place during my lifetime, I shall never see the land again. To an African, the family and the land . . . I need you. I want to marry you."

"I'm sorry." And God knew I meant that.

"I shall finish at the U.N. tomorrow. On the next day, I shall fly to Amsterdam, an open city, where I am told whiskey is cheap and a variety of entertainment is available to a lonely man."

I saw those delicate hands sliding over white women's bodies and in their long, lank hair. But I couldn't imagine him kissing the white lips.

"I shall stay in Amsterdam four or five days and then I shall go to Copenhagen, another open city. My desire for you is total, Miss Angelou. I want your mind, and spirit and your body. After all, I may be an African with a mission, but I am also a man. I must attend a conference in London in ten days, but before the conference, I must try to drive thoughts of you out of my mind." He stopped talking and I waited in the silence for a second before I excused myself and went to the toilet.

Wells had wasted none of its elegance on the women's room. There were two small cubicles for toilets and a small outer area which was only large enough for two people.

A woman bumped into me on her way out. She saw the tears on my face.

"Hey, are you O.K? You sick?"

I shook my head and walked through the open door. She poked her head in. "You sure you don't need any help?"

I shook my head again and thanked her.

The little mirror over the washstand was vague with dust but I looked in it and saw misery in sharp outline. If I went through with the wedding to Thomas, I would load our marriage with such disappointment, the structure couldn't stand. He was too good a man to abuse, yet I knew that I would never forget or forgive the facts. Because of him, I would have lost Make, a life of beckoning adventure and Africa. Africa. I would hate him for that. And Make. Make needed me. I would be a help to him. I was brave. Abbey had once told me I was too crazy to be afraid. I would be a fool to let Make go to a bunch of whorish white women in Amsterdam. In fact, I might be betraying the entire struggle. I wouldn't do that. And then Guy. Guy would have the chance to have an African father. There could be no greater future for a black American boy than to have a strong, black, politically aware father. His being African would add an enriching spice.

Admitting for the first time a decision I had made at the fancy-dress ball, I would accept Make's offer.

I called Abbey from a pay phone. She answered.

"Just wanted to make sure you were there."

"What's happening?"

"Nothing yet, I'll call back."

"Are you all right?"

"Yeah. Really. I'll call you in a few minutes."

Make stood again as I reached the table. I sat down and took the napkin in my hands. The words refused to get themselves in order.

"Mr. Make, I'll do it. I'll do it. I'll go with you."

His face broke open. A brown moon splitting, showing its white core. The room was filled with large even teeth and shining round eyes.

"I'll marry you, Miss Angelou. I'll make you happy. We will be known as the happiest family in Africa." He came around the table and pulled me to my feet to kiss me. I noticed other customers for the first time and drew away.

Make laughed, turning to the tables of black people openly watching us.

"It is all right. She has just said she'll marry me."

Applause and laughter. The folks liked a happy story.

He held my hand as if I had just won a race, "This is the joining of Africa and Africa-America! Two great peoples back together again."

I tried to sit back down. He was going to make a speech. A laugh rumbled up his chest and between the perfect teeth.

"No. I claim my engagement kiss."

His lips were full and soft. Shaken by the physical touching, we took our seats again. The woman who had offered to help me in the toilet came to our table.

"Honey, I should have known you weren't crying out of sadness." She smiled. "You all have a drink with us. We've been married eighteen of the best years of my life."

A man's voice shouted across the room, "Ernestine, just offer the folks a drink and come on back and sit down."

The woman grinned. "See how nice we get along? He orders. I obey. Sometimes."

Make and I laughed as she strutted back to her table.

After a few nervous minutes of finding no way to say all the things which needed to be said, I asked Make if he was free for the afternoon. He said he was. I excused myself and went to the telephone.

"I've done it this time, Ab."

"Done what?"

"It. I've told Vusumzi Make I'll marry him."

"Who?" Her voice was strong with shock.

120

"A South African freedom fighter. He's brilliant, Abbey, and pretty. Beautiful, in fact. And we've fallen in love."

"Well, hell, Maya Angelou, what about Thomas?"

"I want to talk to you about that."

"Seems like to me, you'll have to talk to Thomas."

At the moment that chore didn't seem so onerous.

"I wish you'd come down to Wells and meet him and take him to your house. I have to go back to the office, but I'll come over after work. Will you?"

She didn't use a second to deliberate.

"Of course I'll come. Are you going to wait or do I just walk in and ask for the African who's going to marry Maya Angelou?"

I told Make that my friend, Abbey Lincoln, was coming to pick him up.

He recognized her name immediately and began to tell me how the Max Roach/Abbey Lincoln records were smuggled into South Africa and then passed around like the hot revolutionary material they were. He knew the title of every track and most of the words to all their songs. The man, indeed, was a wonder.

When I looked through the window and saw Abbey double-parking her Lincoln sedan, we left the restaurant. Abbey got out of the car and shook hands with my latest fiancé. They drove away and the rest of the afternoon passed like film in slow motion starring a stranger. I answered telephones, signed letters, spoke to volunteers, but my mind hovered somewhere between the Serengeti plains, Thomas' apartment in Brooklyn and the sweet scent of patchouli which rose each time Mr. Make shifted his heavy body.

Max and Mr. Make were talking and Abbey was preparing dinner when I arrived at the Columbus Avenue apartment. Abbey shouted a welcome from the kitchen and both men embraced me.

Make said proudly, "Ah, here is my beautiful wife."

Max nodded. "Maya, you got yourself one this time. Yeah, you got yourself a man."

I sat through dinner in a stupor. Max and Abbey's place was

121

no more real than my office had been. A man I had met exactly one week earlier was grinning possessively at me across the table. Max, who had seen enough of life to be healthily suspicious, approved of the stranger. Later when I helped Abbey dry the dishes, she said that she thought I was better suited to the unknown Make than to the known Thomas. And anyway, I was just wild enough to make it work.

Make slipped close to me over the ribbing of the corduroy couch.

"I am tired, and would like to rest Max has said I might stretch out in that room." I was supposed to agree. I did want to grab his hand and lug him to bed, but I said, Mr. Make, I . . ."

"Please, we are going to be married, call me Vus."

"Vus, I'm obliged to clear up the matter with Thomas." Make leaned against the back of the sofa and kept quiet for a few minutes.

"Yes. I agree. But when you talk to him I want to be present. He might be difficult."

"I'll speak to him alone tomorrow night. And then . . ."

"Shouldn't I come with you? It might be dangerous."

I refused his offer. Talking with Thomas was my responsibility. My pompous idiocy had gotten me into the mess, and rash emotion was further complicating the jumble. And I felt a little excitement at the coming confrontation.

"Then I shall be the one to talk to Guy. I'm going to be his father and we must begin our relationship properly."

Vus put me into a taxi heading for Brooklyn.

Guy had rocks in the jaws and flint in his eyes. He had called the office and had been told that I had left early. He went to the Killens and they had no news of my whereabouts. Thomas hadn't heard from me and Paule Marshall didn't know where I was. He couldn't find Abbey's number. He chided me. It wasn't fair to insist that he be considerate and phone home if I was going to treat him with casual indifference. It was nearly eleven o'clock.

Three men looked to me for proof of devotion.

My son expected warmth, food, housing, clothes and stability. He could be certain that no matter which way my fortune turned he would receive most of the things he desired. Stability, however, was not possible in my world; consequently it couldn't be possible in his. Too often I had had to decline unplayable hands dealt to me by a capricious life, and take fresh cards just to remain in the game. My son could rely on my love, but never expect our lives to be unchanging.

Thomas wanted equilibrium, also. He was looking for a nice wife, who was a good cook and was neither so pretty or so ugly that she drew attention to herself. I tried his number again. I had to tell him that he hadn't yet found his mate. He didn't answer the ring.

Vus saw me as the flesh of his youthful dream. I would bring to him the vitality of jazz and the endurance of a people who had survived three hundred and fifty years of slavery. With me in his bed he would challenge the loneliness of exile. With my courage added to his own, he would succeed in bringing the ignominious white rule in South Africa to an end. If I didn't already have the qualities he needed, then I would just develop them. Infatuation made me believe in my ability to create myself into my lover's desire. That would be nothing for a stepper.

At dawn Thomas answered the telephone. He said he would pick me up from the office and collect the wedding gifts. We would stop at my house and after dinner with Guy, we would go back to his apartment for "a little you-know-what."

The day jerked itself to evening in stops and starts. Time either wouldn't move at all or it raced like a whirlwind.

At last, and too soon, Thomas stood in my office doorway, smiling, showing his death-white teeth.

"Hey, baby, where's the stuff?"

I said "Hi" and pointed him to the cartons against the wall. While I was saying good night to the office staff, he carried the gifts downstairs, and when I joined him on the pavement he was loading them in the trunk of his car.

123

He was still smiling. I wondered how could anybody say good-bye to a smiling man.

"You like the luggage, baby?"

"Yes. Where did you buy it?"

The question wiped the smile from his face. "Why?"

"Oh, in case I want to add to the set."

He relaxed and the smile returned as full as it was before. "I got them from a fellow I know. And if you want some more, I'll get them for you".

I had suspected that the bags were stolen when they appeared in my office in supermarket cardboard boxes, and Thomas now confirmed my suspicions. I needed all the hurt feelings I could muster for the imminent farewell scene, so I kept quiet and waited.

At home, Guy watched television and Thomas read the sports pages while I cooked dinner. I knew that but for my shocking plans, we were acting out the tableau of our future. Into eternity. Guy would be in his room, laughing at *I Love Lucy* and Thomas would be evaluating the chances of an athlete or a national baseball team, and I would be leaning over the stove, preparing food for the "shining dinner hour." Into eternity.

We ate without excitement and Guy said good night, going back to his room.

Thomas rose to bring in the luggage but I stopped him.

"I have some talk for you. Why don't we have a drink?"

I began talking slowly and quietly. "I've met a South African. He escaped over the desert. He kept himself alive by eating worms. The whites sent him out to die but he survived. He has come to the United States and he deserves our support." I looked at Thomas, who had become a terrapin, his large head withdrawn into his shoulders, his eyes steady and unblinking.

I continued my story, saying that the man was inspired by Dr. Martin Luther King and had come to petition the United Nations on behalf of his people. I used small words and short sentences

124

as if I were telling a fairy tale to a child. Thomas was not en-thralled.

I said, "A large conference is going to be held in London, where other people who have escaped from South Africa will meet and form a joint freedom-fighting organization." So far I was telling the truth. But since I didn't have the courage to tell Thomas I was leaving him, I knew I was building up to a lie.

The man in front of me had turned into a big red rock, and his freckles blotched dark brown on his face.

"Indians from the South Africa Indian Congress and Africans from both South Africa and South-West Africa will take two weeks to work out an accepted charter. As we know, " 'In unity there is strength.' "

There was no light in Thomas' eyes.

We sat in dangerous silence.

I balled up my nerve. "They . . . Anyway, this African I've just met has asked me to attend the conference. They want a black American woman who can explain the philosophy of nonvio-lence." I was getting there.

Thomas twitched his shoulders, raised his body an inch, then slid deeper into the chair. His eyes still reflected nothing.

"I have decided to accept the invitation and deliver a paper on Martin Luther King."

The invention came as a wonderful surprise. I had been search-ing all day and during the preparation of dinner in vain for a way to say what I had to say, and nothing had come to me. Obviously, apprehension had sharpened my imagination.

"I don't know how long I'll be gone, but I may go to Africa after that."

Thomas, in an unexpectedly fast move, sat up straight. He looked at me, his face wise and hard.

"You got another nigger." He hadn't raised his voice. "All that shit was to tell me you got yourself another nigger."

The moment I dreaded and had lied to avoid had arrived.

"Say it. Say it in plain words. Say, 'Thomas' "—he mimicked

125

my speech—" 'Thomas, I got myself another nigger.' Say it."

He was the interrogator and I was the suspect.

"Well, he's not a nigger."

"He's African, ain't he? Then, he's a nigger just like me and just like you. Except you try to act like a goddam ofay girl. But you just as much a nigger as I am. And so is your goddam holy Martin Luther King, another blackass nigger."

He knew I loathed that word and didn't allow its use in my home. Now each time he said "nigger" he sharpened it and thrust it, rapierlike, into my body.

"Thomas"— I forced a sweet calm into my voice—"Thomas, there doesn't seem to be anything more to say."

He denied that we had come to the end of our conversation and the end of the relationship. I was acting above my station, putting on airs like my siditty friends who were talking about freedom and writing stupid books that nobody read. Thinking I was white, raising my son to use big words and act like a white boy. His sister had told him to watch out for me. I didn't mean him no good. I thought I was better than his family.

I didn't move, even to pick up my drink. He spoke, letting the profanity and his dislike of me fill the room.

He would be surprised if that African didn't leave me stranded in London or in Africa, and I'd come back, dragging my ass, trying to make him feel grateful for a chance to fuck me. Well, don't think that he'd be around. Forget his phone number. In fact, tomorrow, he would have his phone number changed.

I noted with relief that he was already talking about tomorrow. His shoulders fell and he leaned back against the chair, his energy spent. I still didn't move.

He rose and walked out of the room and I followed. He was so large, he filled the entry. In a sharp move, he jerked back the curtain which covered the oval window at the door.

"Come here." I was afraid to refuse, so I wedged myself close to him. "Look at that woman."

Across the street a lone black woman walked under hazy street-

126

light carrying two full shopping bags. I didn't know her. Thomas reached into his jacket and pulled out his gun.

"You know something? I could blow that broad's head off, and I wouldn't do a day."

He put the pistol back into its holster, opened the door and walked down the steps to his car.

I made another drink and thanked God for blessing me yet one more time. I had hurt Thomas' ego but I had not broken his heart. He wasn't injured enough to attack me, but he would never want to see me again.

Stanley and Jack Murray accepted my news without surprise. They said they had not expected me to stay. They felt that since I was an entertainer, I would leave the organization whenever I was offered a good night-club contract or a part in a Broadway play. That's why they had brought in other dedicated workers to take over my job. I didn't bother to tell them how wrong they were.

Grace Killens laughed at me.

"You met him last week at our house, didn't you? And this week you're going to marry him. The Wild West Woman." She laughed and laughed.

John took the news solemnly. Concern tightened his face and squeezed his voice into sharpness.

"He's serious about the struggle, but what else do we know? Are you going to be a second or third wife? How is he planning to look after you? Don't forget Guy. You're putting him under a strange man's roof and he's almost a man himself. How does he feel about that?"

Because he was the most important, I had left Guy for the last. Vus had said he wanted to be the first to talk to him and I was happy to accept the much-vaunted masculine camaraderie. Let men talk to men. It was better for a woman, even a mother, to stand back, keep quiet and let the men work out their mannish problems.

Guy was spending the night with Chuck, and Abbey and Max were performing, so Vus and I were given the use of their apartment. He prepared an elaborate dinner of roast beef and sautéed vegetables and poured a delicious wine. I learned that night that he was an expert in extending pleasure.

At the dining table he spread before me the lights and shadows of Africa. Glories stood in thrilling array. Warrior queens, in necklaces of blue and white beads led armies against marauding Europeans. Nubile girls danced in celebrations of the victories of Shaka, the Zulu king. The actual earth of Africa was "black and strong like the girls back home" and glinted with gold and diamonds. African men covered their betrothed with precious stones and specially woven cloth. He asked me to forgive the paucity of the gift he had for me and to understand that when we returned to Mother Africa he would adorn me with riches the likes of which I had never imagined. When he led me into the darkened guest room and placed a string of beads around my neck, all my senses were tantalized. I would have found the prospect of a waterless month in the Sahara not only exciting, acceptable. The amber beads on my nut-brown skin caught fire. I looked into the mirror and saw exactly what I wanted to see, and more importantly what I wanted him to see: a young African virgin, made beautiful for her chief.

The next afternoon I told Guy that the South African we had met at the Killens' house was coming around for dinner. He took the news so casually I thought that perhaps he had forgotten who Make was. He went to his room and began playing records as I fumbled setting the table.

When the doorbell rang, Guy popped out of the back room like a bottle cork and spun through the kitchen.

"I'll get it."

Before I could set the stove burners to safe levels, I heard the rumble of voices, speaking indistinguishable words.

I reached the living room just as Vus was beginning to lower himself into Guy's favorite chair. He stood again and we shook hands. I offered him the so much more comfortable sofa. Guy shook his head and smiled wanly. "This is comfortable, too, Mom."

Since early childhood, Guy had made certain pieces of furniture his private property. In preschool years and until he was eight or so, each night he would lasso chairs or tables with toy ropes before going off to bed, and he would warn his "horses" to stay in the corral. Although he grew out of the fantasy, his sense of property possession remained and everyone respected it.

Vus sat down in Guy's chair, and I thought he was getting off to a miserable start.

Guy offered to bring drinks, and the second he left the room Vus said, "There is no reason to be nervous. We are both men. Guy will understand." I nodded. Vus thought he understood, but I wondered how much of my son's temperament would really escape him.

I sat primly on the sofa across the room. Guy walked in carrying a napkin-covered tray, ice, glasses and a bottle of Scotch.

"Mom, something smells like its sticking." He walked to Vus. "How do you like your drink?"

Vus stood and mixed his own drink from the tray in Guy's hands. The two of them seemed absorbed in an atavistic ritual. I had ceased to be the center of attention.

"Well, I'll go tend to the dinner."

Vus looked up over his drink. "Yes. Guy and I must talk." Guy nodded as if he already knew something.

"Guy, will you please come to the kitchen for a moment?"

He hesitated, reluctant to leave our guest.

"Now, Mom?"

"Yes. Please."

We stood beside the warm stove and I opened my arms to embrace him. He stepped back, wary.

"Please come. I just want to hug you."

His eyes darted and he looked young and defenseless. Unwilling, he walked into my embrace.

"I love you. Please know that." I hadn't meant to whisper.

He extricated himself and went to the door. His face suddenly sad and old.

"You know, Mom. That sounds just like goodbye."

The sensuality between parents and children often is so intense that only the age-old control by society prevents the rise of sexuality. When a single parent is of the opposite sex the situation is more strained. How to feel love and demonstrate affection without stirring in the young and innocent mind the idea of sexuality? Many parents, alarmed at the dreadful possibility of raising incestuous thoughts in their children's minds, withdraw, refusing all physical contact and leaving the children yearning and befuddled with ideas of unworthiness.

Guy and I had spent years skating the thin ice.

During his twelfth summer, we attended a party in Beverly Hills. The children's party had been catered at one end of an Olympic-sized swimming pool, and I drank Margaritas with the adults at the pool's other end.

That evening, when we returned to our house in Laurel Canyon, Guy startled me.

"You know, Mom. Everyone talks about Marilyn Monroe's body. But we were watching today and all the guys said you had a prettier shape than Marilyn Monroe.

After he went to bed, I sat pondering my next move. He was old enough to masturbate. If I began to figure in his sexual fantasies he would be scarred and I would have added one more weight to an already difficult life.

That night I went through my wardrobe separating away the provocative dresses and choosing the staid outfits which were more motherly. The next day I stopped at the Salvation Army with a large package, and never again bought a form-fitting dress or a blouse with a plunging neckline.

I continued preparing the prenuptial feast, assuring myself that Guy would take the news calmly.

When I set the dining table, I consciously deadened my ears

and hummed a song out loud. I was getting a husband, and a part of that gift was having someone to share responsibilities and guilt.

They came to the table and I saw from Guy's face that Vus had not told him of our marriage plans.

We sat to dinner and I ate straw.

The conversation swirled around me, making no contact: Soccer was as violent a sport as American football. Sugar Ray Robinson was a gentleman, but Ezzard Charles was of the people. Malcolm X had the right ideas but Martin Luther King was using tactics which had only been effective in India. Africa was the real "Old World" and America was aptly described by George Bernard Shaw, who said that it was "the only country which had gone from barbarism to decadence without once passing through civilization."

Guy was relaxed and entered into the exchange with his own young wit. They made each other laugh and my stomach churn.

I gathered the dishes, and when Guy rose to help clear the table, Vus stopped him.

"No, Guy, I must speak to you about our future. And I shall speak now. May we go into your room?"

A shadow of panic rushed into Guy's eyes. He turned to me peering, quickly trying to scan my thoughts. In a second he collected himself.

"Of course. Please. Come this way."

He led the big man into his bedroom; after they entered, the door slammed.

I made a clatter of dishes and a rattle of pans, slamming them together and jingling the flatware into cacophonous harmonies, trying to drown out my own thoughts and any sounds which might slide under Guy's door and slither across the kitchen floor and float up to my ears.

Suppose Guy rejected the man and our plans. He could refuse. Because the white world demonstrated in every possible way that he, a black boy, had to live within the murdering boundaries of racial restrictions, I had raised him to believe that he had a say

131

in the living of his life, and that barring accidents, he should have a say in the dying of his death. And now, so armed, he was able to shape not only his future, but mine as well.

The kitchen was clean, every glass dried and the dishes put away. I sat with a cup of coffee at the kitchen table, controlling the opposing urges to walk without knocking into Guy's room or grab my purse and haul out the front door, running to Ray's and a triple Scotch on the rocks.

Laughter from behind the door brought me back to reality. Guy had accepted Vus, which meant I was as good as married and on my way to live in Africa.

They emerged from the room, broad grins stretched their faces. Guy's high-yellow color was reddened with excitement and Vus looked satisfied.

"Congratulations, Mom." This time Guy opened his arms offering me safe sanctuary. "I hope this will make you very happy."

I stood in Guy's arms and Vus laughed. "Now you'll have two strong men to take care of. We three will be the only invaders Mother Africa will willingly take to her breast."

The evening filled with laughter and plans. When Vus left for Manhattan, Guy spoke candidly.

"You would never have been happy with Mr. Allen."

"How do you know?"

"I know."

"Yes, but how? Because he's a bail bondsman?"

"No, because he didn't love you."

"And Mr. Make does?"

"He respects you. And maybe for an African, that's better than love."

"You know a lot, huh?" I didn't try to conceal my pride.

"Yeah. I'm a man."

The next few days glittered, as friends, recovered from shock at my hasty decision, strung out a Mardi gras of parties. Rosa threw a Caribbean fete, where her African, black American and white liberal friends argued and laughed over plates of her famous rice and beans. Connie and Sam Sutton, an unpretentious intellectual couple, invited academic colleagues to a quiet dinner, which in time turned into a boisterous gathering. All over New York City strangers hugged me, patted my cheeks and praised my courage. Old friends told me I was crazy while struggling to control their admiration and envy.

At the end of the string of parties, Vus and I left for England, leaving Guy in the home of Pete and T. Beveridge, who lived a few blocks from my Brooklyn house.

We sat on the plane holding hands, kissing, seeing our future as a realm of struggle and eternal victory. Vus said we would marry in Oxford, such a pretty little town.

I explained that I wanted have my mother and son present at my wedding and asked if we could wait. He patted my cheek and said, "Of course. In London we will say we married in America. When we return to New York we will say we married in England. We will have our wedding according to your wishes and whenever you say. I am marrying you this minute. Will you say yes?"

I said yes.

"Then we are married."

We never mentioned the word marriage again.

10

London air was damp, its stone buildings old and grey. Colorfully dressed African women on the streets reminded me of tropical birds appearing suddenly in a forest of black trees. Vus and I moved into a one-room apartment which the PAC kept near Finsbury Park.

For the first few days, I was happy to stay in bed after Vus left for the conference. I read, rested and gloated over how well fortune was finally treating me. I had a brilliant and satisfying man, and I was living the high life in London, a mighty long way from Harlem or San Francisco's Fillmore District. Evenings, Vus entertained me with a concert of stories. His musical accent, his persuasive hands and the musk of his aftershave lotion, hypnotized me into believing I lived beside the Nile and its waters sang my evensong. I stood with Masai shepherds in the Ngorongoro crater, shooing lions away from my sheep with a wave of an elephant hair whisk. Morning love-making and evening recitals lost none of their magic, but the time between the two events began to lengthen. When I told Vus that I was not used to having so much time on my hands, he said he would arrange for me to meet some of the other wives of freedom fighters attending the conference.

Mrs. Oliver Tambo, the wife of the head of the African National Congress, invited me to lunch. The house in Maida Vale was neat and bright, but the sensation of impermanence in the large rooms was so strong that even the cut flowers might have been rented. She welcomed me and the other guests cordially but with only a part of her attention. I didn't know then that all wives of freedom fighters lived their lives on the edge of screaming desperation.

As we sat down at the table, the telephone rang constantly, interrupting the conversation we were trying to establish. Mrs. Tambo would lower one side of her head and listen and most often allow the rings to wear themselves to silence. A few times she got up, and I could hear the one-sided sound of a telephone conversation.

Lunch was slow-cooked beef and a stiff corn-meal porridge called mealy. She told me that she had gone to the trouble of preparing South African traditional food so that I would not be shocked when I met it again. I didn't tell her that in the United States we ate the same thing and called it baked short ribs and corn-meal mush.

A startlingly beautiful woman spoke to me. Her skin was blue-black and smooth as glass. She had brushed her hair severely, and it lay in tiny ripples back from a clean, shining forehead. Her long eyes were lifted above high cheekbones and her lips formed themselves in a large black bow. When she smiled, displaying white even upper teeth but bare lower gums, I knew she was from Kenya. I had read that the women of that country's Luo tribe have their bottom four teeth extracted to enhance their beauty. She was bright and tough, describing Europe's evil presence in Africa.

Mrs. Okalala from Uganda, a squat tugboat of a woman, said she found it ironic, if not downright stupid, to hold a meeting where people discussed how to get colonialism's foot off the neck of Africa in the capital of colonialism. It reminded her of an African saying: Only a fool asks a leopard to look after a lamb.

Two Somali women wrapped in flowing pink robes smiled and ate daintily. They spoke no English and had attended the lunch for form's sake. Occasionally they whispered to each other in their own language and smiled.

Ruth Thompson, a West Indian journalist, led the conversation, as soon as lunch was finished.

"What are we here for? Why are African women sitting eating, trying to act cute while African men are discussing serious questions and African children are starving? Have we come to London just to convenience our husbands? Have we been brought here only as portable pussy?"

I was the only person shocked by the language, so I kept my reaction private.

The Luo woman laughed. "Sister, you have asked, completely, my question. We, in Kenya, are women, not just wombs. We have shown during Mau Mau that we have ideas as well as babies."

Mrs. Okalala agreed and added, "At home we fight. Some women have died in the struggle."

A tall wiry lawyer from Sierra Leone stood. "In all of Africa, women have suffered." She picked at the cloth of her dress, caught it and dragged it above her knees. "I have been jailed and beaten. Look, my sisters. Because I would not tell the whereabouts of my friends, they also shot me." She wore a garter belt and the white elastic straps on her left leg evenly divided a deep-gouged scar as slick and black as wet pavement. "Because I fought against imperialism."

We gathered around her, clucking sympathy, gingerly touching the tight skin.

"They shot me and said my fighting days were over, but if I am paralyzed and can only lift my eyelids, I will stare the white oppressors out of Africa."

The spirit of overcoming was familiar to me, also. In my Arkansas church we sang,

> "I've seen starlight
> I've seen starlight
> Lay this body down
> I will lay down in my grave
> And stretch out my arms."

Nineteenth-century slaves who wrote the song believed that they would have freedom and that not only would souls cross over Jordan to march into glory with the other saints, but the grave itself would be unable to restrict the movement of their bodies.

When the lawyer dropped the hem of her dress all the women wrapped her 'round with arms, bodies and soft voices.

"Sister, Mother Africa is proud of you."

"A true daughter of a true mother."

The Somali women had also touched the scar. They spoke unintelligible words of sorrow and stroked the Sierra Leonian woman's back and shoulders.

Mrs. Tambo brought out a large bottle of beer. "This is all there is in the house."

The lawyer took the bottle with both hands and raised it to the sky. "The mother will understand." She turned and handed the beer to Mrs. Okalala. "Auntie, as the elder, you must do the honor."

I followed the general movement and found myself with the women bunched together in the center of the small living room. The woman faced us, solemnly.

"To talk to God I must speak Lingala." Except for the Somali women and me, all the women nodded.

She began to speak quietly, near a moan. Her tempo and volume increased into a certain chant. She walked around in rhythm and dribbled beer in the four corners of the room. The women, watching, accompanied her in their languages, urging her on, and she complied. The Somali women's voices were united into the vocal encouragement. I added "amens" and "hallelujahs," knowing that despite the distances represented and the Babel-like sound of languages, we were all calling on God to move and move right now. Stop the bloodshed. Feed the children. Free the imprisoned and uplift the downtrodden.

I told about black American organizations, remembering the Daughter Elks and Eastern Stars, Daughters of Isis and the Pythians. Secret female organizations with strict moral codes. All the women in my family were or had been members. My mother and grandmothers had been Daughter Rulers and High Potentates. Oaths were taken and lifelong promises made to uphold the tenets and stand by each sister even unto death.

The African women responded with tales of queens and princesses, young girls and market women who outwitted the British or French or Boers. I countered with the history of Harriet Tubman, called Moses, a physically small woman, slave, and how she escaped. How she stood on free ground, above a free sky, hundreds of miles from the chains and lashes of slavery and said, "I must go back. With the help of God I will bring others to freedom," and how, although suffering brain damage from a slaver's blow, she walked back and forth through the lands of bondage time after time and brought hundreds of her people to freedom.

The African women sat enraptured as I spoke of Sojourner Truth. I related the story of the six-foot-tall ex-slave speaking at an equal rights meeting of white women in the 1800s. That evening a group of white men in the hall, already incensed that their own women were protesting sexism, were livid when a black woman rose to speak. One of the town's male leaders shouted from the audience: "I see the stature of the person speaking and remark the ferocious gestures. I hear the lowness and timbre of the speaker's voice. Gentlemen, I am not convinced that we are being addressed by a woman. Indeed, before I will condone further speech by that person, I must insist that some of the white ladies take the speaker into the inner chamber and examine her and then I will forbear to listen."

The other men yelled agreement, but the white women refused to be a party to such humiliation.

Sojourner Truth, however, from the stage took the situation in hand. In a booming voice, which reached the farthest row in the large hall, she said:

"Yoked like an ox, I have plowed your land. And ain't I a woman? With axes and hatchets, I have cut your forests and ain't I a woman? I gave birth to thirteen children and you have sold them away from me to be the property of strangers and to labor in strange lands. Ain't I a woman? I have suckled your babes at this breast." Here she put her large hands on her bodice. Grabbing the cloth she pulled. The threads gave way, the blouse and her undergarments parted and her huge tits hung, pendulously free. She continued, her face unchanging and her voice never faltering, "And ain't I a woman?"

When I finished the story, my hands tugging at the buttons of my blouse, the African women stood applauding, stamping their feet and crying. Proud of their sister, whom they had not known a hundred years before.

We agreed to meet often during the conference and share our stories so that when we returned to our native lands we could take back more than descriptions of white skins, paved streets, flushing toilets, tall buildings and ice-cold rain.

A year would pass before I actually went to Africa, but that afternoon in Oliver Tambo's English apartment, I was in Africa surrounded by her gods and in league with her daughters.

The conference ended and Vus had to go to Cairo on PAC business. He took me to London's Heathrow airport and handed me a pile of English pounds.

"Find a good apartment, in Manhattan, and furnish it well. It must be large and central." I was unhappy at the prospect of going back to New York alone, but he assured me that he would return in two weeks or at most a month. After he concluded his business in Egypt he might have to go to Kenya. The thought of his exotic destinations cheered my spirit and strengthened my resolve. I was happy to return to New York and the task of finding an apartment which would fit his exquisite taste.

In one week I found an apartment in Manhattan on Central Park West, packed books and hired a mover. On our moving day, Guy and I sat among the boxes in the Brooklyn living room. He wanted me to tell him about London again. I described the speakers talking in the rain at Hyde Park Corner and the solemn guards at Buckingham Palace, but he wanted to hear about the Africans.

"Tell me how they looked. How did they walk? What were they called?"

The names were beautiful. "There was Kozonguizi and Make-Wane., Molotsi, Mahomo."

Guy sat quietly. I knew he was running the sounds through his mind. After a moment he said, "You know, Mom, I've been thinking of changing my name. What do you think?"

What I thought was that my marriage to Vus had affected him deeply, but I said nothing.

"Johnson is a slave name. It was the name of some white man who owned my great-great-grandfather. Am I right?"

I nodded and felt ashamed.

"Have you chosen a name?"

He smiled, "Not yet. But I'm thinking about it. All the time."

Guy spent the next few weeks adjusting to his new school, and

I used the time seeing my friends and trying to beautify the apartment.

The Harlem Writers Guild members and Abbey listened attentively to my description of Africans in London. They nodded, appreciating the freedom fighters' dedication. They smiled at me, proud that I had been so close to the motherland.

Before Vus returned, I painted the kitchen and put brightly colored wallpaper in the bathroom. The apartment was crisp and elegant.

Vus came home like a soldier returning from a conquered battlefield. His sagas of Cairo were heroic. He had drunk coffee with President Nasser and talked privately with his assistant. Egyptian officials supported the African struggle for freedom, and soon he would take Guy and me to live in Cairo. Excitement shook away Guy's just-forming adult postures. He jumped up, wiggling.

"We're going to Egypt? I'll see the pyramids? Boy, I'm going to be riding camels and everything."

Vus chuckled, happy to be the cause of such elation. Guy finally took his thrills to bed and I rushed into Vus's waiting arms.

The next morning my interior decorating met with stony disapproval. The old sofa was wrong for a man in my husband's position and the secondhand-store bedroom set definitely had to go.

"I am an African. Even a man sleeping in the bush will lay fresh leaves on the ground. I will not sleep on a bed other men have used."

I didn't ask him what he did in hotels. Certainly he didn't call the manager and say, "I want a brand-new mattress. I am an African."

I said, "But if we're going to Egypt we shouldn't buy new furniture."

He answered, "The things we buy will be of such quality they will have a high resale value. And anyway, we're not moving immediately".

I followed him meekly around a furniture store where he selected an expensive bed, a teak coffee table and a giant brown leather sofa.

He paid in cash, pulling bills from a large roll of money. The source of Vus's money was a mystery. He evaded my questions with the agility of an impala. There was nothing for me to do but relax and accept that he knew what he was doing. My son and I were in his care and he looked after us well. He was an attentive father, making solo visits to Guy's school and sitting with him late evenings over textbooks. They laughed often and affectionately together. When other Africans visited, Vus would insist that Guy sit in on the unending debates over violence and nonviolence, the role of religion in Africa, the place and the strength of women in the struggle. I tried to overhear their interesting conversations, but generally I was too busy with household chores to take the time.

It seemed to me that I washed, scrubbed, mopped, dusted and waxed thoroughly every other day. Vus was particular. He checked on my progress. Sometimes he would pull the sofa away from the wall to see if possibly I had missed a layer of dust. If he found his suspicions confirmed, his response could wither me. He would drop his eyes and shake his head, his face saddened with disappointment. I wiped down the walls, because dirty fingerprints could spoil his day, and ironed his starched shirts (he had his shoes polished professionally).

Each meal at home was a culinary creation. Chicken Kiev and feijoda, Eggs Benedict and Turkey Tetrazzini.

A good woman put ironed sheets on the beds and matched the toilet paper to the color of the bathroom tile.

I was unemployed but I had never worked so hard in all my life. Monday nights at the Harlem Writers Guild challenged my control. Heavy lids closed my eyes and the best reading of the best writing could not hold my exhausted attention.

"A bride, you know." Everyone would laugh, except Rosa, who knew how hard I was trying to be a good housewife.

141

"That African's got her jumping." Hands clapped at the humor of it all. But they were speaking more truth then they knew. When I wasn't home tired I was as tight as a fist balled up in anger. My nerves were like soldiers on dress parade, sharp, erect and at attention.

We were living luxuriously but I didn't know how much cash we had, nor could I be sure that the bills were paid. Since I had been sixteen, except for three married years between, I had made and spent my own money.

Now I was given a liberal food and house allowance and a little cash for personal expenditure (taxis and Tampax). Vus collected and paid the bills. The novelty was not amusing and my heart was not at peace.

Members of the South Africa United Front were invited to India to meet Krishna Menon. When Vus left I fumbled around the house for a few days, seeing no one but Guy, trying to accommodate an uncomfortable sense of uselessness. When every window was polished and every closet as orderly as department-store racks, I decided to go to Abbey's house. The most called-upon prerequisite of a friend is an accessible ear.

"He doesn't want me to work, but I don't know what's going on and it's making me feel crazy."

Abbey brushed the nap of her long-haired sofa. "You wanted a man, Maya Angelou. You've got one." She just didn't know how seriously upset I was.

"But, Ab, I didn't give over my entire life. You know that's not right."

She locked her jaws and stared at me for a long time. When she spoke, her voice was hard and angry. "A man's supposed to be in charge. That's the order of nature." She was raising an argument which we had debated for years.

My position had always been that no one was responsible for my life except me. I was responsible for Guy only until he reached maturity, and then he had to take control of his own existence. Of course, no man had ever tried to persuade me differently by offering the security of his protection. "Well, then, I must be outside of nature. 'Cause I can't stand not knowing where my air is coming from."

Abbey made a clucking sound with her tongue, and said, "The worst injury of slavery was that the white man took away the black man's chance to be in charge of himself, his wife and his family. Vus is teaching you that you're not a man, no matter how strong you are. He's going to make you into an African woman. Just watch it." She dismissed the discussion and me. But she didn't know the African women I had met in London or the legendary women in the African stories. I wanted to be a wife and to create a beautiful home to make my man happy, but there was more to life than being a diligent maid with a permanent pussy.

11

The Cultural Association for Women of African Heritage had its second meeting at Abbey's luxury penthouse apartment on Columbus Avenue. Several weeks before, we had agreed on a charter, a policy statement and a name: CAWAH. It sounded exotic. We agreed. The newly founded organization included dancers, teachers, singers, writers and musicians. Our intention was to support all black civil rights groups. The charter, as drawn up by Sarah Wright and signed unanimously by the membership, stated that since the entire power of the United States was arrayed in fury against the very existence of the Afro-Americans, we, members of CAWAH, would offer ourselves to raise money for, promote and publicize any gathering sincerely engaged in developing a just society. It further stated that our members, multitalented, would agree, after an assenting vote, to perform dance concerts, song fests, fashion shows and general protest marches.

Abbey's living room filled with strident voices. Should we or should we not insist that every member show her commitment to being black by wearing unstraightened hair. Abbey, Rosa and I already wore the short-cut natural, but it was the other women, with tresses hanging down like horse's manes, who argued that the naturals should be compulsory.

"I've made an appointment for next Friday. I'm having all this shit cut off because I believe that I should let the world know that I'm proud to be black." The woman placed her hands on the back of her neck and lifted years of hair growth.

I said, "I don't agree." I would miss seeing her long black pageboy.

Abbey said, "I don't agree either. Hair is a part of woman's glory. She ought to wear it any way she wants to. You don't get out of one trick bag by jumping into another. I wear my hair like this because I like it and Max likes it. But I'd dye it green if I thought it would look better."

We all laughed and put that discussion aside, addressing ourselves to plans for an immense fashion show based on an African theme and showing African designs. Abbey said, "In Harlem, I'm sick of black folks meeting in white hotels to talk about how rotten white folks are." So Rosa and I were assigned to find a suitable auditorium for the affair.

Rosa and I met on 125th Street and the first thing she said was "Lumumba is dead." She continued in a horror-constricted voice, saying that she had learned of the assassination from Congolese diplomats, but that there would be no announcement until the coming Friday when Adlai Stevenson, the United States delegate to the United Nations, would break the news.

I said nothing. I knew no words which would match the emptiness of the moment. Patrice Lumumba, Kwame Nkrumah and Sékou Touré were the Holy African Triumvirate which radical black Americans held dear, and we needed our leaders desperately. We had been abused, and so long abused, that the loss of one hero was a setback of such proportion it could dishearten us and weaken the struggle.

We were walking aimlessly, in a fog, when the sound of people talking, moving, shouting, broke into our stupor. We allowed ourselves to be drawn to the corner where the Nation of Islam was holding a mass meeting.

The street corner wriggled with movement as white policemen nervously guarded the intersection. A rapt crowd had pushed as close as possible to the platform where Malcolm X stood flanked by a cadre of well-dressed solemn men. Television crews on flat-bed trucks angled their cameras at the crowded dais.

Malcolm stood at the microphone.

"Every person under the sound of my voice is a soldier. You are either fighting for your freedom or betraying the fight for freedom or enlisted in the army to deny somebody else's freedom."

His voice, deep and textured, reached through the crowd, across the street to the tenement windows where listeners leaned half their bodies out into the spring air.

"The black man has been programmed to die. To die either by his own hand, the hand of his brother or at the hand of a blue-eyed devil trained to do one thing: take the black man's life."

The crowd agreed noisily. Malcolm waited for quiet. "The Honorable Elijah Muhammad offers the only possible out for the black man. Accept Allah as the creator, Muhammad as His Mes-senger and the White American as the devil. If you don't believe he's a devil, look how he's made your life a hell."

Black people yelled and swayed. Policemen patted their unbut-toned holsters.

Rosa and I nodded at each other. The Muslim tirade was just what we needed to hear. Malcolm thrilled us with his love and understanding of black folks and his loathing of whites and their cruelty.

Unable to get close to the platform, we pushed ourselves into Mr. Micheaux's bookshop and watched and listened in the door-way.

"Talk, Malcolm."

Malcolm roared back, his face a golden-yellow in the sun, his hair rusty-red.

"If you want to live at any cost, say nothing but 'yes, sir' and

145

do nothing except bow and scrape and bend your knees to the devil. But if you want your freedom, you'd better study the teachings of the Honorable Elijah Muhammad, and start respecting your women. Straighten out your home affairs and stop cheating on your wives. You know who you're really cheating?"

Female voices shot up like arrows over the crowd. "Tell these fools, brother Malcolm." "Tell them to stop acting like little boys." "Explain it. Explain it on down." "Break it down."

Malcolm took a breath and leaned toward the microphone. "You are cheating your fathers and mothers and grandfathers and grandmothers and-you-are-cheating-Allah."

A man on the platform lifted his hands, showing copper palms, and chanted in Arabic.

After a burst of applause, Malcolm paused and looked solemnly at the crowd. People stopped moving; the air became still. When he spoke again his tone was soft and sweet.

"Some of you think there are good whites, don't you? Some good white folks you've worked for, or worked with or went to school with or even married. Don't you?"

The listeners exchanged a grumble of denial.

Malcolm continued speaking low, nearly whispering. "There are whites who give money to the SCLC, the NAACP and the Urban League. Some even go so far as to march with you in the streets. But let me tell you who they are. Any white American who says he's your friend is either weak"—he waited for the word to have its effect and when he spoke again his voice growled—"or he's an infiltrator. Either he'll be too scared to help you when you need help or he's getting close to you so he can find out your plans and deliver you back in chains to his brothers."

The street corner exploded with sound as anger and recognition collided. When Malcolm finished speaking the crowd yelled their approval of the fire-hot leader. Rosa and I waited in the bookstore until most of the people left the corner.

We walked without speaking to Frank's Restaurant. Again there was no need to talk. Malcolm's words were harsh, but too close to the bitter truth to argue. Our people were alone. As always, alone. We could not expect protection from whites even if they happened to be our relatives. Slave-owning fathers had sold black sons and daughters. White sisters had put their black sisters in slave coffles for a price.

Rosa and I drank at the bar, not looking at each other.

"What can we do?"

"What do you think?" Rosa turned to me sadly as if I had failed her. She had been counting on me to be intelligent. She continued, frowning, "What the shit do you think? We've got to move. We've got to let the Congolese and all the other Africans know that we are with them. Whether we come from New York City or the South or from the West Indies, that black people are a people and we are equally oppressed."

I ordered another drink.

The only possible action that occurred to me was to call the members of CAWAH and throw the idea out for open discussion. Among us we would find something to do. Something large enough to awaken the black American community in New York.

Rosa didn't think much of my idea but she agreed to go along.

About ten women met at my house. Immediately the tone was fractious and suspicious. How did Rosa know Lumumba was dead? There had been no announcement in the newspapers.

Rosa said she had gotten her news from reliable sources.

Some members said that they thought our organization had been formed to support the black American civil rights struggle. Weren't we trying to swallow too much, biting into Africa? Except for Sékou Touré and Tom Mboya, when had the Africans backed us?

One woman, a fashion model, hinted that my husband and Rosa's diplomat boyfriend made us partial to the African cause. Abbey said that was a stupid attitude, and what happens in Africa affects every black American.

One woman said the only thing Africans had really done for us was to sell our ancestors into slavery.

147

I reminded the conservatives in our group that Martin Luther King had said that he found great inspiration and brotherly support on his recent trip to Africa.

Rosa spoke abruptly. "Some of us are going to do something. We don't know just what. But all the rest of you who aren't interested, why'n the hell don't you get your asses out and stop taking up our time?"

As usual when she got excited, her West Indian accent appeared and the music in her voice contradicted the words she chose.

Abbey got up and stood by the door. A rustle of clothes, the scraping of shoes, and the door slammed and six women were left in the living room.

Abbey brought brandy and we got down to business. After a short, fierce talk our decisions were made. On Friday, we would attend the General Session of the United Nations. We would carry black pieces of cloth, and when Adlai Stevenson started to make his announcement on Lumumba's death, we six women would use bobby pins and clip mourning veils to the front of our hair and then stand together in the great hall. It wasn't much to do but it was dramatic. Abbey thought some men might join us. She knew Max would like to come along. Amece, Rosa's sister, knew two West Indian revolutionaries who would like to be included. If men joined us, we would make elasticized arm bands, and at the proper moment, the men could slip the black bands up their sleeves and stand with the women. That was the idea. No mass movement but still a dramatic statement.

As the meeting was coming to end, I remembered a piece of advice Vus had given a few young African freedom fighters:

"Never allow yourself to be cut off from the people. Predators use the separation tactic with great success. If you're going to do something radical go to the masses. Let them know who you are. That is your only hope of protection."

I quoted Vus to the women and suggested that we let some folks in Harlem know what we intended to do. Everyone agreed.

We would go to Mr. Micheaux; he could pass the word around Harlem faster than an orchestra of conga drums.

The next afternoon we went back to the bookstore, where posters of blacks covered every inch of wall space not taken up by shelves: Marcus Garvey, dressed in military finery, drove forever in an open car on one wall. W. E. B. DuBois gazed haughtily above the heads of book browsers. Malcolm X, Martin Luther King and an array of African chiefs stared down in varying degrees of ferocity.

Mr. Micheaux was fast moving, quick talking and small. His skin was the color of a faded manila envelope. We stopped him on one of his spins through the aisles. He listened to our plans impatiently, nodding his head.

"Yeah. The people ought to know. Tell them yourselves. Yeah, you tell them." His short staccato sentences popped out of his mouth like exploding cherry bombs. "Come back this evening. I'll have them here. Not nigger time. On time. Seven-thirty. You tell them."

He turned, neatly avoiding customers in the crowded aisle.

A little after seven o'clock at the corner of Seventh Avenue, we had to push our way through a crowd of people who thronged the sidewalks. We thought the Muslims, or the Universal Improvement Association, were holding a meeting, or Daddy Grace and his flock were drumming up souls for Christ. Of course, it was a warm spring evening and already the small apartments were suffocating. Anything could have brought the people into the streets.

Mr. Micheaux's amplified voice reached us as we neared the bookstore.

"A lot of you say Africa ain't your business, ain't your business. But you are fools. Niggers and fools. And that's what the white man wants you to be. You make a cracker laugh. Ha, ha." His voice barked. "Ha, ha, crackers laugh."

Because of my height, I could see him on a platform in front of the store. He held on to a standing microphone and turned his body from left to right, his jacket flapping and a short-brim brown hat shading his face from view.

"Abbey, these people"—the human crush was denser nearer to the bookstore—"these people are here to hear us."

She grabbed my hand and I took Rosa's arm. We pressed on.

"Some of your sisters are going to be talking to you. Talking to you about Africa. In a few minutes, they're gonna tell you about Lumumba. Patrice Lumumba. About the goddam Belgians. About the United Nations. If you are ignorant niggers, go home. Don't stay. Don't listen. And all you goddam finks in the crowd —run back and tell your white masters what I said. Tell 'em what these black women are going to say. Tell 'em about J. A. Rogers' books, which prove that Africans had kingdoms before white folks knew how to bathe. Don't forget Brother Malcolm. Don't forget Frederick Douglass. Tell 'em. Everybody except ignorant niggers say 'Get off my back, Charlie. Get off my goddam back.' Here they come now." He had seen us. "Come on, Abbey, come on, Myra, you and Rosa. Come on. Get up here and talk. They waiting for you."

Unknown hands helped us up onto the unstable platform. Abbey walked to the microphone, poised and beautiful. Rosa and I stood behind her and I looked out at the crowd. Thousands of black, brown and yellow faces looked back at me. This was more than we bargained for. My knees weakened and my legs wobbled.

"We are members of CAWAH. Cultural Association for Women of African Heritage. We have learned that our brother, Lumumba, has been killed in the Congo."

The crowd moaned.

"Oh my God."

"Oh no."

"Who killed him?"

"Who?"

"Tell us who."

Abbey looked around at Rosa and me. Her face showed her nervousness.

150

Mr. Micheaux shouted. "Tell 'em. They want to know."

Abbey turned back to the microphone. "I'm not going to say the Belgians."

The crowd screamed. "Who?"

"I won't say the French or the Americans."

"Who?"

It was a large hungry sound.

"I'll say the whites killed a black man. Another black man."

Mr. Micheaux leaned toward Abbey. "Tell 'em what you all are going to do."

Abbey nodded.

"On Friday morning, our women and some men are going to the United Nations. We are going to sit in the General Assembly, and when they announce the death of Lumumba we're going to stand up and remain standing until they put us out."

The crowd agreed loudly.

"I'm coming."

"I'll be there."

"Me too."

"Yeah, stand up and be counted."

"That's right!"

A few dissenting voices were heard.

"Bullshit. Is that all?"

"They kill a man and you broads are going to stand up? Shit." And, "They'll shoot your asses too! Yes, they will."

The opposition was drowned out by the larger encouragement.

Mr. Micheaux took the microphone.

"Come here, Myra." The little man could spell my name but he never pronounced it correctly. "You talk."

He turned to the crowd. "Here's a woman married to an African. Her husband just barely escaped the South African white dogs. Come on, Myra. Say something."

I repeated what had already been said at least once. Repetition was a code which everyone understood and appreciated. We had a saying: "Make everything you say two-time talk. If you say it once, you better be able to repeat it." Black ears were accustomed to the call and response in jazz, in blues and in the prose of black preachers.

Mr. Micheaux took the microphone from me and called Rosa. She looked out at the faces and spoke very quickly.

"We'll be there. Any of you who wants to come will be welcome. We are going to meet at eight-thirty in front of the U.N. We'll make up extra veils and arm bands and our members will be waiting to distribute them. Come all. Come and let the world know that no longer can they kill black leaders in secret. Come."

She gave the microphone to Mr. Micheaux and beckoned to me and Abbey. We were helped off the stage. The crowd parted, and made an aisle of sounds.

"We'll be there."

"Eight-thirty on Friday."

"See you, sister. See you at the U.N."

"God bless you."

We sat quiet in the taxi and held on to each other. The enormity of the crowd and its passionate response had made us mute. We agreed to meet the next day.

I went back to an empty house. Guy's dinner dishes drained on the sideboard and a note propped on the dining-room table informed me that he was attending a SANE meeting and to expect him at ten-thirty.

Rosa phoned. We had to draw money from CAWAH. Her niece Jean was going downtown to a fabric outlet in the morning. She would buy black tulle and elastic. Rosa would pick up bobby pins from Woolworth's. We ought to meet at her house to make the arm bands and stick the pins in the veils. I agreed and hung up. Abbey phoned. Would I call women of CAWAH and would I check with the Harlem Writers Guild, and just to be on the safe side, wouldn't it be a good idea to make up a hundred veils and arm bands? I agreed.

Guy came home, full of his meeting. SANE was planning a demonstration on Saturday in New Jersey. He and Chuck would like to go. If the Killens and I gave permission for them to miss a school day, they would join a march on Friday, walking across the George Washington Bridge. He would be O.K., Mom. They would carry sleeping bags, and a lot of peanuts, and after all, hadn't I said I wanted him to be involved? "Dad," would certainly agree if he wasn't in India. My generation had caused the atomic bomb to be dropped on Hiroshima, the year he was born. So he could say correctly that he was an atomic baby. He and Chuck had talked. The bomb must never be used again. Human beings had been killed by the hundreds of thousands, and millions mutilated, and did I want to see the photographs of Hiroshima again?

I gave him permission to go to New Jersey.

Jean, Amece and Sarah cut the bolt of black tulle. Rosa sewed strips of elastic to half the large squares while Abbey and I gathered bobby pins into the remainder.

Jean pinned a veil to her hair and the stiff material stood out like a softly pleated fan. Her eyes and copper-colored skin were faintly visible through the material. She looked like a young woman, widowed by an untimely accident. We looked at her and approved. Our gesture was going to be successful.

On Friday morning, I stepped over Guy's sleeping bag, which he had laid open on the living-room floor. It wouldn't be kind to awaken him, since he would be sleeping rough that evening after his march. He knew I had planned to leave the house early for the United Nations. I placed a five-dollar bill on the plaid sleeping bag and left the apartment.

Abbey's house was a flurry of action. CAWAH women were busy, drinking coffee, laying the veils in one box, talking, putting the arm bands in another box, eating sweet rolls a teacher had brought, smiling and flirting with Max, who walked around us like a handsome pasha in a busy harem. We left for the elevators, carrying the boxes, and jumpy with excitement.

Max and Abbey could take four in their car. The rest would find taxis. We agreed to meet on the sidewalk in front of the U.N. Amece and Rosa had the veils, so they rode with Max. The teacher, the model, Sarah and I would travel together. Jean and the other friends would get their own taxis. Finding a cab so early on Friday on New York's Upper West Side was not easy. Business people had radio-controlled taxis on regular calls, and many white drivers sped up when black people hailed them, afraid of being ordered north to Harlem and/or of receiving small tips.

At ten minutes to nine our taxi turned off 42nd Street onto First Avenue. Sarah and I screamed at the same time. The driver put on brakes and we all crashed forward.

"What the hell is going on here?" The cabbie's alarm matched our own. People stood packed together on the sidewalk and spilled out into the street. Placards stating FREEDOM NOW, BACK TO AFRICA, AFRICA FOR THE AFRICANS, ONE MAN, ONE VOTE waved on sticks above the crowd.

We looked out the windows. Thousands of people circled in the street and all of them were black. We paid and made our way to the crowd.

"Here she is. Here's one of them."

"Sister, we told you we'd be here. Where you been?"

"How do we get inside? The police said . . ."

"They won't let us in."

The shouts and questions were directed at me. I began a chant and used it moving through the anxious crowd: "I'll see about it. I'll take care of it. I'll take care of it. I'll see about it." Not knowing whom to see, or really how I would take care of anything.

Rosa was waiting for me in front of the severely modern building by the large glass doors.

"Can you imagine this crowd? So many people. So many." She was excited and her Caribbean was particularly noticeable. "And the guards have refused entrance."

"Rosa, you said you'd get tickets from the African delegations."

"I know, but only the Senegalese and my friend from Upper Volta have shown up." She had to shout, because the crowd had begun to chant.

She leaned toward me, frowning, "I've only got seven tickets."

154

The people on the sidewalk shouted. "Freedom!" "Freedom!" "Lumumba! Lumumba!"

She said, "Little Carlos is here. The Cuban, you know. He took the tickets and went in with Abbey, Max, Amece and others. He'll bring the tickets back and take in six more. It's the only way." Carlos Moore was an angry young man who moved through Harlem's political sky like a luminous meteor.

I looked over at the black throng. Many had never been in midtown Manhattan, thinking the blocks south of Harlem as dangerous as enemy territory and no man's land. On our casual encouragement, they had braved the perilous journey.

Carlos came trotting through the double doors. "Sister, you have arrived." He grinned, his little chocolate face gleeful. "I am ready for the next group. Let's go! Now!"

I turned, and without thinking about it, plucked the first people in the crowd.

"Give me your placards. You're going in." I held the ungainly weighted sticks and Carlos shouted to the chosen men and women. "Follow me, brothers and sisters. Stay close to me." They disappeared into the dim foyer, and I redistributed the placards.

Rosa had walked away into the crowd. I took her example and moved through the people near the building.

"What's going on, sister?"

"The crackers don't want to let us in, huh?"

"We could break the motherfucker wide open."

"Shit, all we got to do is die. And we gonna do that any goddam way."

I stopped with that group. "Nothing could please the whites more than to have a reason to shoot down innocent black folks. Don't give them the pleasure."

An old woman grabbed my sleeve. "God will bless you, honey. If you keep the children alive."

She sounded wise and was about the age of my grandmother. "Yes, ma'am. Thank you." I took her hand and pulled her away from the seething mass. She would go in with the next group. We walked to the steps together. I turned and raised my voice to explain what had obviously happened.

Informers had alerted the police that Harlem was coming to the U.N. So security had been increased. In order to get into the building we had to exercise restraint. The cops were nervous, so to prevent some trigger-happy idiot from shooting into the crowd, we had to remain cool.

The people assented with a grace I found assuring. The old woman and I reached the top steps as Carlos came through the doors. "Six more. And we move. Now!"

Carlos gathered the next five people along with the old lady and led them into the building.

For the next thirty minutes, as Carlos siphoned off groups of six and led them into the building, more cadres of police arrived to stand armed and confused on the sidewalks and across the street, while plain-clothed white men took photographs of the action.

A marcher grabbed my sleeve. "What you folks think you're doing? You told us to come down here and now you can't get us in." The man was furious. He continued, "Yeah, that's black folks for you. Running around half shaved and grinning."

I wanted to explain how some fink had put us in the cross, but Rosa appeared, taking my other sleeve.

"Come on, Maya. Come on now." Her urgency would not be denied. I looked at the angry man and lied. "I'll be right back".

Inside the gleaming hall, unarmed security guards stood anxiously at their posts. Near the wide stairs leading to the second floor, Carlos was hemmed in by another group of guards.

"I've got my ticket. This is mine." Frayed stubs protruded from his black fist. "They were given to me by a delegate."

Rosa and I pushed into the circle, forcing the guards away. Rosa took his arm. "Come on, Carlos, we've got to go."

We walked together straight and moderately slowly, controlling the desire to break and run, keening into the General Assembly.

Although we were beyond the guards' hearing, Carlos whispered, "The Assembly has started. Stevenson is going to speak soon."

Upstairs, more guards stood silent as we passed. Two black men were waiting by the entry to the hall, anxiety flushing their faces.

"Carlos! We thought they had you, man."

"They'll never have me, mon. I am Carlos, mon."

His assurance had returned. Rosa smiled at me and we entered the dark, quiet auditorium. Miles away, down a steep incline, delegates sat before microphones in a square of light, but the upper balcony was too dim for me to distinguish anything clearly.

After a few seconds, the gloom gave way, and the audience became visible. About seventy-five black people were mixed among the whites. Some women had already pinned veils over their faces.

Amece, Jean and the teacher sat together. Max and Abbey were across the aisle near Sarah and the model. An accented voice droned unintelligibly.

"Uh, uhm, mm, um."

The little white man so far away leaned toward his microphone, his bald forehead shining-white. Dark-rimmed glasses stood out on the well-known face.

A scream shattered his first word. The sound was bloody and broad and piercing. In a second other voices joined it.

"Murderers."

"Lumumba. Lumumba."

"Killers."

"Bigoted sons of bitches."

The scream still rode high over the heads of astounded people who were rising, clutching each other or pushing out toward the aisle.

The houselights came on. Stevenson took off his glasses and looked to the balcony. The shock opened his mouth and made his chin drop.

A man near me screamed, "You Ku Klux Klan motherfuckers."

157

Another yelled, "Murderers."

African diplomats were as alarmed as their white counterparts. I was also shaken. We had not anticipated a riot. We had been expected to stand, veiled and mournful, in a dramatic but silent protest.

"Baby killers."

"Slave drivers."

Terrorized whites in the audience tried to hustle away from the yelling blacks. Security guards rushed through the doors on the upper and lower levels.

The garish lights, the stampede of bodies and the continuing high-pitched scream were overpowering. My knees weakened and I sat down in the nearest seat.

A woman in the aisle beside me screamed at the guards, "Don't dare touch me. Don't put your hands on me, you white bastard!"

The guards were shouting, "Get out. Get out."

The woman said, "Don't touch me, you Belgian bastard."

Below, the diplomats rose and formed an orderly file toward an exit.

When the piercing scream stopped I heard my own voice shouting, "Murderers. Killers. Assassins."

Two women grappled with a guard in the aisle. Carlos had leaped onto a white man's back and was riding him to the floor. A stout black woman held the lapels of a white man in civilian clothes.

"Who you trying to kill? Who you trying to kill? You don't know me, you dog. You don't know who you messing with."

The man was hypnotized and beyond fear, and the woman shook him like a dishrag.

The diplomats had vanished and except for the guards the whites had disappeared. The balcony was ours. Just as in the Southern segregated movie houses, we were in the buzzards' roost again.

Rosa found me and I got up and followed her. We urged the people back to the safety of the street. The black folks strode proudly past the guards, through the hall and out the doors into sunshine.

The waiting crowd, enlarged by latecomers and more police, had changed its mood. Insiders had told outsiders that we had rioted, and now an extravagant disorder was what the blacks wanted, while the law officers yearned for vindication.

"Let's go back in." "Let's go in and show them bastards we mean business." "This ain't no United Nations. This is just united white folks. Let's go back in."

A cadre of police stood on the steps, their eyes glittering. By law, they were forbidden inside the U.N. building, but they were eager to prevent our reentry.

Some folks screamed at the silent seething police.

"You killed Lumumba too. You shit."

"I wish I had your ass on 125th Street."

"Take off your pistol. I'll whip your ass."

Carlos rushed to me.

"We're going to the Belgian Consulate. Walk together." Rosa's voice was loud. "Forty-sixth Street. The Associated Press Building. Let us go. Let's go."

The crowd began to move between a corridor of police which stretched to the street. Up front, someone had started to sing.

"And before I'll be a slave, I'll be buried in my grave . . ."

The song rippled, now high, now low. Picked up by voices and dropped but never discarded.

"And go home to my God and be free."

Mounted police, sitting tall on hot horses, looked down as we crossed First Avenue, singing.

Rosa and I were walking side by side in the last group as we turned into 43rd street. I said, "That scream started it. Wonder who screamed."

She frowned and laughed at the same time. "Amece, and she almost killed Jean."

The marchers around us were singing

159

"No more slavery,
No more slavery,
No more slavery over me."

Rosa continued, "Amece said she looked down and saw Stevenson and thought about Lumumba. She reached to caress her daughter, but Jean jumped and Amece screamed. Unfortunately, she had her arm around Jean's neck. So when Jean jerked, Amece tightened her grip and kept screaming. Nobody was going to hurt her baby. So she screamed." Rosa laughed. "Nobody but Amece. She nearly choked Jean to death."

The crowd was trooping and chanting.

Six mounted police climbed the sidewalk and rode through the stragglers. People jumped out of the way as the horses bore down on them.

A wiry black man unable to escape was being pressed against the wall of a building. I flung myself toward him slapping horses, jutting my elbows into their flanks.

"Get away. Move, dammit."

The man was flat against the wall, ignoring the horses, staring up at the policemen. I reached him and took his hand.

"Come on, brother. Come on, brother."

We walked between the shifting horses and back to Rosa, who had halted the group.

Rosa was grinning, her face filled with disbelief. "Maya Angelou, I thought you were scared of animals. You went into those horses, kicking ass!"

She was right. I had never owned a pet. I didn't understand the intelligent idiocy of dogs or cats; in fact, all animals terrorized me. The day's action had taken away my usual self and made me uncommon. I was literally intoxicated with adventure.

We approached the corner of 46th and Sixth Avenue, and the intersection reminded me of a South American news telecast. For the moment, heavily armed police and angry people seemed to neutralize the scene. Bright sunlight left no face in shadow and

160

the two groups watched each other warily, moving dreamily this way and then that. That way and this. Policemen's hands were never far from their pistols, and plain-clothed officers spoke into the static of walkie-talkies. Black demonstrators edged along the sidewalk, rumbling and carrying battered and torn placards.

Police cars were parked double in the street and a captain walked among his men, talking and looking obliquely at the crowd, trying to evaluate its mood and its intention.

When Rosa dashed away from me and into the shuffling crowd, a beribboned officer came over.

"You're one of the leaders?" His pink face was splotched with red anger.

Following the Southern black advice "If a white man asks you where you're going, you tell him where you've been," I answered, "I'm with the people."

"Where is your permit? You people have to have a permit to demonstrate."

Three black men suddenly appeared, placing themselves between the policemen and me.

"What do you want with this black lady?"

"Watch yourself, Charlie. Don't mess with her."

Instantly more police surrounded my protectors, and black people from the dragging line, seeing the swift action, ran over to encircle the newly arrived police.

I had to make a show of confidence. I looked into the officer's face and said, "Permit? If we left it to you whites we'd be in the same shape as our folks in South Africa. We'd have to have a permit to breathe."

A man standing by my side added, "Naw. We ain't got no damn permit. So you better pull out your pistols and start shooting. Shoot us down now, 'cause we ain't moving."

The policemen, eager to accept the man's invitation, snorted and fidgeted like enraged horses. The officer reigned them in with his voice. He shouted, "It's all right, men. I said, it's all right. Back to your stations."

161

There was a brief period of hateful staring before the cops returned to the street and we rejoined the larger group of black people shuffling along the pavement.

Rosa found me. "Carlos is inside." Her eyes were narrowed. "Somebody said he's been in there over a half-hour. The Belgian Consulate is on the eleventh floor. Maybe the cops have got him."

The knowledge of what police do to black men rose wraithlike before my eyes. Carlos was little and pretty and reminded me of my brother. The cops did have Bailey and maybe he was being clubbed or raped at that very minute. I saw a horrifying picture of Bailey in the hands of madmen but there was nothing I could do about it.

I could do something about Carlos.

I said, "I'm going in. You keep the people marching."

I searched the faces nearest me.

Vus once told me, "If you're ever in trouble, don't under any circumstances ask black middle-class people for help. They always think they have a stake in the system. Look for a *tsotsi*, that's Xhosa for a street hoodlum. A roughneck. A convict. He'll already be angry and he will know that he has nothing to lose."

I continued looking until I saw the man. He was taller than I, rail-thin and the color of bitter chocolate. One deep scar ran from the flange of his left nostril to his ear lobe and another lay between his hairline and his left eyebrow.

I beckoned to him and he came toward me.

"Brother, my name is Maya. I think Carlos Moore is in this building somewhere. He's the leader of this march. The cops may have him and you know what that means."

"Yeah, sister, yeah." He nodded wisely.

"I want to go in and see about him and I need somebody to go with me."

He nodded again and waited.

"It'll be dangerous, but will you go?"

"Sure." The planes on his face didn't change. "Sure, Sister Maya. Let's go." He took my elbow and began to propel me to the steps.

162

I asked, "What's your name?" He said, "Call me Buddy."

Rosa's voice came to me as we went through the revolving doors. "Be careful, Maya."

The lobby was busy with police, guards and milling white men. Although my escort was pushing me quickly toward the bank of elevators, I had time to look at the building's directory. Above the eleventh-floor listing of the Belgian Consulate were the words AMERICAN BOOK COMPANY, 10TH FLOOR. A fat, florid police officer stepped in front of me and my companion.

"Where are you going?"

The *tsotsi* spoke. "None of your goddam business."

I poked his side and said sweetly, "I'm going to the American Book Company."

The cop and the *tsotsi* stared knowingly at each other. Loathing ran between the two men like an electrical current.

"And you. Where do you think you're going?"

"I'm going with her. Every step of the way."

The cop heard the challenge and narrowed his eyes and I heard the protection and felt like a little girl. The pudgy cop followed us to the elevators and I pushed the tenth-floor button, holding on to the black man's hand. The ride was tense and quick. We walked out into the hall and turned to watch the officer's face until the doors closed.

I said, "Let's find the stairs."

Around the corner we saw the exit sign.

"Buddy, you go through and let the door close, then see if you can open it again."

He walked out onto the landing and waited until the door slammed shut. I stepped back as he turned the knob and opened the door from his side.

"Come on. Let's get up there."

We raced up the steps to the eleventh floor. He grabbed the knob, but the door wouldn't open.

"That cracker cop. He beat us to it. Stay here."

He turned and trotted up another flight. I heard him mutter. "This damn door is locked too."

He came down the steps heavily.

"What you wanna do now?"

I couldn't think at the moment. I had only a vague plan to reach the eleventh floor and "see about Carlos." My mind had not budged beyond the possibility of achieving that feat. I looked stupidly at Buddy, who was waiting for an answer. After a few seconds, my voice surfaced. "I guess there's nothing else to do but go back to the street. I'm sorry."

I expected to see disgust or at least derision on my accomplice's face, but he displayed no emotion.

"All right, sister. Let's go."

We walked back down to the tenth floor and I pushed the door, but it resisted. I must have gasped, because he pushed me aside and grabbed the knob. "Let me do it." He took the knob and leaned his body against the metal panel, but the door wouldn't give. Panic accelerated my blood. Like an idiot I had given myself to death. The cops could open the door any minute and blow my brains out. No one would see and no one would be able to protect me. I saw an image of my son in his classroom. Who would tell him, and how would he handle the news? My new husband would receive a telegram in India. What would he think of a wife so frivolous as to commit suicide? My poor mother . . . The man beside me, whom fear had caused me to forget, took my shoulders in his hands.

"Sister. Sister. You ain't got nothin' to worry about. I'm here."

He released me and stood on the landing's edge. "They'll have to walk over my dead body to get to you."

Buddy ran down the steps. I heard him stop on the ninth floor, then his footsteps descended and stopped again and again. In a few seconds he called, "Sister Maya, come on. I got a door. Come on." I met him on the sixth-floor landing. My heart was fluttering so I could hardly catch my breath. The hallway and the elevator looked to me like Canada must have to escaping slaves. We were in the lobby before my embarrassment returned. My hand on his arm turned him around. "Buddy, I apologize for panicking a while ago. I'm going to tell my husband about you."

He looked at me, and shook his head. "Sister, in this country a Negro is always about to get killed, so that ain't nothing. But you tell your husband that a black man was ready to lay down his life for you. That's all."

He took my elbow and guided me past the still-waiting police and to the door. I walked right into Rosa's arms.

"Girl, what happened? Carlos came out just after you went in. A bunch of us were getting ready to go get you." We hugged tightly. I said, "Rosa, you've got to meet this brother," but when I turned to introduce Buddy, he had disappeared into the thinning crowd.

Rosa continued, "You were in there nearly twenty minutes." That was astounding news. I had been bold, blatant and audacious. I had been silly, irresponsible and unprepared. My body had been enclosed with panic and my mind immobilized with fear. A stranger had shown the courage of Vivian Baxter and the generosity of Jesus. And all that had happened in twenty minutes.

Television and radio reporters were walking among the remaining protesters seeking interviews.

One woman spoke into a microphone. "Yes, we're mad. You people pick us off like we're jack rabbits. You dad-gummed right, we're mad." A man walking behind her added, "Lumumba was in the Congo. The Congo is in Africa and we're Africans. You get that?"

CAWAH members had agreed to make no public statements, so we turned our faces when the journalists approached. The line of marchers was exhausted. People had begun to peel away. Their shoulders sagged and they walked heavily. They knew that their latest protest had done no good. They had been Joshua's band, shouting and screaming, singing and yelling at the walls, but Jericho had remained upright, unchanged.

That night I went to Rosa's for dinner and to watch the evening news. The cameras caught black bodies hurtling out of the U.N. doors, and marchers chanting along 46th Street.

Angry faces in profile glided across the screen, shouting accusations. When an unknown, well-dressed man came into view, and speaking pompously, said that he took full responsibility for the demonstration, Jean responded by calling him a sap sucker and turning off the television.

The echo of the day's excitement and the wonder of CAWAH's power to bring all those people from Harlem kept us quiet for a few minutes. When conversation did return we talked about our next moves. The day had proven that Harlem was in commotion and the rage was beyond the control of the NAACP, the SCLC or the Urban League. The fury would turn on itself if it was not outwardly directed. There would be an increase of stabbings and shootings as black people assaulted each other, discharging tension, and blindly looking for a surcease of pained lives.

Rosa and I said, "the Black Muslims" and grinned, because we thought alike and at the same time. Of course, the Muslims, with their exquisite discipline and their absolute stand on black-white relations, would know how to control and use the ferment in Harlem. We should go straight to Malcolm X and lay the situation in his lap. It would be interesting to see what he would do. And it would be a relief to shift the responsibility.

The next day, Guy jumped with excitement. "Mom, you're great. Really great. I wish I had been there. Boy, I wish I could have seen Stevenson's face. Boy, that's fantastic."

John Killens phoned. "Why didn't you let me know you people were going to have a riot? I'm always ready for a riot. You know that, angel."

When I explained that we had only expected a few people, he grunted and said we had fallen into the same trick bag whites are in. We underestimated the black community.

Two days later, Rosa and I walked into the Muslim Restaurant. Making the appointment had been the easiest part. I simply telephoned the Mosque and asked if Mr. Malcolm X could spare a half-hour for two black ladies. After a brief pause I was given a time and a place. Putting my thoughts in respectable order was more difficult, because after I knew Malcolm would see us I became appalled at our presumption.

We told a waitress that we had come to see Mr. Malcolm X. She nodded and walked away, disappearing through a door at the end of the long counter. We stood nervously in the center of the room. In a moment Malcolm appeared at the rear door. His aura was too bright and his masculine force affected me physically. A hot desert storm eddied around him and rushed to me, making my skin contract, and my pores slam shut. He approached, and all my brain would do for me was record his coming. I had never been so affected by a human presence.

Watching Malcolm X on television or even listening to him speak on a podium had been no preparation for meeting him face to face.

"Ladies, *Salaam aleikum.*" His voice was black baritone and musical. Rosa shook hands, and I was able to nod dumbly. Up close he was a great red arch through which one could pass to eternity. His hair was the color of burning embers and his eyes pierced. He offered us a chair at a table and asked a nervous waitress for tea, which she brought in trembling cups.

Rosa was more contained than I, so she began explaining our mission. The sound of her voice helped me to shake loose the constriction of muteness. I joined the telling, and we distributed our story equally, like the patter of a long-time vaudeville duo.

"We—CAWAH . . ."

"Cultural Association of Women of African Heritage."

"Wanted to protest the murder of Lumumba so we—"

"Planned a small demonstration. We didn't expect—"

"More than fifty people—"

"And thousands came."

"That told us that the people of Harlem are angry and that they are more for Africa and Africans"

"than they ever let on . . ."

167

Malcolm was leaning back in his chair, his chin tilted down, his attention totally ours. He straightened abruptly.

"We know of the demonstration, but Muslims were not involved. New York *Times* reporters telephoned me and I told them, 'Muslims do not demonstrate.' And I'll tell you this, you were wrong."

Rosa and I looked at each other. Malcolm X, as the most radical leader in the country, was our only hope, and if he didn't approve of our action then maybe we had misunderstood everything.

"You were wrong in your direction." He continued speaking and looking straight into our eyes. "The people of Harlem are angry. And they have reason to be angry. But going to the United Nations, shouting and carrying placards will not win freedom for anyone, nor will it keep the white devils from killing another African leader. Or a black American leader."

"But"—Rosa was getting angry—"what were we supposed to do? Nothing? I don't agree with that." She had more nerve than I.

"The Honorable Elijah Muhammad teaches us that integration is a trick. A trick to lull the black man to sleep. We must separate ourselves from the white man, this immoral white man and his white religion. It is a hypocrisy practiced by Christian hypocrites."

He continued. White Christians were guilty. Portuguese Catholic priests had sprinkled holy water on slave ships, entreating God to give safe passage to the crews and cargoes on journeys across the Atlantic. American slave owners had used the Bible to prove that God wanted slavery, and even Jesus Christ had admonished slaves to "render unto their masters" obedience. As long as the black man looked to the white man's God for his freedom, the black man would remain enslaved.

I tried not to show my disappointment.

"Thank you. Thank you for your time. Mr. X— oh, I don't know your last name. I mean, how should you be addressed?"

"I am Minister Malcolm. My last name is Shabazz. But just call me Minister Malcolm."

Rosa had stood, irritation on her face.

Malcolm said, "I know you're disappointed." His voice had softened and for a time the Islamic preacher disappeared. "I'll tell you this. By twelve o'clock, some Negro leaders are going to be like Peter in your Christian Bible. They will deny you. There will be statements given to the press, not only refuting what you did, but they will add that you are dangerous and probably Communists. Those Negroes"—he said the word sarcastically—"think they're different from you and that the white man loves them for their difference. They will sell you again and again into slavery. Now, here's what we, the Nation of Islam, will not do. We will not ask the people of Harlem to march anywhere at any time. We will not send black men and black women and black children before armed and crazy white devils, and we will not deny you. We will do two things. We will offer them the religion of Islam the Prophet Muhammad and the Honorable Elijah Muhammad. And we will make a statement to the press. I will say that yesterday's demonstration is symbolic of the anger in this country. That black people were saying they will not always say 'yessir' and 'please, sir.' And they will not always allow whites to spit on them at lunch counters in order to eat hot dogs and drink Coca-Colas." He stood; our audience was over. Suddenly he was aloof and cool, his energy withdrawn. He said, *"Salaam aleikum"* and turned to join a few men who had been waiting for him at the counter.

We left the restaurant in a fog of defeat. Black despair was still real, the murders would continue and we had just used up our last resource. When Rosa and I embraced at the subway there was no elation in our parting.

That evening the radio, television and newspapers bore out Malcolm's predictions.

Conservative black leaders spoke out against us. "That ugly demonstration was carried out by an irresponsible element and does not reflect the mood of the larger black community."

"No good can come from yesterday's blatant disrespect at the U.N.." "It was undignified and unnecessary."

Malcolm X was as good as his word. He said, "Black people are letting white Americans know that the time is coming for ballots or bullets. They know it is useless to ask their enemy for justice. And surely whites are the enemies of blacks, otherwise how did we get to this country in the first place?

12

Vus was back in New York, a little heavier and more distracted. He said the Indian curries had been irresistible and his meetings succeeded but raised new questions which he had to handle at once. He was out of the house early and came home long after dark. Guy was engaged in the mysteries which surround fifteen-year-old boys: The cunning way girls were made. The delicious agony of watching them walk. The painful knowledge that not one of the beauteous creatures would allow herself to be held and touched. Except for the refrigerator, the telephone was his only important link to life. One morning I realized that weeks had passed since I had participated in a conversation with anyone. When Max invited me over to read a script with Abbey, I accepted gladly. He had composed the music for Jean Genet's play, *The Blacks*, which was to open Off-Broadway in the late spring. When I walked into their apartment, a small group of musicians was tuning up beside the piano. I was introduced to the production team.

Sidney Bernstein, the producer, was a frail little man, who sat smiling timidly, his eyes wandering the room unfocused. The energetic and intense director, Gene Frankel, snapped his head from right to left and back again in small jerks, reminding me of a predatory bird, perched on a high bluff. The stage manager, Max Glanville, a tall sturdy black man, was at ease in the room.

He sat composed while his two colleagues twitched. When Frankel said he was ready to hear the music, there was impatience in his voice.

Sidney smiled and said there was plenty of time.

Abbey and I sat opposite each other holding copies of the marked script. We divided the roles evenly and when the music began, we read, sometimes against the music, over it, or waited in intervals as the notes took center stage. Neither of us was familiar with the play, and since its structure was extremely complex, and its language convoluted, we read in monotones, not even trying to make dramatic sense. Finally, we reached the last notes. The evening had seemed to be endless. Gene Frankel was the first to stand. He rushed up to Max, took his hand, looked deep into his eyes, "Great. Great. Just great. We've got to be going. O.K. Thank you, ladies. Thank you. Great reading." Frankel turned around like a kitten trying to catch its tail. "O.K., Sidney? Let's go. Glanville." He turned again. "Musicians? Oh yeah, thanks, guys. Great."

In a second he was at the door, his hand on the knob. Sidney went to the musicians, shaking hands, giving each a bit of a wispy grin. He thanked Max and Abbey and me. "The music was perfect." Glanville looked at his white partners slyly and smiled at us. His leer said he was leaving with them only because he had to, and we would understand.

"O.K., folks. Thanks. Thanks, Max. We'll be talking to you." When the door closed behind them I laughed, partly out of relief. Max asked what was funny. I said the play and the producers.

"You mean you didn't understand it." All of a sudden he was angry and he began to shout at me. He said *The Blacks* was not only a good play, it was a great play. It was written by a white Frenchman who had done a lot of time in prison. Genet understood the nature of imperialism and colonialism and how those two evils erode the natural good in people. It was important that our people see the play. Every black in the United States should see it. Furthermore, as a black woman married to a South African

171

and raising a black boy, I should damn well understand the play before I started laughing at it. And as for ridiculing the white men, at least they were going to put the play on, and all I could do was laugh at them. I ought to have better sense.

The musicians made a lot of noise packing up their instruments. Abbey sat quiet, looking at Max; I got up and gathered my purse. I wanted at least to reach the door before the tears fell.

"Good night."

Abbey called, "Thanks, Maya. Thanks for reading." I was nearly at the elevator before I heard a door and Max's voice at the same time.

"Maya, wait." He walked toward me. I thought that he was sorry to have spoken so harshly. "Take this." He handed me a wrapped package. "Read it." He was nearly barking. "Read it, understand it. Then see if you'll laugh." I took the manuscript and he spun around and went back into his apartment.

Vus studied political releases, Guy did schoolwork and I read *The Blacks*. During the third reading, I began to see through the tortuous and mythical language, and the play's meaning became clear. Genet suggested that colonialism would crumble from the weight of its ignorance, its arrogance and greed, and that the oppressed would take over the positions of their former masters. They would be no better, no more courageous and no more merciful.

I disagreed. Black people could never be like whites. We were different. More respectful, more merciful, more spiritual. Whites irresponsibly sent their own aged parents to institutions to be cared for by strangers and to die alone. We generously kept old aunts and uncles, grandparents and great-grandparents at home, feeble but needed, senile but accepted as natural parts of natural families.

Our mercy was well known. During the thirties Depression, white hobos left freight trains and looked for black neighborhoods. They would appear hungry at the homes of the last hired and the first fired, and were never turned away. The migrants were given cold biscuits, leftover beans, grits and whatever black folks could spare. For centuries we tended, and nursed, often at our breasts, the children of people who despised us. We had cooked the food of a nation of racists, and despite the many opportunities, there were few stories of black servants poisoning white families. If that didn't show mercy, then I misunderstood the word.

As for spirituality, we were Christians. We demonstrated the teachings of Christ. We turned other cheeks so often our heads seemed to revolve on the end of our necks, like old stop-and-go signs. How many times should we forgive? Jesus said seven times seventy. We forgave as if forgiving was our talent. Our church music showed that we believed there was something greater than we, something beyond our physical selves, and that that something, that God, and His Son, Jesus, were always present and could be called "in the midnight hour" and talked to when the "sun raised itself to walk across the morning sky." We could sing the angels out of heaven and bring them to stand thousands thronged on the head of a pin. We could ask Jesus to be on-hand to "walk around" our deathbeds and gather us into "the bosom of Abraham." We told Him all about our sorrows and relished the time when we would be counted among numbers of those who would go marching in. We would walk the golden streets of heaven, eat of the milk and honey, wear the promised shoes and rest in the arms of Jesus, who would rock us and say, "You have labored in my vineyard. You are tired. You are home now, child. Well done." Oh, there was no doubt that we were spiritual.

The Blacks was a white foreigner's idea of a people he did not understand. Genet had superimposed the meanness and cruelty of his own people onto a race he had never known, a race already nearly doubled over carrying the white man's burden of greed and guilt, and which at the same time toted its own insufficiency. I threw the manuscript into a closet, finished with Genet and his narrow little conclusions.

Max Glanville called two days later.

"Maya, we want you in the play." The play? I had jettisoned Genet and his ill-thought-out drama.

Glanville's voice reached through the telephone. "There are two roles and we're just not sure which one would suit you best. So we'd like you to come down and read for us."

I thanked him but I said I didn't think so and hung up. I reported the call to Vus only because it gave me a subject to introduce into dinner conversation. However, he jarred me by laughing. "Americans are either quite slow or terribly arrogant. They do not know or care that there is a world beyond their world, where tradition dictates action. No wife of an African leader can go on the stage." He laughed again. "Can you imagine the wife of Martin King or Sobukwe or Malcolm X standing on a stage being examined by white men?" The unlikely picture made him shake his head. "No. No, you do not perform in public."

I had already refused Glanville's invitation, but Vus's reaction sizzled in my thoughts. I was a good actress, not great but certainly competent. For years before I met Vus, my rent had been paid and my son and I had eaten and been clothed by money I made working on stages. When I gave Vus my body and loyalty I hadn't included all the rights to my life. I felt no loyalty to *The Blacks*, since it had not earned my approval, yet I chafed under Vus' attitude of total control. I said nothing.

Abbey had been asked to take a role in the play. I told her that Vus had said he wouldn't allow me to. She said Max thought the play was important, and since Vus respected Max, maybe they ought to talk. Abbey hung up and in moments Max called, asking for my husband.

I heard Vus hang up the telephone in the living room. He walked into the kitchen. "I'm meeting Max for a conference." Every meeting was a conference and each conversation a discussion of pith. I nodded, and kept on washing dishes.

Vus came home and asked for the manuscript. I recovered the play from the back of the closet and gave it to him. Guy and I played Scrabble on the dining-room table while Vus sat under a lamp in the living room. He would rise from time to time and pass through to the kitchen getting a fresh drink. Then he would return silently to the sofa and *The Blacks*.

Guy went off to bed. Vus still read. I knew he was going back and forth through the script. He hardly looked up when I said good night.

I was in a deep sleep when he shook me awake. "Maya. Wake up. I have to talk to you." He sat on the side of the bed. The crumpled pages were spread out beside him.

"This play is great. If they still want you, you must do this play." I came awake like my mother—immediately and entirely aware.

I said, "I don't agree with the conclusion. Black people are not going to become like whites. Never."

"Maya, you are so young, so, so young." He patronized me as if I were the little shepherd girl and he the old man of Kilimanjaro.

"Dear Wife, that is a reverse racism. Black people are human. No more, no less. Our backgrounds, our history make us act differently."

I grabbed a cigarette from the night stand, ready to jump into the discussion. I listed our respectfulness, our mercy, our spirituality. His rejoinder stopped me. "We are people. The root cause of racism and its primary result is that whites refuse to see us simply as people."

I argued, "But the play says given the chance, black people will act as cruel as whites. I don't believe it."

"Maya, that is a very real possibility and one we must vigilantly guard against. You see, my dear wife"—he spoke slowly, leaning his big body toward me—"my dear wife, most black revolutionaries, most black radicals, most black activists, do not really want change. They want exchange. This play points to that likelihood. And our people need to face the temptation. You must act in *The Blacks*."

He continued talking in the bed and I fell asleep in his arms.

The next morning Abbey and I went down to the St. Mark's Playhouse on Second Avenue. Actors sat quietly in the dimly lit seats, and Gene Frankel paced on the stage. Max Glanville had seen us enter. He nodded in recognition and walked to the edge of the stage. He stopped Gene in mid-step and whispered. Frankel lifted his head and looked out.

"Maya Make. Maya Angelou Make. Abbey Lincoln. Come down front, please." We found seats in the front row.

Glanville came back and sat down. "Abbey, we want you to read the role of Snow. But, Maya, we've not decided whether you should do the Black Queen or the White Queen."

I said, "Of course the Black Queen."

"Just read a little of both roles." He got up and went away, returning with an open manuscript.

"Read this section." He flipped pages. "And then read this underlined part."

I stepped up on the low stage and without raising my head to look at the audience began to read. The section was short and I turned the script to the next underlined pages and recited another monologue without adding vocal inflection.

There was scattered applause when I finished and a familiar husky voice shouted, "You've got all the parts, baby." Another voice said, "Yes, but let's see your legs."

Godfrey Cambridge flopped all over a seat in the third row and Flash Riley sat next to him.

I joined them and we talked about Cabaret for Freedom, while Frankel, Bernstein and Glanville stood together on the stage muttering.

Frankel shouted, "Lights" and the house lights came on. He walked to the edge of the stage. "Ladies and gentlemen, I'd like to introduce you to each other, and please mark your scripts. Godfrey Cambridge is Diouf. Roscoe Lee Brown is Archibald. James Earl Jones is Village. Cicely Tyson is Virtue. Jay Riley is the Governor, Raymond St. Jacques is the Judge. Cynthia Belgrave is Adelaide. Maya Angelou Make is the White Queen. Helen Martin is Felicity, or the Black Queen. Lou Gossett is Newport News. Lex Monson is the Missionary. Abbey Lincoln is Snow and Charles Gordone is the Valet. Max Roach is composer, Talley Beatty is choreographer and Patricia Zipprodt is costume designer. Ethel Ayler is understudying Abbey and Cicely. Roxanne Roker understudies Maya and Helen."

I looked around. Ethel and I exchanged grins. We had been friends years before during the European tour of *Porgy and Bess*.

Frankel continued, "We've got a great play and we're going to work our asses off."

Rehearsals began with a playground joviality and in days accelerated into the seriousness of a full-scale war. Friendships and cliques were formed quickly. The central character was played by Roscoe Lee Brown, and within a week he became the chief figure off stage as well. His exquisite diction and fastidious manners were fortunately matched with wit. He was unflappable.

James Earl Jones, a beige handsome bull of a man watched Frankel with fierce stares, reading his lips, scanning his hairline and chin, ear lobes and neck. Then suddenly James Earl would withdraw into himself with a slammed-door finality.

Lou Gossett, lean and young, skyrocketed on and off the stage, innocent and interested. For all his boyish bounding he had developed listening into an art. Cocking an ear at the speaker, his soft eyes caring and his entire body taut with attention.

Godfrey and Jay "Flash" Riley competed for company comedian. When Flash won, Godfrey changed. The clowning began to disappear and he sobered daily into a drab, studious actor.

Cicely, delicate and black-rose beautiful, was serious and aloof. She sat in the rear of the theater, her small head bent into the manuscript, saving her warmth for the character and her smiles for the stage. Raymond, looking like a matinee idol, and Lex were old-time friends. They studied their roles together, breaking each other up with camped-up readings. Helen and Cynthia were professionals; just watching them, I knew that they would have their lines, remember the director's blocking and follow the steps of Talley's choreography without mistakes in a shorter time than anyone else. Charles Gordone, a finely fashioned, small yellow man, made slight fun of everything and everyone, including himself as another target for sarcasm.

There was some resistance to Frankel's direction on the grounds that, being white, he was unable to understand black motivation. In other quarters there was a submission which bordered on obsequiousness and which brought to mind characterizations of Stepin Fetchit.

Each day, tension met us as we walked into the theater and lay like low morning fog in the aisles.

Abbey and I, with the solidarity of a tried friendship, read and studied together, or joined by Roscoe, lunched at a nearby restaurant where we discussed the day's political upheavals. We three would not have called ourselves solely actors. Abbey was a jazz singer, I was an activist, and although Roscoe had played Shakespearean roles and taught drama, he had also been a sprinting champion and an executive with a large liquor company. Early on, we agreed that *The Blacks* was an important play but "the play" was not the only thing in our lives.

My marriage was only a few months old, Vus was still an enigma I hadn't solved and the mystery was sexually titillating. I was in love. Guy's grades had improved but he was seldom home. When I offered to invite the parents of his new friends over for dinner, he laughed at me.

"Mom, that's old-timey. This isn't Los Angeles, this is New York City. People don't do that." He laughed again when I said people in N.Y.C. have parents and parents eat too.

"I haven't even met most of those guys' folks. Look, Mom, some of them are seventeen and eighteen. How would I look if I said, 'My mom wants to meet your mom'? Foolish."

The Harlem Writers Guild accepted that most of my time would be spent at the theater, but that did not release me from my obligation to attend meetings and continue writing.

178

By the first week's end, Frankel had completed the staging and Talley was teaching the actors his choreography. The set was being constructed and I was laboring over lines.

Raymond, Lex, Flash, Charles and I played the "whites."

We wore exaggerated masks and performed from a platform nine feet above the stage. Below us, the "Negroes" (the rest of the company) enacted for our benefit a rape-murder by a black man (played by Jones) of a white woman (a masked Godfrey Cambridge). In retaliation we, the colonial power—royalty (the White Queen), the church (Lex Monson), the law (Raymond St. Jacques) the military (Flash Riley) and the equivocating liberal (Charles Gordone)—descended into Africa to make the blacks pay for the crime. After a duel between the two queens, the blacks triumphed and killed the whites one by one. Then in sarcastic imitation of the vanquished "whites," the black victors ascended the ramp and occupied the platform of their former masters.

The play was delicious to our taste. We were only acting, but we were black actors in 1960. On that small New York stage, we reflected the real-life confrontations that were occurring daily in America's streets. Whites did live above us, hating and fearing and threatening our existence. Blacks did sneer behind their masks at the rulers they both loathed and envied. We would throw off the white yoke which dragged us down into an eternal genuflection.

I started enjoying my role. I used the White Queen to ridicule mean white women and brutal white men who had too often injured me and mine. Every inane posture and haughty attitude I had ever seen found its place in my White Queen.

Genet had been right at least about one thing. Blacks should be used to play whites. For centuries we had probed their faces, the angles of their bodies, the sounds of their voices and even their odors. Often our survival had depended upon the accurate reading of a white man's chuckle or the disdainful wave of a white woman's hand. Whites, on the other hand, always knew that no serious penalty threatened them if they misunderstood blacks.

Whites were safely isolated from our concerns. When they chose, they could lift the racial curtain which separated us. They could indulge in sexual escapades, increase our families with mulatto bastards, make fortunes out of our music and eunuchs out of our men, then in seconds they could step away, and return unscarred to their pristine security. The cliché of whites being ignorant of blacks was not only true, but understandable. Oh, but we knew them with the intimacy of a surgeon's scalpel.

I dressed myself in the hated gestures and made the White Queen gaze down in loathing at the rotten stinking stupid blacks, who, although innocent, like beasts were loathsome nonetheless.

It was obvious that the other actors also found effective motivation. The play became such a cruel parody of white society that I was certain it would flop. Whites were not so masochistic as to favor a play which ridiculed and insulted them, and black playgoers were scarce.

James Baldwin was a friend of Gene Frankel's and he attended rehearsals frequently. He laughed loudly and approvingly at our performances and I talked with him often. When I introduced him to Vus they took to each other with enthusiasm.

At dress rehearsal, on the eve of opening night, black friends, family and investors who had been invited hooted and stamped their feet throughout the performance. But I reckoned their responses natural. They were bound to us, as fellow blacks, black sympathizers or investors.

Vus and Guy grinned and assured me that I was the best actor on the stage. I accepted their compliments easily.

On the morning of opening night, the cast gathered in the foyer, passing jitters from hand to hand, like so many raw eggs. I looked around for Abbey but she hadn't arrived.

When we walked into the dark theater, Gene Frankel bellowed from the stage.

"Everybody down front. Everybody."

He was having a more serious nervous attack than we who had to face the evening audience. I snickered. Roscoe Brown turned to me and made a face of arch innocence.

We filled the front rows, as Frankel paced out the length of the stage. He stopped and looked out at the actors.

His voice quivered. "We have no music. No music and Abbey Lincoln will not be opening tonight. Max Roach has taken his music out of the show."

He threw out the information and waited, letting the words rest in our minds.

Anxious looks were exchanged in the front row.

"Abbey's understudy is ready. She's been rehearsing all morning."

We turned and saw Ethel sitting poised stage left. Frankel added, "We can go on. We have to go on, but there is a song and the dance, for which we don't have a damn note."

Moans and groans lifted up in the air. We had endured the work, the late nights and early mornings of concentration, the long subway trips, the abandoned families, Talley Beatty's complex choreography and the director's demanding staging.

Max Roach was a genius, a responsible musician and my friend. I knew he had to have a reason.

I got up and went outside to the public telephone.

Max answered, sounding like a slide trombone. "The son of a bitches reneged. We had an agreement and the producers reneged on it."

"And Abbey is out of the play?"

"You goddam right."

"Well, Max, you won't hate me if I stay?"

"Hell no. But my wife will not get up on that stage."

Frankel had said we would open with or without the music.

I asked, "Max, would it be all right if I wrote the tunes? We can get along with two tunes."

"I don't give a damn. I just don't want to have that bastard using my music.

"I'll still be your sister."

Max was an attentive brother but he could be a violent enemy.

"Yeah. Yeah. You're my sister."

The telephone was slammed down.

If I stopped to think about my next move, I might convince myself out of it. Black folks said, "Follow your first mind."

I beckoned Ethel from the aisle. She rose and we walked into the lobby. Ethel had musical training and I had composed tunes for my album and for Guy. Together we could easily write the music for just two songs.

Ethel had the air of a woman born pretty. The years of familial adoration, the compliments of strangers, and the envy of plain women had given her a large share of confidence.

"Sure, Maya. We can do it. It's just two songs, right? Let's get to the piano."

We walked down the stage to where Frankel was in conference with Talley and Glanville.

"We'll write the music."

"What?"

"We'll write it this afternoon."

I added, "And teach it to the cast."

Frankel nearly jumped into Sidney Bernstein's arms. "Did you hear that?"

Bernstein smiled and waggled his head happily.

"I heard. I heard. Let's let them do it. If they say they can do it, let's let them do it. Nice girls. Nice ladies. Let them do it."

Sidney's small frame shook with eagerness. "Dismiss the cast. Let them have the theater."

Frankel nodded.

Ethel and I sat close on the piano stool. The old *Porgy and Bess* companionship was still good between us. We agreed that the key of C, with no flats or sharps, would be easier for nonsinging actors to learn. Ethel played a melody in the upper register and I added notes. We spoke the lyrics and adjusted the melody to fit. Within an hour, we had composed two tunes. The cast returned from the break. They stood around the piano and listened to our melodies. I turned at the first laughter, ready to defend our work, but when

I looked at the actors I saw that their laughter was with me and themselves. Ethel Ayler and I had not done anything out of the ordinary. We had simply proved that black people had to be slick, smart and damned quick.

That night the play began on a pitch of high scorn. The theater became a sardonic sanctuary where we sneered at white saints and spit on white gods. Most blacks in the audience reacted with amusement at our blasphemous disclosures, although there were a few who coughed or grunted disapproval. They were embarrassed at our blatancy, preferring that our people keep our anger behind masks, and as usual under control.

However, whites loved *The Blacks*. At the end of the play, the audience stood clapping riotously and bellowing, "Bravo," "Bravo." The cast had agreed not to bow or smile. We looked out at the pale faces, no longer actors playing roles written by a Frenchman thousands of miles distant. We were courageous black people, looking directly into enemy eyes. Our impudence further excited the audience. Loud applause continued long after we left the stage.

We howled in our dressing rooms. If the audience missed the play's obtrusive intent, then the crackers were numbly insensitive. On the other hand, if they understood, and still liked the drama, they were psychically sick, which we suspected anyway.

We were a hit, and we were happy.

Blacks understood and enjoyed the play, but each night in the theater whites outnumbered my people four to one, and that fact was befuddling. Whites didn't come to the Lower East Side of New York to learn that they were unkind, unjust and unfair. Black orators, more eloquent than Genet, had informed white Americans for three centuries that our living conditions were intolerable. David Walker in 1830 and Frederick Douglass in 1850 had revealed the anguish and pain of life for blacks in the United States. Martin Delaney and Harriet Tubman, Marcus Garvey and Dr. DuBois, and Martin King and Malcolm X had explained with anger, passion and persuasion that we were living precariously on the ledge of life, and that if we fell, the entire structure, which had prohibited us living room, might crumble as well.

So in 1960, white Americans should have known all they needed to know about black Americans.

Why, then, did they crowd into the St. Mark's Playhouse and sit gaping as black actors flung filthy words and even filthier meanings into their faces? The question continued to stay with me like a grain of sand wedged between my teeth. Not painful but a constant irritant.

At last, a month after we had opened, I was given an answer. That evening the cast had changed into street clothes and gathered in the lobby to meet friends. A young white woman of about thirty, expensively dressed and well cared for, grabbed my hand.

"Maya? Mrs. Make?" Her face was moist with tears. Her nose and the area around it, were red. Immediately, I felt sorry for her.

"Yes?"

"Oh, Mrs. Make." She started to sob. I asked her if she'd like to come to my dressing room. My invitation was like cold water on her emotion.

She shook her head, "Oh no. Nothing like that. Of course not, I'm all right."

The rush of blood was disappearing from her face, and when she spoke again her voice was clearer.

"I just wanted you to know . . . I just wanted to say that I've seen the play five times." She waited.

"Five times? We've only been playing four weeks."

"Yes, but a lot of my friends . . ."—now she was in control of herself again—"a lot of us have seen the play more than once. A woman in my building comes twice a week."

"Why? Why do you come back?"

"Well"—she drew herself up—"well, we support you. I mean, we understand what you are saying."

The blur of noise drifted around us, but we were an isolated inset, a picture of American society. White and black talking at each other.

184

"How many blacks live in your building?"

"Why, none. But that doesn't mean . . ."

"How many black friends do you have? I mean, not counting your maid?"

"Oh," she took a couple of steps backward. "You're trying to insult me."

I followed her. "You can accept the insults if I am a character on stage, but not in person, is that it?"

She looked at me with enough hate to shrivel my heart. I put my hand out.

"Don't touch me." Her voice was so sharp it caught the attention of some bystanders. Roscoe appeared abruptly. Still in character, giving me a little bow, "Hello, Queen."

The woman turned to leave, but I caught her sleeve. "Would you take me home with you? Would you become my friend?"

She snatched her arm away, and spat out, "You people. You people." And walked away.

Roscoe asked, "And pray, what was that?"

"She's one of our fans. She comes to the theater and allows us to curse and berate her, and that's her contribution to our struggle."

Roscoe shook his head slowly. "Oh dear. One of those."

The subject was closed.

13

The lipstick smudge was not mine, nor did the perfume come from my bottles. I laid Vus's shirt across the chair and hung his suit from the doorknob. Then I sat down to wait for him to come from the shower.

We had not discussed infidelity; I had simply never thought of it. But the third time Vus's clothes were stained with the evidence of other women's make-up I had to face the possibility.

He came into the bedroom, tying the belt of his silk paisley dressing gown.

"Dear, shall we go out to breakfast? I have a meeting downtown. We could go to Broadway and then—".

"Vus, who is the woman? Or rather, who are the women?"

He turned to me and dropped his hands to his side. His face as blank as a wooden slat.

"Women? What women?" The round eyes which I loved were glazed over, shutting me out. "What stupidness are you talking about?"

I kept my voice low. I was asking because I was my mother's daughter and I was supposed to be courageous and honest. I didn't want an honest answer. I wished for him to deny everything, or to hand me any contrived explanation.

"The lipstick. It's fuchsia. It's not mine. This time the perfume is Tweed. I have never worn that scent."

"Ah," he smiled, stretching and opening his fine lips, allowing me a flash of even teeth. "Ah, my darling, you're jealous." He walked over and took my hands and pulled me up from the chair. He held me close and his belly shook against mine. He was laughing at me.

"My darling wife is a little jealous." His voice and body rumbled. He released me and looked into my eyes.

"My dear, there are no other women. You are the only love in my world. You are the only woman I've ever wanted and all that I have."

That was what I wanted to hear, but as a black American woman, I had a history to respect and a duty to discharge. I looked at him directly.

"Vus, if you fell in love with Abbey, or Rosa or Paule, I could understand. I would be hurt but not insulted. They are women who would not intend to hurt me, but love is like a virus. It can happen to anybody at any time. But if you chippie on me, you could get hurt, and I mean seriously."

Vus pulled away. We were face to face, but he had withdrawn into his privacy.

"Don't you ever threaten me. I am an African. I do not scare easily and I do not run at all. Do not question me again. You are my wife. That is all you need to know."

He dressed and left without repeating his breakfast invitation.

I walked around the house thinking of my alternatives. Separation was not possible. Too many friends had advised me against the marriage, and my pride would not allow me to prove them right. Guy would never forgive me if I moved us one more time and I couldn't risk losing the only person who really loved me. If I caught Vus flagrantly betraying me, I would get a gun and blow his ass away or wait until he slept and pour boiling lye in his mouth. I would never use poison, it could take too long to act.

I hung his suit near an open window and washed the lipstick stain from his shirt.

There was a sad irony in the truth that I was happier in the dusty theater than in my pretty apartment on Central Park West.

Despite the clash of cultures, Guy and Vus were building a friendship. My son was making a strenuous effort to understand the ways of "Dad." He was interested in knowing what it must have been like to be a black male growing up in Africa. Vus was pleased by Guy's interest and accepted his free, curious upbringing, although it was alien to his own. When Guy questioned his stepfather's announcements, Vus took the time to explain that an African youngster would never ask an adult why he had done or said a certain thing. Rather, African youths courteously accepted grown-up statements, then went off on their own to find the answers that suited them. They sat together, laughing, talking and playing chess. They were pleased with the dinners I prepared, but when I called their attention to the fresh flowers on the table or a new dress I was wearing, their reactions were identical.

"How very nice, my wife."

"Lovely, Mom. Really very lovely."

"Guy, your mother makes a beautiful house for us."

They treated me as if I were the kind and competent family retainer.

Guy had forgotten the years when I had encouraged him to interrogate me, question my rules, try to pick apart my every conclusion. There had been no father to bring balance into the pattern of my parenting, so he had had the right to question and I had the responsibility of explaining. Now Vus was teaching him to be an African male, and he was an apt student. Ambiguity stretched me like elastic. I yearned for our old closeness, and his dependence, but I knew he needed a father, a male image, a man in his life. I had been raised in a fatherless home, so I didn't even know what fathers talked about to their daughters, and surely I had no inkling of what they taught their sons.

I did know that Guy was treating me in a new and unpleasant way. My face was no longer examined for approval, nor did he weigh my voice for anger. He laughed with Vus, and consulted Vus. It was what I said I wanted, but I had to admit to myself that for my son I had become only a reliable convenience. A something of very little importance.

At home, Vus read American, European and African papers, clipping articles which he later copied and sent to colleagues abroad. He spent mornings at the United Nations, buttonholing delegates, conspiring with other African freedom fighters and trying to convince the press that South Africa in revolution would make the Algerian seven-year-war appear like a Sunday School picnic. He talked to everyone he thought influential—bankers, lawyers, clergymen and stockbrokers. I decided to accept that the make-up which smudged his collars and the sweet aromas which perfumed his clothes came from brushes with the secretaries of powerful men.

I started going to the theater early and returning home reluctantly.

Backstage, Roscoe Lee Browne and I acted out a two-character drama which brought color into my slowly fading life. Our strongest expressions were silent, and physical touching was limited to scrupulous pecks on each other's cheeks. More picturesque than handsome, his attentions held no threat or promise of intimacy.

Although the other cast members appeared oblivious to the measure of my misery, he noticed but was too discreet to embarrass me with questions.

When I sat in my dressing room, working the crossword puzzle, or pressing a poem into shape, Roscoe's light step would sound beyond the door.

"Hello, my dear. It's outside. By the door."

I would jump to catch the sight of him, but the hallway was always empty, save a neat posy resting against the wall, or one flower wrapped in flimsy green paper.

The constancy and delicacy of Roscoe's concern made him the ideal hero for fantasy and the necessary contrast to my real life. He was all pleasure and no offense, excitement without responsibility. If we had embraced or if we once discussed the torment of my marriage, our private ritual of romance would have failed, overburdened by ordinariness. If one is lucky a solitary fantasy can totally transform one million realities.

My controlled paranoia prevented me from realizing the seriousness of a phone call I received one evening.

When I picked up the receiver, a man's throaty voice whispered "Maya Make? Vusumzi Make is not coming home."

The statement surprised me but I wasn't alarmed. I asked, "Did he ask you to tell me that? Why didn't he call? Who are you?"

The man said, "Vusumzi will never come home again." He hung up the telephone.

I walked around the living room trying to sort out the message. The English was labored but I could not place the origin of the heavy accent. Vus knew so many foreigners, the man could have been from any country in the world. He also knew many women, and just possibly an African diplomat suspected that his wife and Vus were having an affair. He telephoned, not so much to threaten Vus, as to awaken my suspicions. He had wasted his money and his time. When I left for the theater, Vus hadn't returned home.

During the play the memory of the telephone call lay just under the remembered lines. Helen Martin and I were engaged in the play's final duel when the idea came to me that Vus might be in danger. The angry husband could have already hurt him. Maybe he had been caught with the man's wife and had been shot or stabbed. I finished the play, and only Roscoe took notice of my distraction. Each time I looked at him, he raised an eyebrow or pursed his lips, or gave me a questioning glance.

After the final ensemble stare into the audience, I turned and rushed for my dressing room, but Roscoe caught up with me in the corridor behind the stage.

"Maya, are you all right?"

The care on his face activated my tears. "It's Vus. I'm worried."

He nodded. "Oh yes, I see." He couldn't possibly see and I couldn't possibly tell him. We walked into the lobby en route to the dressing rooms, and Vus stepped out of the crowd of playgoers.

"Good evening, my dearest." He was whole and he was beautiful.

Roscoe smiled as they shook hands. He said, "Mr. Make, our Queen is a great actress. Tonight she excelled herself." He inclined his head toward me and walked away. I knew that Vus didn't approve of public displays of emotion, so I hugged him quickly and went to change into street clothes.

I couldn't hold my relief. In the taxi I rubbed his large round thigh, and put my head on his chest, breathing in his living scent. "You are loving me tonight." He chuckled and the sound rumbled sweetly in my ear.

He made drinks at home and we sat on the good sofa. He took my hand.

"You are very nervous. You have been excited. What happened at the theater?"

I told him about the telephone call and his face changed. He began chewing the inside of his bottom lip; his eyes were deep and private.

190

I faked a light laugh and said, "I thought some irate husband had caught you and his wife *in flagrante,* and maybe he . . ."

I shut up. I sounded silly even to myself. Vus was far away.

When he spoke his voice was cold and his speech even more precise than usual.

"We must have the number changed. I'm surprised it took them so long."

I didn't understand. He explained. "That was someone from the South African police. They do that sort of thing. Telephone the wives of freedom fighters and tell them their husbands or their children have been killed." He grunted, "I guess I should be insulted that they are just beginning on you. It indicates that they have not been taking me seriously." He turned his large body to face me. "Tomorrow, I'll have the number changed. And I will step up my campaign."

The telephone incident brought me closer to the reality of South African politics than all the speeches I had heard. That voice stayed in my ear like the inane melody of a commercial jingle. When I least expected it, it would growl, "Maya Make? Vusumzi Make will never come home again."

I wanted to stay at Vus's side, go everywhere with him. My concern followed him in the street, in taxis, trailed him into the U.N. Even when we were at home, I wasn't satisfied unless we were in the same room. Vus's attempts to reassure me were futile. Worry had come to live with me, and it sat in the palms of my hands like beads of sweat. It returned even as I wiped it away.

The second telephone call came about two weeks later.

"Maya Make? Do you know your husband is dead?" The voice was different but the accent was the same. "His throat has been cut." I slammed down the telephone, and a second later I picked it up and screamed obscenities over the buzz of the dial tone. "You're a lying dog. You racist, Apartheid-loving, baby-killing son of a bitch." When I replaced the telephone, I had used every profane word I knew and used them in every possible combination. When I told Vus he said he'd have the number changed again. He worried that such tactics threw me. I could expect those and worse. I decided if the phone calls continued, I would handle them and keep the news to myself.

Having a live-in father had a visible effect on my son. All his life Guy had been casual to the point of total indifference about his clothing, but under Vus's influence, he became interested in color-coordinated outfits. Vus took him to a tailor to be fitted for two vested suits. He bought splendid shoes and button-down shirts for my fifteen-year-old, and Guy responded as if he had been waiting for such elegance all his life.

The telephone calls resumed. I was told that I could pick up my husband's body at Bellevue, or that he had been shot to death in Harlem. Whenever I was home alone, I watched the telephone as if it were a coiled cobra. If it rang, I would grab its head and hold on. I never said hello but waited for the caller's voice. If I heard "Maya Make," I would start to quietly explain that South Africa would be free someday and all the white racists had better be long-distance swimmers or have well-stocked life rafts, because the Africans were going to run them right to the ocean. After my statement I would replace the receiver softly and think, That ought to get them. Usually, I could spend an hour or so complimenting myself on my brilliant control, before worry would snake its way into my thoughts. Then I would use the same telephone to try to locate Vus.

Mburumba Kerina, of the South-West Africa People's Organization, was his friend and lived in Brooklyn. I would call and Jane, Kerina's black American wife, would answer.

"Hi, Jane. It's Maya."

"Oh hello, Maya. How are things?"

"O.K. and with you?"

"Oh nothing. And with you?"

"Nothing." Then she would shatter my hopes that my husband was at her house. "How is Vus?"

"Oh fine. And Mburumba?"

"Just fine. We ought to get together soon."

"Yes, very soon. Well, take care."

"You too. Bye."

"Bye."

Jane never knew how I envied her unusual assurance. She was younger than I and had been working as a guide at the U.N. when she met Kerina. They fell in love and married, and she settled into the nervous life of a freedom fighter's wife as coolly as if she had married the minister of a small-town Baptist church.

When I found Vus after numerous phone calls, I gave reasons contrived for my interruptions.

"Let's go to dinner after the play."

"Let's go straight home after the play."

"Let's go to a bar after the play."

Vus was a master of intrigue, so I suppose that I never fooled him with my amateur cunning, but he was simply generous enough to pretend. One afternoon I answered the telephone and was thumped into a fear and subsequent rage so dense that I was made temporarily deaf.

"Hello, Maya Make?" Shreds of a Southern accent still hung in the white woman's voice.

"Yes? Maya Make speaking." I thought the woman was probably a journalist or a theater critic, wanting an interview from Maya Angelou Make, the actress.

"I'm calling about Guy." My mind shifted quickly from a pleasant anticipation to apprehension.

"Are you from his school? What is the matter?"

"No, I'm at Mid-town Hospital. I'm sorry but there's been a serious accident. We'd like you to come right away. Emergency ward."

She hung up. I grabbed my purse and the keys, slammed the door, raced down the stairs and was standing on the pavement before I realized I didn't know the address of the hospital. Fortunately, a taxi had stopped by a traffic light. I ran over and asked the driver if he knew where the Mid-town Hospital was located. He nodded and I got into the cab and said, "Please hurry. It's my son."

My watch said it was eleven, so Guy was in school and couldn't have been hurt in a traffic accident. Maybe there had been a gang fight. The cabbie cut in front of cars, causing other drivers to honk their horns and screech their tires, but it seemed that time and the taxi were crawling.

I paid with bills I never saw and ran through the doors of the Emergency entrance. A young black nurse at the desk looked at me wearily.

"Yes?"

I told her that my son had been hurt, and I wanted to know how badly, and where was he and could I see him? I told her his name, and she began to run her finger down a list. She continued examining the next page. She didn't find Guy's name. I told her I had received a phone call. She said they had not admitted a Guy Johnson and was I sure of the hospital? I heard the caller's voice. "I'm at Mid-town Hospital . . ."

She was lying. She was in the South African service. The thoughts slammed into my consciousness like blows to the heart. For the first time since I heard "I'm calling about Guy" I became aware of thinking.

I went to a pay phone and called Guy's school. After a few minutes I learned that he was in history class.

I walked up Central Park West toward the apartment, too angry to savor relief. I thought of the greedy immorals who lay claim to a people's land by force, and denied the existence of other human beings because of their color. I had opposed the racist regime on principle because it was ugly, violent, debasing and murderous. My husband had his own reasons for trying to bring down the government of Verwoerd and I had supported him. But as I walked under the green trees, and smelled the aroma of young summer flowers, I felt a spasm of hate constrict my throat and tighten my chest. To break a mother's heart for no gain was the most squalid act I could imagine. My defiance from now on would be personal.

.   .   .

Ethel Ayler had a co-starring role in a new Broadway play, so she was leaving *The Blacks*. We talked backstage on her last night.

Ethel said, "Maya, Sidney ought to pay us something for our music." I agreed.

We had tried to squeeze money out of the producer on three or four occasions, but each time we mentioned being paid for composing the two songs, he had laughed and invited us to lunch or dinner. Now when Ethel was closing we decided to make a last attempt. We changed clothes quickly and rushed into the lobby, where we saw Sidney Bernstein standing alone.

Ethel and I walked over to him. Ethel said, "Sidney, you know this was my last night. I start rehearsing *Kwamina* tomorrow."

Sidney turned and gave Ethel an insipid little smile, "Yeah, Ethel, congratulations. I hope it'll be a hit."

I said, "So does she, Sidney. But we want to talk to you about money. You have to pay us something for composing the music for this show."

He raised his chin and looked in my face. He didn't even try to dilute his scorn.

"Get off my back, will you? You didn't compose anything. I saw you. You just sat down at the piano and made up something."

Ethel and I stared at him, then at each other. The people Sidney had been waiting for arrived, collected him and, laughing, walked down the stairs.

I saw Ethel control her features. She closed her lips and made her eyes vacant. When she shrugged her shoulders I thought I knew what she was going to say.

"He's a fool, Maya. Forget him." I had anticipated correctly. She held her cosmetic case delicately in her left and waved at me elegantly with her right. "Take it easy, Maya. Let's keep in touch." She walked away. A Broadway success was her future, so she could ignore Sidney Bernstein's unfairness, However, I couldn't. And the statement that I had composed nothing, I had simply sat down at the piano and made the music up, clogged the movement of my brain.

Vus and James Baldwin were waiting at the bottom of the stairs, so I dropped the befuddlement on them.

What did it mean? The stupid bastard was of a piece with the other arrogant thieves who took the work of black artists without even threatening them with drawn pistols. I wasn't locked into *The Blacks.*

Vus still paid most of the bills, so I wasn't dependent on the job, and since I had no theatrical ambition I didn't have to be afraid that the producers would bad-mouth me off and on Broadway. Vus and Jim stayed quiet.

Vus took my shoulders in his hands and pressed his thumbs into the soft muscles at the joint of my arms. The pain made me forget about Sidney Bernstein, Ethel Ayler, the music and *The Blacks.* I stopped crying and he released me.

"My dear. You will never return to this theater. You have just closed."

I looked at Jim Baldwin. Vus's statement was as shocking as Bernstein's rejection. I knew that Jim would understand that I couldn't simply not return to the the theater. He would explain that as a member of Equity, the theatrical union, I was obliged to give at least two weeks' notice. Jim was silent. Although we three stood in arm's reach of each other, he watched Vus and me as if we were screen actors and he was sitting apart in a distant auditorium.

I said, "I can't close without giving notice. My union will have me up on charges. Bernstein can sue me . . ."

Vus walked away to the pavement's edge and hailed a taxi. I whispered to Jim, "Tell him I can't do that. Please explain. He doesn't understand."

Jim grinned, his big eyes flashing with enjoyment. "He understands, Maya. He understands more about what Bernstein has done than you. Don't worry, you'll be all right."

We crowded into the back seat of the cab. Vus leaned toward the driver.

"Take us, please, to the nearest Western Union office."

The driver hesitated for a few seconds, then started his motor and drove us to Broadway. On the ride, Vus and Jim leaned across me, agreeing on the bloody arrogance of white folks. It was ironic that the producer of a play which exposed white greed so eloquently could himself be such a glutton. Whether we were in the mines of South Africa, or the liberal New York theater, nothing changed. Whites wanted everything. They thought they deserved everything. That they wanted to possess all the materials of the earth was in itself disturbing, but that they also wanted to control the souls and the pride of people was inexplicable.

We walked into the Western Union office. Jim and I stood talking while Vus filled out a form.

He handed it to the telegraph operator. When the man finished copying the message, Vus paid and then, taking the form back, he walked over to us and read aloud: "Mrs. Maya Angelou Make will not be returning to *The Blacks* or the St. Mark's Playhouse. She resists the exploitation of herself and her people. She has closed. Signed, Vusumzi Linda Make, Pan African Congress, Johannesburg, South Africa. Currently Petitioner at United Nations."

Vus continued. "That will be the last you will hear of those people, my dear. Unless Bernstein wants an international incident."

Jim laughed out loud. "See, Maya Angelou, I told you, you have nothing to worry about."

We walked out of the office, and linking arms, strolled into the nearest bar.

The fat Xhosa, the thin New Yorker and the tall Southerner drank all night and exchanged unsurprising stories on the theme of white aggression and black vulnerability. And somehow we laughed.

I sat beside the telephone the next day. The hangover and drama of leaving the show made me quick and ready to blast the ears of Bernstein, or Frankel or Glanville or anyone who would dare call me about Vus's telegram. The telephone never rang.

14

Black and white activists began to press hard on the nation's conscience. In Monroe, North Carolina, Rob Williams was opposing a force of white hatred, and encouraged black men to arm and protect themselves and their homes and families. Mae Mallory, a friend from the U.N. protest, had joined Rob. Julian Mayfield, the author of *The Big Hit* and *Grand Parade*, wrote a stinging article on Williams' position and then traveled South to lend his physical support. Stokely Carmichael and James Foreman founded a new group, Student Nonviolent Coordinating Committee, an offshoot of the Southern resistance organizations, and were taking the freedom struggle into hamlets and villages, where white hate was entrenched and black acceptance of inferior status a historic norm. Malcolm X continued to appear on national television. Newspapers were filled with reports of tributes to Martin Luther King and editorials honoring his nonviolent ideology. The white liberal population was growing. White students joined black students in Freedom Rides traveling on public conveyances to Southern towns which were racist strongholds.

Ralph Bunche was the U.S. ambassador to the U.N. and had received the Nobel Prize for his work as mediator in the Palestine conflict. When his son was denied membership in the all-white Forest Hills Tennis Club, Dr. Bunche made a statement which revealed his insight. The internationally respected representative, who had a complexion light-colored enough to allow him to pass for white, said, "I know now that until the lowliest Negro sharecropper in the South is free, I am not free."

Ossie Davis' play *Purlie Victorious* opened on Broadway, and his wife Ruby Dee, as the petite Lutie Belle, had white audiences howling at their own ignorance and greed. Paule Marshall's *Soul Clap Hands and Sing* was published, and readers were treated to well-written stories of black hope, despair and defeat. John Killens' *And Then We Heard the Thunder*, exposed the irony of black soldiers fighting for a white country in a segregated army. Baldwin's *The Fire Next Time* was an unrelenting warning that racism was not only homicidal but it was also suicidal. In Little Rock, Daisy Bates had led nine children into a segregated white high school and when the Arkansas governor, Orval Faubus, ordered local police to prevent the students' entry, President Dwight Eisenhower sent federal troops to keep the peace.

Harry Belafonte and Miriam Makeba were performing fundraising concerts for the freedom struggle. Max and Abbey traveled around the country doing their "Freedom Now Suite."

Guy was totally occupied with school, SANE, Ethical Culture and girls. Vus traveled to and from East Africa, West Africa, London and Algeria, and I sat at home. I had no job and only the spending money Vus had left. My departure from the SCLC had been so hasty, I was embarrassed to go back and offer my services even as a volunteer. I was not a Muslim nor a student, so there was no place for me either in Malcolm X's organization or in SNCC. I withdrew from my friends and even the Harlem Writers Guild.

At last Vus returned from his latest extended trip. As usual, he brought gifts for me and Guy, and stories which had us tense with excitement and open-mouthed with admiration. My present was a blouse and an orange silk sari. He was delicate and assured when he wrapped the cloth around my hips and draped the end over my shoulders. I didn't ask where or how he had learned the technique. I was becoming a good African wife.

We walked into the lobby of the Waldorf-Astoria Hotel and the quiet was intimidating. Tuxedoed white men held the elbows of expensively dressed white women, and they made no noise as they glided over the carpeted floor. I held on to Vus's arm and, dressed in my orange sari, stretched my head and neck upward until I added a few more inches to my six-foot frame. Vus had taught me a little Xhosa, and I spoke clearly and loudly in the click language. When we entered the elevator I felt all those white eyes on my back. I was an African in the bastion of white power, and my black King would protect me.

The Sierra Leone's ambassador's suite was festive with brown- and black-colored people in African dress and the melodies of Ghanaian High Life music. Vus took me to the ambassador, who was standing with a group of women near the window.

The ambassador saw Vus and beamed. "Ah, Mr. Make. Welcome. Ladies, I would like you to meet our revolutionary brother from South Africa, Vusumzi Make." Vus smiled and bowed, the light catching his cheekbones, and causing his hair to glisten.

He straightened up and spoke, "Your Excellency, I present my wife, Maya Angelou Make."

The ambassador took my hand. "She is beautiful, Make." He also bowed. "Madam Make, we have heard of you in Africa. Mr. Make has done the continent a great service. Welcome."

I shook hands with the ambassador and each of the women and suddenly found the crowd had dispersed. I saw Vus near a table where a uniformed bartender mixed drinks. The ambassador was dancing with a pretty little woman in a very low-cut cocktail dress and I was left at the window. A roving waiter offered a tray of drinks. I chose a glass of wine and looked down on the lights of New York.

Strange languages swirled around me, and the smell of a spice, known among Arkansas blacks as bird pepper, became strong in the room. I stopped the waiter and took a glass of Scotch from his tray. Vus had taken over from the ambassador and now he was dancing with the little sexy woman, holding her too close, gazing too deeply in her eyes. I found the waiter in a group of laughing guests, took another Scotch and went back to the window to drink and think.

I had a fresh haircut and was wearing the prettiest outfit I owned. I could speak French and Spanish very well and could talk intelligently on a number of subjects. I knew national politics intimately and international subjects moderately well. I was married to a leading African freedom fighter and had daubed French perfume on my body, discreetly. Yet, no one talked to me. I had another drink.

The lights on the street had begun to blur, but I could see clearly that Vus was still dancing with the woman. I would have known what to do if the party had been given by Afro-Americans, or even if there had been a few Afro-American guests. Or if the African guests had all been female. But Vus was successfully teaching me that there was a particular and absolute way for a woman to approach an African man. I only knew how a wife addressed an African husband. I didn't know how to start a conversation with a male stranger, but I did know I was certainly getting drunk. If I could eat soon, I could stop the fast-moving effect effect of alcohol on my brain and body. I headed for the kitchen.

I nearly collided with the ambassador. He backed away and smiled. "Madam Make, I hope you're enjoying yourself."

I made myself smile. "Thank you, Your Excellency," and continued.

A black woman in a housedress was bent over, taking baking tins from the oven. When she straightened and saw me, she made her face and voice flat.

"Can I help you, ma'am?" Her Southern accent was strong.

"I just wanted a bite of something. Anything."

"Ma'am, they will be serving in a few minutes."

"Are you the ambassador's wife?" My question might have sounded stupid, considering the way she was dressed. But I knew that sometimes the chores of party-giving could increase so that guests arrived before the last tasks were done and the hostess had the time to change.

The woman laughed loudly. "Me? God, no. Madam Ambassador? Me?" She laughed, opening her mouth wide, her tongue wiggled. "No, ma'am. I am a Negro. I am the cook." She turned back to the stove, her body shaking with glee. She muttered. "Me?"

I waited until she turned to me again.

"May I give you a hand? I am also a cook." The laughter left her face as she examined me. Her gaze slid from my hair and gold earrings, to my necklace and dress and hands.

"No, honey. Maybe you can cook, but you ain't no cook."

I pulled out a chair from the dinette table and sat down. She was right about my profession, but we were both black, both American, and women.

I said, "I'm married to an African, who is out there dancing the slow grind with some broad. And nobody's talked to me. So . . ."

She put her hands on her hips and shook her head. She said, "Honey, mens, they ain't gone change. You need a little sip." A drink was the last thing I needed, but she reached down alongside the refrigerator and pulled out a bottle of gin from her purse. She poured lavishly into a coffee cup. I took it while she sloshed a little gin into her cup and raised it to me.

"Honey, we women got to stick together. I mean." She swallowed the gin, made a face and growled and I followed her example.

"Sit down and take it easy." She turned and stirred a pot of bubbling sauce, still talking to me over her shoulder.

"What you going to do about it? You welcome to sit in here, but sooner or later, you're going to have to go out there and face him. But help yourself to the gin."

I did.

The cook was ladling chili into a large Chinese bowl when Vus came through the kitchen door. The steam and the booze unfocused my eyes. When I saw him loom through the mist, I started laughing. He reminded me of Aladdin's Djinn, only bigger.

Maybe the cook's gin bottle was a lamp, and I had certainly been rubbing it.

Vus stood over me, asking what I was laughing about. But each time I inhaled so that I could explain, Vus seem to grow larger as if he were somehow connected to my breathing, and laughter would contract my chest and I couldn't say a word.

Vus walked out of the room, and the cook came to me.

"That was your husband?" I nodded, still laughing.

"Well, child, you better get to stepping. He's fat. When a fat man gets mad, huh. I don't care if he's African or not. Ain't no fat man in the world wants to be laughed at." She handed me my purse. The sound of her voice had a small sobering effect, but when I tried to tell her why I had been laughing, I began to giggle again.

"You better go out of here, child, before that man comes back. I saw his face and it wasn't funny."

Finally, her advice reached my active brain. I got up, thanked her and walked from the kitchen through the living room door out into the hall. I pressed the elevator button and as the doors opened Vus burst out of the apartment, saw me and came running down the hall, shouting, telling me to wait. We both stepped into the half-filled elevator.

Vus began to talk. I was his wife, the wife of an African leader. I had embarrassed him. Sitting in the kitchen, getting drunk with the cook. When he tried to talk to me, I had laughed in his face. No African lady would bring such disgrace on her husband. I looked at the other people in the elevator, but they averted their white faces. As neither Vus nor I existed in their real world, they simply had to wait until we reached the ground floor and then our sounds and shadows would disappear.

Vus kept up his tirade as the elevator stopped on our descent, picking up people from other floors. When we reached the lobby, the other passengers scattered like snowflakes. I walked, with my head high, toward the front entrance. Vus was following me, talking, ranting, saying what shame I had brought onto his head, to his name, to his family. What a disappointment I was. How disrespectful I was to a son of Africa.

Deciding not to go out into the street, I turned sharply from the revolving doors and headed back to the elevators. Vus's voice, which had been a rumbling monotone, suddenly lifted.

"Where are you going? Not back to the party. I forbid you. You are my wife. We are going home." At the elevator, I made a quick pivot and walked in the direction of the registration desk, Vus following in my wake, still talking.

The desk clerks, dressed as formally as expensive morticians, thrust long mournful faces at me. I walked past them haughtily. Vus grabbed for my arm but only brushed my sleeve. I snatched away from him and lengthened my stride. When I reached the front doors the second time I looked over my shoulder and saw that his face was bathed in sweat. With an oblique turn, I dodged a small group of white men entering the lobby and increased my speed. Vus's breath came harder and his sentences were short explosions. "Stop! Foolish woman! Moron! Idiot!" I might be all those things or none, but he wasn't going to catch me. I began to sprint. I ran around the sofas, making guests draw their legs out of the way. Vus was lumbering less than a foot behind me. A desk clerk's face suddenly appeared at my side, anxious and gulping. We could have been two underwater swimmers in a clear pool. With just a little energy, I quickly outdistanced him. Vus shouted, "Don't touch her. She's my wife." He stressed the possessive.

A conservatively dressed black man stood in my way. I ran straight toward him but at the last second I veered, and he pulled his attaché case up, and cradled it in his arms. I heard his sigh of relief after I passed him.

When I reached the bank of elevators again, I looked back. Vus was nearly in arm's reach. The desk clerk followed him, and behind the desk clerk, a uniformed policeman and a grey-suited man, whom I took to be the manager, brought up the rear. The cop's presence gave me added energy. This seemed as a good a time as I was ever likely to get. I would show that if I didn't have to dodge bullets, if it was a fair race, just me and him, I could outrun any New York policeman. I hitched my purse in my armpit and stretched my legs.

Shouts floated around the lobby "Stop her!" and Vus's "Don't touch her" and "Who is she?"

Startled guests stood together under the crystal chandelier, as we wound through the lobby. I screamed back, "All of you can go to hell."

An empty revolving-door section was moving slowly, so I dove into it and pushed quickly. I heard a thud, and when I stepped out onto the pavement, I looked through the side window. I saw Vus, the clerk and the policeman had hit the door at the same time and tumbled into a heap on the floor. At that moment I turned and saw a woman get out of a taxi. Before she could slam the door, I ran and jumped into the cab.

It wouldn't be wise to go home, so I gave the driver Rosa's address on Riverside Drive.

I sat drinking black coffee and watching Rosa laugh at my description of the race in the Waldorf Astoria lobby. I had sobered. My actions were unforgivable. I had shown all those white folks that black people had no dignity. I had embarrassed my husband, who was risking his life for our people. He had called me an idiot and he was right. Rosa kept laughing, but for me there was nothing funny anymore.

Vus telephoned the next morning and came to collect me.

He brought flowers for Rosa and perfume for me. We kissed; he declared his love. He didn't mention my outrageous display and I said nothing about his vulgar flirtation. We were completely reconciled.

The sheriff's deputies appeared armed and solemn at my apartment one winter afternoon. When they were assured that I was Mrs. Make, one man handed me a piece of paper while the other tacked a notice on the front door. They moved with the precision of practice and were gone before I could sort out my questions. I stood in the hall reading the form and then looked at the notice. We had been evicted for nonpayment of the rent. We had to be out of the apartment in twenty-four hours, or the sheriff's deputies would put our furniture on the street.

Guy was still at school. Vus was at the U.N. I calmly made a pot of coffee and sat down in the kitchen to think. I had never been put out of a house in all my life. My mother would throw one of her famous tantrums if she heard about my eviction. My son was certain to be embarrassed and made more insecure. My friends would pity me and my enemies would shake their heads and smirk.

I read the form again. I was holding the third and last notice, which meant that Vus had collected the other two and said nothing to me. Then the responsibility was his. I had played the cared-for housewife, who made no money. I hadn't asked for the position, but had accepted the role marriage had forced upon me. I convinced myself that I was without blame, and the total responsibility of how and where Guy and I lived lay in Vus's lap.

I could borrow money from the Killens or my mother or Rosa, but according to the eviction notice it was too late to pay back rent. We had no recourse save to vacate the premises.

I went to the local supermarket and collected cartons. When I returned the eviction notice seemed to have become enlarged. It covered the door from ceiling to floor. After rereading it, I went inside and began packing. I put all our clothes in suitcases and the steamer trunk I had brought from California. I culled the best pots and skillets from kitchen cupboards and placed them in cardboard boxes. The furniture, the expensive sofa, good beds and chairs had been Vus's selection, so their disposal or arrangement could wait.

There was a frantic sound of the scraping of the key and the jerking open of the door. Guy and Vus arrived together. They crowded each other in the foyer.

Guy spoke first. "Mom, did you see this door? Did you see the . . . ?" I sat on the sofa watching them untangle themselves. Vus came into the living room followed by Guy. "Have you spoken to anyone?"

It was a strange question. I didn't know what he meant, so I shook my head. When Guy asked me, not Vus, what we were going to do, I knew that although I had relinquished my responsibility, and although Guy had seemed to accept Vus as head of our family, in a critical moment he turned back to me.

Vus asked Guy to please go to his room. For the first time in months, Guy studied my face. I nodded and he went into his room reluctantly and left his door ajar.

Vus sat down with a heaviness which could not be credited to his bulk alone.

His first statement struck me as being as strange as his first question. "I have a lot of money, so there's nothing to worry about."

In a few hours, we would be on the street. It was enough that we would have no place to sleep, but our address and telephone number would cease to belong to us. In fact, we were soon to lose everything which identified us to our community except our names, and Vusumzi Make sat facing me, saying, "There's nothing to worry about."

The tiny lines around his eyes deepened and he began to pull viciously at the hairs on his chin. He didn't hear me offer to make a drink or a fresh pot of coffee, so I didn't repeat the offer.

After a few minutes he hauled himself out of the chair and picked up his brief case. He turned at the door and looking in my direction, but without actually looking in my eyes, spoke. "As I say, there is nothing to worry about." He opened the door, walked out, and eased it closed, quietly.

Guy came out of his room, agog with worry.

"Mom, what's going to happen? The thing said twenty-four hours. Where are we going? How did this happen? What did you do?"

The sight of my long tall beautiful boy brought back the memory of an ancient incident.

My then husband, Tosh, Guy, who was seven, and I were riding in our truck one lovely Sunday morning. We had just finished our weekly outing at the San Francisco city dump where Tosh and Guy threw office trash and home garbage onto the acrid ever-going burning heap of refuse. We had been in a high mood on the return home. Guy made puns and Tosh laughed at them. I felt secure. I had a loving husband and my husband had a job. My son, who was healthy and bright, received love and the necessary, to me, amount of chastisement. What more could I, a young uneducated black girl expect? I was living in my earthly paradise.

We waited at the intersection of Fulton and Gough for the lights to change. Suddenly, a car lurched into the passenger side of the truck. I was thrown forward, my forehead struck the windshield and my teeth crunched against the top of the cab's dashboard. When I regained consciousness, Tosh was blowing his breath in my face and murmuring. I asked about Guy and Tosh said that as the car hit, I grabbed for Guy and folded him in my arms. Now he was standing on the corner unhurt.

I got out of the truck and walked over to my son, who was being consoled by strangers. When I bent down at his side, he took one glance at my battered face and instead of coming into my arms, he began to scream, strike out at me and back away.

Tosh had to come to talk him into the taxi. For days, he moped around the house avoiding my gaze. Each time I turned quickly enough to catch him looking at me, I shivered at the hateful accusation in his eyes.

We had not caused the accident. Tosh had been the driver, and I was the most injured person. But I was the mother, the most powerful person in his world who could make everything better. Why had I made them worse? I could have prevented the accident. I should not have allowed our truck to be at that place at that time. If I hadn't been so neglectful, my face would not have been cut, my teeth would not be broken and he would not have been scared out of his wits.

Now, eight years later, Guy was asking himself why had I, by neglecting my duty, why had I put his pride in jeopardy? Had I thought that being married removed my responsibility to keep the world on its axis and the universe in order?

Guy stood flexing and tightening his fists, as if he were squeezing and releasing, then squeezing the questions again. I remained quiet, relishing a small but savory knot of satisfaction. He had shifted his loyalty to Vus, leaving me only the leftovers of attention. Now in the crisis, I became the important person again.

When he realized that I was not going to speak, he sat down on the sofa beside me. Suddenly I didn't know what to say. If, when he reentered the room, I had given an explanation or posed a few alternatives, our lives would have continued in the same rhythms indefinitely. But I had waited too long to speak.

I watched my son. When he slid on the sofa, opened his long arms to embrace me and said, "It'll be okay, Mom. We'll live through this one, too," I began to cry. My teenager was growing up.

Vus returned after nightfall. He had arranged for the sale of our furniture, and a mover would arrive the next morning to take our personal belongings to a hotel where he had rented and paid for a furnished apartment. He had also started the ball rolling for us to go to Egypt. He delivered the news to me but winked at Guy and cocked his head. Guy looked back at Vus with a blank stare and said, "That's great, Dad," and walked into his room.

For three weeks, in the musty hotel off Central Park West, we lived a life alien to everything I had known. Retired people, sick and discarded, shuffled along the hallways, whispering passionately to themselves. At all hours they inched frail feet along the lobby's worn carpet. They never looked up, or spoke to anyone, just continued traveling, staying close to the walls, their heads down, pushing the dank air.

Guy began to speak in a lower register and Vus and I whispered even in the bedroom. Our comings and goings were furtive and quiet. Only Rosa visited me during those weeks. I didn't want anyone else to know that we had moved underground and joined a pack of tragic moles.

I kept telling myself it was only for three weeks. A person could stay on a torture rack, or fast, for three weeks. It was just as well that we left New York with no fanfare, and no sad farewells. Vus went to Egypt to prepare a place for us while Guy and I traveled to San Francisco. I needed to see my mother. I needed to be told just one more time that life was what you make it, and that every tub ought to sit on its own bottom. I had to hear her say, "They spell my name W-O-M-A-N, 'cause the difference between a female and a woman is the difference between shit and shinola."

At the airport she looked worn, although she was wearing too much nut-brown powder and the lipstick was so thick that when we kissed hello, our lips made a sucking sound. Her happiness at seeing us was brief.

On the way home she confirmed the suspicions which arose the moment I had seen her. She drove her big car poorly and talked about trifling matters. Vivian Baxter was very upset.

She settled Guy into his old room on the downstairs floor of the big Victorian house, and asked me to join her in the kitchen. She began to talk, over tall and strong drinks.

She had sent me a photograph of her new husband. He was a dark-brown good-looking man, and she had raved about him in her letters to me. They had sailed together and played on the beaches of Tahiti and Fiji and in the bars of Sydney, Australia. Their marriage sounded like a frolic: Two lovers in a boat put out on a calm sea. But as she talked, seated at her kitchen table, I saw that the relationship was floundering, and she was straining every muscle to keep it afloat.

"He means well, baby, and he tries to do well, but it's the drink. He just doesn't know how to control it."

Her face was sad and her voice trembled as she put fresh ice and Scotch in our glasses. Her husband was away on a long trip and she was finding it hard to manage her loneliness.

The next few weeks brought a change in our relationship which I never expected: We reversed roles. Vivian Baxter began to lean on me, to look to me for support and wisdom, and I, automatically, without thinking about it, started to perform as the shrewd authority, the judicious one, the mother. Guy was disconcerted by the new positions in the family. He became rigidly courteous, smiled less and assumed a sober stateliness which sat awkwardly on the shoulders of a teenage boy.

Vus called from Cairo to say that our tickets were waiting at a local travel agency, and it was impossible to hide my relief.

When I told Mother that we would be leaving soon, she came out of her doldrums for a few hours of celebration. She was thankful, she said, not only for my support but that she had raised a woman who could stand up to a crisis. She reminded me that there were too many old females and not nearly enough women. She was proud of me and that was my going-away gift.

We left San Francisco with her assurance that she would work out the difficulties in her own life and we were not to worry. Her last bidding was not easily carried out. I sat through the entire journey, from San Francisco to Los Angeles to London to Rome, with the concern for my mother riding in my lap. Only when we left Rome's Fiumicino Airport did I start to think about Egypt, Vus and the life my son and I were beginning.

Whether our new start was going to end in success or failure didn't cross my mind. What I did know, and know consciously, was that it was already exciting.

15

Our plane landed at Cairo on a clear afternoon, and just beyond the windows, the Sahara was a rippling beige sea which had no shore. Guy and I went through customs, each peering through a frosted glass for a sight of Vus.

Barefoot men in long soiled nightdresses walked beside us, talking Arabic, asking questions. When we shook our heads and shrugged our shoulders, gesturing our lack of understanding, they fell about laughing, slapping their sides and doubling over. Laughter in a strange language has an unsettling effect. Guy and I walked close together, shoulders touching, into the main terminal.

211

The room was cavernous, and nearly empty, and Vus was not there. A porter asked in his version of English if we wanted a taxi. I shook my head. I had money, nearly a thousand dollars in travelers' checks, but I wasn't about to get into a taxi in an unknown country. Then I realized with a numbing shock that I had no address. I couldn't take a taxi if I wanted it.

I thought about Guy and caught the gasp before it could surface.

"Mom, what are we going to do? You gave Dad the arrival time, didn't you?"

"Of course. We'll just go over there and sit down." I didn't comment on the accusation in his voice, but I recorded it. We had lugged our baggage through a group of laughing porters and janitors when two black men in neat Western suits approached.

"Sister Maya? Sister Make?"

I nodded, too relieved to speak.

"Welcome to Cairo. And Guy? Welcome."

We shook hands and they mentioned their multisyllabic names. Vus was in a meeting with a high official and would join us as soon as possible. He had asked them to pick us up and bring us to his office.

They helped us into a ramshackle Mercedes Benz as if they were placing royalty in a state carriage. My son and I rose to the occasion. Neither of us said a word when, on the outskirts of Cairo, the driver neatly swerved to avoid hitting a camel, although I did push my elbow into Guy's side as we passed the beautiful white villas of Heliopolis. The shiny European cars, large horned cows, careening taxis and the throngs of pedestrians, goats, mules, camels, the occasional limousine and the incredible scatter of children made the streets a visual and a tonal symphony of chaos.

When we entered the center of Cairo, the avenues burst wide open with such a force of color, people, action and smells I was stripped of cool composure.

I touched the man in the front passenger seat and shouted at him, "What's going on? Is today a holiday?"

212

He looked out the open windows, and turned back to me shaking his head.

"The crowd? You mean the crowd?"

I nodded.

"No." He smiled. "This is just everyday Cairo."

Guy was so happy, he laughed aloud. I looked at the scene and wondered how we were going to enjoy living in a year-long Mardi Gras.

Emaciated men in long tattered robes flailed and ranted at heavily burdened mules. Sleek limousines rode through the droppings of camels that waved their wide behinds casually as they sashayed in the shadow of skyscrapers. Well-dressed women in pairs, or accompanied by men, took no notice of their sisters, covered from head to toe in voluminous heavy black wraps. Children ran everywhere, shouting under the wheels of rickety carts, dodging the tires of careening taxis. Street vendors held up their wares, beckoning to passers-by. Young boys offered fresh-fruit drinks, and on street corners, men stooped over food cooking on open grills. Scents of spices, manure, gasoline exhaust, flowers and body sweat made the air in the car nearly visible. After what seemed to be hours, we drove into a quiet, by comparison, neighborhood. Our escorts parked the car, then led us through a carefully tended front garden and into a whitewashed office building. They placed our luggage by the door of the lobby, then shook hands with Guy and me, and assuring us that Vus would arrive soon, left us in the lobby.

Africans came and went, nodding to us in passing. Just as exhaustion began to claim my body, Vus entered through the open doors. He shouted when he saw us, and came rushing to hold me and Guy in his arms. He grinned freely, and he looked about ten years old. I had no doubt, for the moment, that we were going to make each other frivolously happy. Cairo was going to be the setting for two contemporary lovers.

Vus released me and hugged Guy, chuckling all the while. He

213

was a sexy brown-skin Santa Claus, whose love and largesse were for us alone.

"Come, let's go home. We live across the street." I spoke to Guy and pointed to the luggage. Vus shook his head and said, "They will be brought to us." We walked through the garden, arms linked, and headed for number 5 Ahmet Hishmat.

Vus led us up the stairs of the large marble-fronted building. On the steps, a black man dressed in dirty clothes grinned and bowed: "Welcome, Mr. Make." Vus put some coins in the man's outstretched hand and spoke to him in Arabic. As we walked into the building's cool dark corridor, Vus told us the man was Abu, the *boabab* or doorman, and he would deliver our bags. At the end of the corridor, he unlocked a carved door and we entered a luxurious living room. A gold-and-red-striped satin sofa was the first object which caught and held my attention.

A muted tapestry hung on the wall above another rich-looking sofa. In the middle of the room a low table of exquisite parquetry rested on an antique Oriental rug.

Vus wondered aloud if I liked the room and Guy made approving sounds, but I couldn't imagine how a landlord could leave such important and expensive pieces in a rented apartment.

Guy shouted from a distance. "You should see this, Mom."

Vus took my elbow and directed me into the next room, where a Louis XVI brocaded sofa and chairs rested on another rich rug. The dining room was filled with French antique furniture. The large bedrooms held outsize beds, armoires, dressing tables and more Oriental rugs.

I grinned because I didn't know what else to do. When we reached the empty kitchen, a little sense returned to me.

A soot-encrusted lamp sat on a ledge with stacked plates, a pile of cheap cutlery and thick glasses.

Vus coughed, embarrassed. "They use this"—indicating the lamp—"to cook on. It's a Sterno stove. Uh . . . I didn't get around to fixing up the kitchen yet. Anyway, regular stoves are very, very expensive. I thought I'd wait until you arrived."

214

"You mean, we own all that crap?" I must have shouted because Guy, who was crowded into the small room with us, frowned at me, and Vus gave me a haughty, angry look.

"I have tried to make a beautiful house for you, even to the point of ignoring my own work. Yes, I've postponed important PAC affairs to decorate this apartment, and you call it crap?" He turned and walked through the door. Guy shook his head, disgusted with my lack of gratitude and grace, and followed Vus out of the kitchen. Their silent departure succeeded in humbling me. Vus was a generous man. Indeed, I had only seen that kind of furniture in slick magazine advertisements, or in the homes of white movie stars. My husband was lifting me and my son into a rarified atmosphere, and instead of thanking him for the elevation, I had been sour and unappreciative.

A profound sense of worthlessness had made me pull away from owning good things, expensive furniture, rare rugs. That was exactly how white folks wanted me to feel. I was black, so obviously I didn't deserve to have armoires, shiny with good French veneer, or tapestries, where mounted warriors waged their ancient battles in silk thread. No, I decided to crush that feeling of unworthiness. I deserved everything beautiful and I merited putting my long black feet on Oriental carpets as much as Lady Astor. If Vus thought he wanted his wife to live beautifully, he was no less a man (and I had to get that under the layers of inferiority in my brain) than a Rockefeller or a Kennedy.

The luggage had been placed in the middle of the floor of the first living room. I heard Vus's and Guy's voices from the balcony, so I went to join them with a smile warm enough to melt the snows on Mount Everest.

"This is the most gorgeous house I've ever seen." Vus nodded and smiled at me as if I were a recalcitrant child who had recovered her good manners following a foolish tantrum. Guy grinned. He had known his mother would come through. We stood looking down on the back of a man who was bent weeding what Vus said was our private garden. We had a doorman and our own gardener. That information was a fair-sized lump, but I swallowed it.

The first weeks in Cairo were occupied with introductions to freedom fighters from Uganda, Kenya, Tanganyika, North and South Rhodesia, Basutoland and Swaziland. Diplomats from already-independent African countries dropped by our apartment to meet Vus Make's American wife, who was trying to be all things to everybody.

Jarra Mesfin, from the Ethiopian Embassy, and his wife Kebidetch Erdatchew came early and stayed late. Joseph Williamson, the Chargé d'Affaires from Liberia, and his wife A. B. invited us to the Residency.

I was the heroine in a novel teeming with bejeweled women, handsome men, intrigue, international spies and danger. Opulent fabrics, exotic perfumes and the service of personal servants threatened to tear from my mind every memory of growing up in America as a second-class citizen.

Vus, Guy and I had lunch near the pyramid of Giza, where we watched camel riders lope around the bottom of the Sphinx. Car radios, nearly turned to their highest pitch, released the moaning Arabic music into the dusty air.

I had hired Omanadia, a short stubby older woman from Sudan, as cook-housekeeper after Vus said my reluctance to have a servant in the house was not proof of a democratic spirit, but rather of a bourgeois snobbism, which kept a good job from a needy worker. Anyway, she was a cook and knew how to manage the little Sterno lamp which remained my only stove.

Guy was enrolled in the American College at Mahdi, and was picked up daily in a bus for the fifteen-mile ride out of Cairo to his school. He might have felt the need to show off for his schoolmates and new teachers, or the abrupt cultural change may have prompted him, but whatever the reason or reasons, he did extremely well in his studies. There was no need to urge him to do his homework, and the mood which had visited him in the more recent months in New York and San Francisco was dispelled. In Cairo, he had a clarity, was cheerful, garrulous and my young son again. We engaged each other in a contest to see who would have the largest Arabic vocabulary and speak with the best accent.

There was an Afro-Asian Solidarity Conference in downtown Cairo and Vus thought I'd like to attend.

The sight of the huge auditorium made me catch my breath. Long tables, banked at an easy incline, held headsets and microphones, and men of every color, wearing various national outfits, wandered the aisles, conversing loudly in many languages strange to my ear. The arrangement of seats, the microphones and the multinationals reminded me of the General Assembly of the United Nations, my heart thumped and I reached for Vus, who, hating public displays of attachment unless he initiated them, stepped away, but stayed close enough to whisper.

"They don't make you nervous, do they?"

I straightened myself and pulled as far from him as he had withdrawn from me. "Not at all. I don't frighten easily."

That was more mouth than truth, but I put my head up and walked down into the mingle of men. Vus caught my arm and stopped me.

"I want to introduce you to your fellow countryman." I looked around to see a thin young man, dressed in a well-cut suit, smiling at me. He was of one piece. His eyes were almond shaped, his face long and gently molded into an oval, his smile was long and thin, and he was the color of a slightly toasted almond. Vus said, "This is David DuBois. He is a journalist in Cairo, and my very good friend. David, meet my wife, Maya."

His first words were a healing balm spread on an ache I had not distinguished. "Hello, Maya Angelou Make. I've heard about you. All Egypt will be happy to welcome you. And they say you can sing, too."

The voice of an adult American black man has undeniable textures. It has a quality of gloss, slithery as polished onyx, or it can be nubby and notched with harshness. The voice can be

217

sonorous as a bass solo or light and lyrical as a flute. When a black man speaks in a flat tone, it is not only intentional but instructional to the listener.

I had forgotten how much I loved those sweet cadences. I said, "I surely want to thank you. I'm glad to be here."

We smiled at each other and embraced. Maybe he had missed hearing a black American woman's voice.

The cocktail parties at home increased. Vus had to make contacts, and he also had to entertain them, their wives and friends. When he was in Cairo, the house throbbed with activity. I learned to cook elaborate dinners without pork and served chilled fruity unalcoholic punches when our guests were Moslem. Roast hams, rice with ham, spinach with salt pork and peas with pig knuckles, with Scotch and gin, were served to African and European guests.

I began to notice the undeniable link between Vus's journeys and our entertainment schedule. When he returned from Algeria, which was independent and militantly anticolonial, his spirits were high and he strutted through the house with an air of insouciance. At those times, he wanted to be alone with me and Guy. He would describe the successful Algerian revolution as if the seven-and-a-half-year rebellion had taken place in South Africa rather than at the continent's most northerly tip. Guy would listen, his eyes gleaming, his face immobile, as Vus told us proudly of his conversations with Ben Bella or Boumedienne. Trips to Ghana also resulted in proud reports of the Nkrumah government and homey conversations. We three would play Scrabble and listen to music. Then in our dim bedroom, he would take me into his arms delicately. My body was the prayer wheel where he placed all his supplications. Love-making became a high celebration, rich and sacred, a sacramental communion.

Conversely, when he had traveled into southern Africa, without passports or documents, when he doffed the tailored suits and handmade shoes, and wore the open sandals and blankets of tribesmen in order to reach a stranded party of escapees, he returned to Cairo quickened, tense with wakefulness. The whites of his eyes were always shot with red lines, and his attention was abstracted with what he had seen, and where he had been.

He was hardly in the house before he would pick up the telephone.

"Are you free this evening? Come over. My wife will cook her famous Afro-American food. We'll drink and eat. Come."

The invitation would be repeated several times before he would ask if I had something I could prepare in a hurry. Invitees would troop into the apartment, eat and drink copiously, talk loudly with each other and leave. Occasionally during the gatherings, David DuBois and I would find a quiet corner and talk about our folks back home.

David's journalistic assignments involved all of Europe, Africa and Asia, and marriage had broadened my interests to include the mercurial politics of those areas as well. However, while the conversations around us swelled with concern over Goa and India, Tshombe and the Belgian-owned Union Minière, the Lebanon and Middle East crisis, we wondered how the black parents in America could let their little children walk between rows of cursing, spitting white women and men, en route to school? What would happen to the children's minds when uniformed police sicked dogs on them just because they wanted to get to class?

At a certain point, we always stopped the self-pitying and reassured ourselves that our people would survive. Look what we had done already.

David and I would begin to hum softly, one of the old spirituals. (He always insisted on starting with his favorite, "Glory, Glory, Hallelujah, When I Lay My Burden Down.")

Surely exhibitionism was a part of our decision to sing in a room of talkers, but a deeper motivation was also present. The lyrics and melody had the power to transport us back into a womblike familiarity. Admittedly, Africa was our place of genesis, long, long ago, but more recently, and more dearly known were the sounds

219

of black America. When David and I lifted the song, diplomats and politicians, women on the make, and men on the run, freeloaders and revolutionaries, stopped haranguing, flirting, jibing, imploring, pontificating, explaining, and turned to listen. First half-heartedly, informed by the knowledge that we were airing melodies written by the last large group of people enslaved on the planet, courtesy forced them to attend. After a few verses, the music made its own demands. They could not remain ignorant of its remarkable humanity. I could not read their minds, but their faces were wide open with allegiance to our songs. Vus, conscious of their attentiveness, paid tribute to our survival and by joining in helped David and me to reestablish for ourselves a connection to a bitter, beautiful past.

16

Omanadia came to the balcony on a lovely summer afternoon.

"Madame?"

I had arisen from a nap in the cool bedroom. I felt refreshed and indulgent. "Yes, Omanadia?" She could not have the rest of the day off, if that was what she wanted. I needed a little more pampering.

"Madame, I stopped the rug man again. You were sleeping."

"What rug man?" I was awake, but slow.

"The man collecting for the rugs. He hasn't been paid for two months. And the two furniture collectors." She laughed roguishly. "The other maids down the street tell me when they're on Ahmet Hishmat, so I don't open the door."

Because of her age and sharp tongue, Omanadia was the bane and the pet of shopkeepers, younger servants and doormen. She knew all the gossip and most of the facts concerning people in our neighborhood.

"Omanadia, how much do we owe?"

She tried to keep a straight face, but her eyes danced. "How much, madame? But Mr. Make would not like me to say. He is the man, madame."

"How much, Omanadia?"

She made her fingers an abacus. We had only paid a tenth of the price on the rugs. We owed over half the cost of the bedroom furniture. We had not paid anything on the embroidered bed linens or towels. The two living rooms and the dining-room set were way overdue for payment, and our rent was two months in arrears. I thanked her and told her to take the rest of the afternoon off.

The specter of the New York City deputy sheriff stood in the doorway, hid just behind the heavy drapes, waited nearly visible in my well-tended flower garden. Eviction in New York was bad, but at least I was at home, where my friends would have helped if I called on them. And always there was Mom. I could have gathered my son and flown back to San Francisco. But if we were thrown out into the streets of Cairo . . . along with the other homeless waifs, whom could I ask for help? When I was young, poor and destitute I had resisted welfare in the U.S. I certainly wasn't about to ask for assistance in a country which was having trouble feeding its own nationals.

I had to get a job.

David answered his telephone and when I said I had an emergency, he agreed to meet me at a tearoom in downtown Cairo.

The restaurant was luminous with crystal chandeliers, polished mahogany counters and jeweled women drinking Turkish coffee from dainty china cups. It was the wrong setting for my pitiable tale.

David had chosen a table in the center of glitter, and when he held out a chair for me, I decided to lie—to tell him the emergency was contrived, that I just wanted a chance to get out of the house. Or that I was planning a banquet and couldn't decide on a menu. He ordered whiskey and I prattled about embassy parties, and dinner near the pyramids, and how well I was learning Arabic, and how Guy was settling down in his new school.

I noticed he hadn't smiled once. When I finally stopped chattering, he asked quietly, "The emergency. What is the emergency?"

"Nothing really." We had had no time to build a friendship. I was about to use him simply because we were both black Americans. My mother's saying, "We're colored but we're not cousins," echoed in my mind. I shouldn't presume that our uniqueness gave me license to ask him for a favor.

"Does it have to do with Vus?" He looked at me directly and I thought, Doesn't everything have to do with Vus?

I said, "I'm getting a little bored sitting at home. I've worked all my life. So really, I thought maybe you might know how I could get a job. Just to have something to do."

He relaxed and grinned. "You want a job? Nice women don't work in Cairo. I thought you knew that. Why don't you join one of the women's organizations? Or set up a club among the wives of African diplomats. You could write some articles for black American newspapers. The *Amsterdam News* or something. Nothing to do?" He laughed. "Girl, I thought you were serious."

I was more than serious, I was desperate. And putting on silly airs, I had appeared to David like the frivolous women I scorned.

"David, I'm broke. Every piece of furniture in that house was bought on installment. The rent is past due, and Guy's school fees are in arrears. I don't have enough money to go back home and I can't stay here unless I get a job." The smile faded from his face and he nodded. "O.K., O.K. I figured it was something like that. Maybe. Maybe, I can get something for you. I'll do what I can. What about Vus? Will he let you work?"

"If I can get a job, I'll handle the rest of it. I've been through too much to turn back now. I've been a frycook, a waitress, a strip dancer, a fund-raiser. I had a job once taking the paint off cars with my hands. And that's just part of it."

David shook his head. "Black women. Huh, huh. O.K. Let's have another drink. I'll call somebody I know this afternoon."

I left the restaurant emboldened by alcohol and a lot of boastful conversation and I felt as secure as the cared-for women still pointing honey-filled baclavas into their red mouths.

Two days later, David took me to meet Zein Nagati, president of the Middle East Feature News Agency. Dr. Nagati was a very large handsome man in rumpled tweeds who had the air of a university professor.

He spoke rapidly, never repeating himself, as if he was used to talking to efficient shorthand secretaries.

He had started a magazine called the *Arab Observer*. It was not strictly speaking an official organ of the Egyptian government; that is, it did not come directly under the heading of the Ministry of Information. Its editorial position, however, would be identical with the national politics. He was hiring a Hungarian layout artist, and already had twelve reporters working. DuBois said I was an experienced journalist, wife of a freedom fighter and an expert administrator. Would I be interested in the job of associate editor? If so I should realize that since I was neither Egyptian, Arabic nor Moslem and since I would be the only woman working in the office, things would not be easy. He mentioned a salary that sounded like pots of gold to my ears and, standing, he reached for my hand.

"Very good, Mrs. Make. You'll begin on Monday. I'll be there to introduce you, and DuBois can show you around. *Salaam.*"

He picked up his brief case, inclined his head to me, shook hands with David and left the room.

I wanted to speak but I felt I had fallen into a deep trench with steep muddy sides.

When I regained a degree of consciousness, David was talking.

"You won't find it that hard. I'll help. Call me at any time. You've done reporting, and you've run offices. Anyway, you wanted a job."

He offered to show me his office, which was in the same building, and then take me to lunch. I followed him meekly, but I don't remember seeing his desk or meeting any other person. We went to the Cairo Hilton, but I could have eaten air sandwiches and a salad made of clouds. My thoughts nibbled on

David's exaggerations to Dr. Nagati based on the lies I had told him. And the larger chunk in my throat which prevented me from swallowing solid food consisted of wondering what cleverness I could devise which would allow me to tell Vus and keep both the job and my husband.

David dropped me off at Ahmet Hismat and patted me on the shoulder. "Girl, you realize, you and I are the only black Americans working in the news media in the Middle East?"

I gave him a phony smile and got out of the taxi with that new mind full of responsibility.

In the United States, when I faced any new situation I knew what to do. I had half educated myself by spending nights and long days in libraries. I had given my son a fair smattering of general information from borrowed books. But in Egypt I faced the dilemma without help. Only the American Embassy would have a collection in English, and since I had spoken so harshly to Africans about the United States' racist policy, going there was out of the question.

I fingered the books Vus and I had brought from the States. George Padmore's *Africa and World Peace*, DuBois' *Souls of Black Folks*, collections of Langston Hughes's and Paul Laurence Dunbar's poems and Baldwin's *Nobody Knows My Name*.

The Baldwin book gave me heart. Nobody seemed to know my name either. I had been called everything from Marguerite, Ritie, Rita, Maya, Sugar, Bitch, Whore, Madam, girl and wife. Now in Egypt I was going to be called "associate editor." And I would earn the title, if I had to work like a slave. Well not quite, but nearly.

Guy brought home another notice for fees from school, and I told him I had made arrangements to pay. The evidence of his complete trust was the fact that the question on his face disappeared in seconds.

Vus returned on Sunday morning, rested and handsome. He was the only person I ever knew who could finish a ten-hour plane trip looking as fresh as new money. We exclaimed over our gifts;

he brought a Zulu necklace for me and a chess set for Guy. We had a large Sunday dinner, and Guy left for the movies with some school friends.

We spent a lovely hour in the bedroom, reacquainting our bodies, and then I brought hot tea and cakes to the living room. Vus joined me in his robe and slippers.

I began cautiously.

"I saw David DuBois. We went to tea."

"Oh great. How is he?"

"I asked him to help me find a job."

Vus sputtered, then rubbed his mouth with a napkin.

His next reaction startled me. He began to laugh. At first a few chuckles but they increased to a hearty guffaw, then he lost his breath again. When he calmed down his first words were "You black women. Who knows what to do with you?" His laughter was more restrained. "Black and American. You think you can come to Egypt and just go get a job? That's foolish. It shows the nerve of the black woman and the arrogance of the American. I must say, my dear wife, those are not very attractive qualities. Don't pout, Maya, you know I love you. There are simply some things which do not become you. I gave you Gamal Nasser's book, didn't you read it? The UAR is committed to upgrading its citizens economically as well as politically. As my wife, and a foreigner as well, you would never find a job. Besides, I look after you. I like you to look after me and Guy, and . . ."—here he rubbed his chin lovingly—"and maybe we'll have a child, a little brother for Guy."

There is a silent scream, which tears through the veins, separating the muscles, pinching the nerves, yet the body seems to remain immobile. We had never talked about having children. I had one son. I seemed to have given an order to my body that one was enough, because although I used no contraceptives, I had only been pregnant the one time.

He was still playing with his chin, pulling at the sparse hairs.

"Vus, the rent is past due. The collectors have been here for

225

payment on the furniture and the rugs. Guy's school has sent two notes home. I've fired the gardener and paid Omanadia out of my food money. I have to go to work."

"But I will see that everyone is paid. I always do, don't I?" I wouldn't answer and I wouldn't remind him of the New York eviction.

He raised his voice. "I don't throw away money, you know that. I only receive an allowance for the office and living expenses. Travel is costly. Printing charges are high. I must keep up my appearance. And so must you. We are freedom fighters. We are not beggars."

Craft and cunning were necessary and even as I schemed, I doubted if I was smart enough.

"Vus, you say you need me. You need a woman, not just a hostess. Your struggle is my struggle. I need to be more involved than serving dinner to refugees and keeping your house."

He started to interrupt but I continued. "If I work, you can spend the living allowance on the office. Instead of a quarterly newsletter, you could send out a monthly. We would be able to buy some warm coats for the new escapees. My salary could take care of the house expenses."

He listened and his eyes shone for a second, then the light went out.

"Darling, you are a wonderful woman. Excuse the harsh words. You're not arrogant. You are thoughtful. I appreciate your idea. But it's not possible. You'll never find work in Cairo."

"Vus, I have a job. Associate editor of the *Arab Observer*. I start tomorrow."

I watched the disbelief on his face turn to anger, then to rage.

"You took a job without consulting me? Are you a man?"

He stood and began to pace over the expensive rug. His tirade carried him from the sofa to the entry, over to the large chair and back to stand in front of me. His vilification included my insolence, independence, lack of respect, arrogance, ignorance, defiance, callousness, cheekiness and lack of breeding. I sat, watching him, listening and thinking. He was right. Somewhere in his swarm of words he had my apt description. I also understood that maybe I had gone too far. Even an American black man would have found such a headstrong wife unsuitable, and how much more an African husband, steeped in a tradition of at least the appearance of male authority. I realized that I had handled the thing badly. I should have been more delicate. I should have allowed Vus time to see me depressed and mournful. Then he could have coerced from me the reason for my mood. I could have so manipulated the situation, that he would, himself, have suggested that maybe I should find a little something to do. A small part-time job. Perhaps a little secretarial work in the afternoon. With the awareness of my unfortunate mismanagement came the shocking knowledge that I was no longer in love.

The man standing over me venting his fury, employing his colorful vocabulary was no longer my love. The last wisps of mystery had disappeared. There had been physical attraction so strong that at his approach, moisture collected at every place where my body touched itself. Now he was in hand's reach, and tantalization was gone. He was just a fat man, standing over me, scolding.

His anger was finally spent, his energy flagged. I waited until he backed away and sat down in the chair facing me. He was exhausted from the outpouring of reproach and I was benumbed by the loss of love. We sat looking at each other, at the floor, at the tapestries, at each other again.

He was the first to speak. His voice was soft.

"You must call David and explain that you acted as an American woman, but that I returned home and reminded you that now you are an African wife."

I knew that neither threats nor inducements would cause me to give up the job.

I made my voice silken soft. "I have given my word. Not only to David but to Dr. Zein Nagati. He is a friend of Gamal Abdel Nasser and he knows that I am your wife. He said they need me. It might reflect badly on your name if I withdraw now."

Vus stood again. "You see? You see how your foolish headstrong American ways have endangered the struggle?"

He tried to build up to the earlier anger but was too tired to do so. He went back to the bedroom and reappeared dressed. He walked past me and out of the house, slamming the door.

I stayed in the pretty living room, thinking. I had a son to raise, and a lovely house. I had a job for which I was unqualified. I had an angry husband, whom I no longer loved. And I was in Cairo, Egypt, where I had no friends.

The doorbell rang, and thinking Vus had stalked out leaving his keys, I opened it. David DuBois stood smiling in the dim light. I grinned because he looked like Deliverance itself.

"Girl, I thought you might be getting nervous about tomorrow. So I came 'round to tell you everything's going to be all right."

We sat in the living room talking lightly about journalism and expectations. I wanted to unburden my aggravation. To tell him that I not only didn't know how to be an associate editor, but that my husband was bitterly opposed to my being anything but his obedient wife.

Vus walked in on our inane chatter. When he saw David his face lightened, the heavy cheeks lifted and he smiled delightedly.

They embraced as he called David "My brother." David must have noticed that he didn't speak to me.

"Vus, you must be proud of your wife. I mean about the job."

Vus cooled, and drew himself inward. "Job?" He said the word as if he had never used it before.

David looked at me, caught the misery which I didn't try to hide. He turned back to Vus. "When you were away she telephoned me. I took her out to tea and she said you were working so hard, stretching yourself so thin, that she was beginning to worry about your health. She said that as your wife she had to carry some of the load. That no one man could continue to do all you do without help."

Vus's body began to relax. His shoulders eased down to their natural position, a slow smile began to slacken his tightened features.

With words David was stroking away his hostility. "She said that most African men, in your position, would never allow their wives to work, but that you were a revolutionary, and that the success of the African conflict was your goal. And you meant to reach it by any means necessary."

Vus nodded. "True. True."

David was persuasive, convincing and a liar. He was also my supportive, fast-thinking inventive brother.

I was surprised to find when Vus and I went to bed, that being in the arms of a stranger in no way lessened my physical pleasure.

Vus insisted on accompanying me downtown to the *Arab Observer* offices. When we entered the enormous loftlike room, David called from a far corner. He greeted Vus first, then me. He introduced Vus first to my colleagues, and all the men shook hands, asked after each other's health and thanked God in Arabic. I was outside their ceremony like a foundling on an orphanage doorstep. After they finished saluting and bowing and grinning, David beckoned to me and I was presented.

Although I sensed little cordiality, I relaxed, because at least the men were not antagonistic. Vus's presence had assured them that I was not an audacious woman challenging their male community. I belonged to a man who, probably in straitened circumstances, was putting his wife to work. By introducing Vus first, David had followed established ritual and dissipated the hostility before it could collect.

I had to admit that although Vus's decision to escort me to my job (my father never accompanied me on the first day of school) infuriated me, his attendance had been a godsend.

I was shown my desk and a servant brought us all small cups of coffee from a brazier near the window. The coffee-drinking ceremony finally finished, Vus shook hands again with all the men, nodded to me and left the office. David stayed a few minutes, then shook hands around the room. When he took my hand, he said quietly, "You've made a good impression. I'll call you later."

229

I had said nothing, done nothing, shown no intelligence, wit or talent. Was I to assume that was the good impression?

Ignorance held me in my chair for at least an hour. Men, whose names I had already forgotten, or hadn't heard clearly at the first introduction, passed my desk, their hands full of papers and their eyes averted. The servant brought me cup after cup of sweet sluggish coffee, which I drank dutifully.

Suddenly there was a great sound of swishing papers, thumping feet, the tacking of typewriters. Dr. Nagati had arrived. He bobbed his head to the now industriously bustling reporters and came directly to my desk.

"Mrs. Make?" I stood.

"How are you getting on? David was here? You've been introduced? Good." He raised his voice, and speaking in Arabic, caused the employees to gather around him. Again, I stood outside the circle of men, not understanding as he continued to speak in an explosive tone. He slid into English without changing the force of speech.

"Mrs. Make?" It was a shouted order to come to attention, in a full-dress parade.

"Yes, Dr. Nagati?" I edged through the passage now made for me to face the great man. He looked down at me and tried a smile, which failed.

"This man handles British news. This one is in charge of European, this one is editor of Soviet news, this one American, this one Asian, and you will write about Africa. You will also look at all their copy, and they will look at yours. The *Arab Observer* will be a weekly, starting next week. We print in the basement of this building. You will go downstairs now with me and meet the typesetters."

Without another word, he walked away. It only took me a second to realize that he expected me to follow.

We walked into the dimly lit and dusty room on the lower floor. Dr. Nagati raised his voice, hollering in Arabic. Men in traditional galabias appeared like phantoms out of the gloom. All at once bright lights exposed the farthest recesses.

I was introduced in English as Mrs. Make, the new associate editor. The men shook my hand and welcomed me in Arabic. I smiled and wished Dr. Nagati would stay in the building forever, or at the very least return with me to the upstairs offices. We took our leave of the printers, and he talked until we reached the door leading out of the building. The magazine must be ready for distribution next week. It must have grace and be beautiful. Its news must be timely and accurate. I must remember that although none of the men had worked with women before, except possibly secretaries, they were all cultured and capable. Speaking of secretaries, he would be sending a few over later in the week.

"Goodbye, Mrs. Make. I'm sure you'll do well." He pushed the door open and disappeared through it, while my mouth was hanging open wide enough to allow in a swarm of flies.

I directed myself back to my desk. At least I knew that I was expected to cover the African affairs. It would be necessary to collect all newspapers, magazines, journals and essays. A large map and a set of the Oxford English Dictionary would help. Now, now that I no longer desired Vus, I needed him. Every fact he'd ever learned was filed neatly in his orderly brain. He knew tribes, leaders, topography, weather and the political stances of all countries on the continent.

Two reporters, the coffee bearer and I reached my desk at the same time. The server set down the small cup and walked away, as both the journalists drew up chairs. When I sat down, they told me their names again, and began to chat with me, quite cozily. We agreed tacitly that our first introduction had never happened. They offered to show me the Telex machine and how I could acquire background material on any news release. They proposed that I move my desk into the adjoining room, where there was a library with hundreds of books in English. The grin began in my stomach or behind my kneecaps or under my toenails. It undulated in sweet waves, overrunning my body with warmth and well-being. I thought of Brer Rabbit. Like all Southern black children, I had heard folk tales since my early youth, and a favorite came back to me as I sat in that wide-open newsroom in Cairo.

For years Brer Rabbit had been stealing carrots from a garden, and after many attempts, after many elaborate but ineffectual snares, the owner of the plot finally succeeded in catching him.

The man was red as blood with anger. He shook the rabbit until his tail nearly fell off. He said, "Rabbit, I've got you now. And I'm going to do the worst thing in the world to you. I mean the baddest thing. I mean the meanest thing. I'm going to make you cry and scream and wish that God never put breath in your body."

The rabbit started crying. "Please, Mr. Farmer. Don't do the worst thing to me. Do anything but that. But I don't think you know what the worst thing is. So just do me as you want to do me." The rabbit started shuffling and grinning. "But don't do the worst thing."

The farmer looked at the rabbit suspiciously. He asked, "What is the worst thing?" Rabbit said, "I won't tell you." The farmer began to lie. "You can tell me, little rabbit. I won't do it. I promise you."

The rabbit began to relax. He asked the farmer. "Do you swear if I tell you, that you won't do it to me?"

The farmer put his hand on his heart and swore. The rabbit relaxed even more.

He said, "Farmer, you've got a big black iron pot. You can fill it with lard and light a fire under it and cook me in boiling oil, and I wouldn't care."

The farmer was doubtful, but the rabbit kept talking. "You can skin me alive and use my fur to make a coat for your little girl, and that would be all right with me." The farmer looked at the rabbit with disbelief, but the rabbit continued. "You can cut off all my feet and give them to your friends for good luck and I'd like that. But the worst thing . . ."

The farmer was getting excited. "Tell me, little rabbit, what is the worst thing?"

The rabbit began to tremble, his voice got so little the farmer could barely hear him. "See that briar patch over there?" He pointed to a clump of nettles, "Please don't throw me over there."

232

The farmer's face became hard. He asked the rabbit, "Are you sure that's the worst thing?" Rabbit said, "They stick in my sides like burning needles, they pop in my eyes like thorns, they hold me like chains and lash my body like whips. Please don't throw me in the briar patch."

The farmer picked up the rabbit by the ears, he lifted him high in the air and he began to swing him around over his head, all the time asking, "Are you sure?" And the rabbit answered, crying, "It's the worst thing!"

Finally, when the farmer had the rabbit turning at a fast speed, he pointed him toward the briar patch and let go. Brer Rabbit landed on his feet. His eyes were dry and bright. His ears perked up and waved. Brer Rabbit grinned at the farmer, his teeth shining white as buttermilk. He said, "Home, at last. Home at last. Great God Almighty, I'm home at last."

I smiled sweetly as the men shoved and pulled my desk into the library. When they left, and I stood before the crowded bookshelves, reading unfamiliar titles and the names of authors unknown to me, still I felt just like Brer Rabbit in the briar patch.

17

For two weeks I stayed in the room, using each free moment to cull from the shelves information about journalism, writing, Africa, printing, publishing and editing. Most of the books had been written by long-dead authors and published years before in Britain; still, I found nuggets of useful facts.

The arrival of secretaries forced me back into the larger room with my male colleagues, but by that time I had a glimmering of journalistic jargon. I began to combine a few news items taken directly from the Telex, and insert some obscure slightly relevant background information. Then I would rehead the copy and call it my own.

233

I stayed at the *Arab Observer* for over a year and gradually my ignorance receded. I learned from Abdul Hassan how to write an opinionated article with such subtlety that the reader would think the opinion his own. Eric Nemes, the layout artist, showed me that where an article was placed on a page, its typeface, even the color of ink, were as important as the best-written copy. David DuBois demonstrated how to select a story and persevere until the last shred of of data was in my hands. Vus supplied me with particulars on the politically fluid, newly independent African states. I received a raise from Dr. Nagati, the respect of my fellow workers and a few compliments from strangers.

Weekdays began with a family breakfast served by Omanadia. Vus read the newspaper, Guy's face was buried in a book and I scanned work I always brought to the table. Often after we left the house, going separate ways, I would think that we had again lost the art of talking together. We had ceased to find amusement in one another.

Guy's life was becoming intricately complicated. He was asked to cope with adolescent sexuality, the enigmatic Arabic language, a body which seemed to be stretching to touch the clouds and another joyless home. In attempting to protect himself he withdrew into books or threw himself into the wild, raucous Cairo streets.

I offered to give parties for his Arabic friends so that he could spend more time in the house. He refused politely but coolly, saying that neither he nor his acquaintances wanted to be shut up indoors. They'd rather be in the *souks* and back streets, the old town and the great Al Tahrir Square, and don't worry about him, he was just fine.

Neither of us could successfully masquerade our unhappiness from the other. We had been too close, too long. We accepted with mutual respect the other's pretense at contentment.

Vus's work doubled.

The number of men escaping from South Africa was escalating. Some only reached Northern Rhodesia, where they stayed hidden until arrangements could be made for their further escape. A few men lodged in Ethiopia, but they had to be moved, and Vus's responsibility was to find friendly nations where the now-homeless wanderers could stay. All needed clothes, food, housing. Some wanted military training, while others asked for medical or legal education. Vus's concern in their behalf never wavered.

Although the romance in our marriage had evaporated, I still admired and appreciated him. I even loved him, I simply was not in love with him. There was ample evidence that he had other romantic interests anyway. Often, he returned home very late, reeking of perfume, heavy lidded and offering no explanation. On a few evenings, he didn't return at all. I said nothing. I had my work, my house and had made two friends. A.B. Williamson, the round pretty wife of the Liberian Chargé d'Affaires, and Kebidetch Erdatchew, wife of the Ethiopian Embassy's First Secretary. On the surface, we seemed to have nothing in common save our gender and blackness. Kebidetch was thin, small and married to a son of the royal Selassie House. She was as beautiful as antique gold and as reserved as a vault and lent credence to the common African saying that the loveliest women on the continent were to be found in Ethiopia.

Her own beauty was legendary. One day in Addis Ababa, the regal Jarra Mesfin saw her from a passing car and determined, at that hasty glance, that he would find her, woo her and wed her. The ensuing courtship and marriage became the subject of popular songs sung in the streets and cafés of Ethiopia. Seven years later, they still shared languid looks across crowded rooms. They were childless and lived in Zamalek in a quiet luxurious apartment, with an ancient manservant they had brought from Ethiopia.

A.B. (friends called her Banti) had been raised in the underdeveloped Grand Bassa region of Liberia. Her family sent her to Monrovia, the capital city, for further education. Her pert looks and witty good humor won her friends and marriage to a bright young lawyer, whose career was just beginning to rise.

The couple lived in the Ambassador's Residence with their own three children, Banti's younger sister, the teenage daughter of a friend, two Liberian maids, a nanny, an Egyptian laundryman, a doorman and a cook. The building shivered with sound. Noisy children played tag games on the graceful staircase. West African High Life music boomed from the large record player, young girls giggled over young-girl secrets in the ceremonial drawing room, and Banti moved her short chubby body through the house, her laughter adding one more spice to the already aromatic cacophony.

Kebi, Banti and I met several times at diplomatic receptions, and at my house during one of our costly parties, but we didn't cross the threshold from courteous acquaintance into friendship until one night at the Liberian Residence when an overflow of visitors filled every inch of space in the building's first floor. African, Asian and European diplomats with their wives mingled with Egyptian government officials and their wives. Waiters, hired for the occasion, prodded through the throng, shoving trays of drinks toward the crowded guests.

I was sitting with a Yugoslavian woman in the informal lounge when I heard Vus's voice part the general murmur of the crowd in another room.

"I speak for the Xhosa, the Zulu, the Shona and the Lesotha. You are a foolish people. Foolish." I jumped up, and remembering my manners just in time, excused myself. (Vus was cozying up the Yugoslavians at that time.) I nudged my way through the flock of people. Vus's tone was becoming louder.

"A foolish, small-minded greedy nation. You are mean and stupid. Stupid." I had arrived sooner than I expected, because as I pushed forward, people nearer the action pulled away, impossibly dispersing. I saw Vus standing face to face with a white man, whose red cheeks and popped eyes were his only evidence of life. He stood stone-stiff; he might have died erect, and been left on the spot to be viewed like a statue. Vus's face, however, was alive with contempt, and his right arm was raised. He was poking the white man's chest with his forefinger.

"Tell them, tell the savages of your country, that Mother Africa will no longer allow them to suck from her breast."

I knew that Vus was intoxicated with either alcohol or rage or a dangerous combination of the two. All sounds had diminished to a low, steady, disapproving undertone. I felt as powerless as if I were mute or hypnotized.

"I speak for Southern Africa. For South-West Africa. For Mozambique, Angola . . ."

"And Ethiopia." The sound came from the rear, and grew louder as the speaker neared Vus. "He speaks for the Amharas and the Gullas and for the Eritreans." Jarra appeared, having pressed his way through the pack of bodies. He stood beside Vus. There was another movement, I saw another separation and Kebi appeared to stand near Jarra. Her movement gave me the courage to edge nearer Vus, but we acted with different motives. She was displaying her support of Jarra; I was hoping that my presence would provoke Vus into gathering his control. We five stood in the center of the room, like warring tribes in a forest clearing, and we had reached a stalemate. Joe Williamson's already high-pitched voice soared over the crowd.

"Brothers. Brothers." Joe stepped up to Vus and Jarra, daintily, like a proud bantam rooster. "Argument is one thing. Riot is another. This is not an occasion for either."

Without changing tone he spoke in Liberian patois, "Ole man say in my country, 'Hurry, hurry, get dere tomorrow. Take time, get there today.' Or better yet, 'We come to party to show our teeth. We go to war to show our arms.' "

Vus turned to look at Joe, and I held my breath. Joe was the doyen of the African diplomatic corps; he had been supportive of Vus and all the other freedom fighters and was highly respected in Cairo, and I liked him. If Vus turned on Joe, I could cross him off our list of acquaintances, because Vus's tongue could be sharp as an assagai, and Joe was a proud man. Vus smiled and shook his head. He said, "Bro Joe, you should be president of this entire continent."

Jarra, taking his cue from Vus's relaxation, said, "Speak for the rest of Africa, Vusumzi, not Ethiopia. However, maybe the emperor will make him a *ras.* " They laughed.

The gathering seemed to exhale at the same time. All of a sudden, music could be heard. The knots of people disbanded. Vus, Joe and Jarra walked away together and the man who had been the object of Vus's tirade disappeared. Only Kebi, Banti, who had been standing behind her husband, and I were left in the middle of the floor. Kebi looked at us, lifted her eyebrows and gave a tiny shrug of her frail shoulders. Banti put her hands on her hips and grinned roguishly. I thought of us as foot soldiers, bringing up the rear in a war whose declaration we had not known, left on the battlefield after a peace was achieved, in which we had not participated. I laughed out loud. Banti and Kebi chuckled. We moved nearer and, smiling, touched each other's shoulders arms, hands and cheeks. Brought to friendship by the frustrated lashing out of one man, a near-stranger's defense of the first man, and by the clever, humorous mediation of a third man, we three women were to be inseparable for the next year and a half.

I never learned what fuse ignited the conflagration. At home, Vus answered my query: "He was wrong, and too cowardly to say what he meant."

"Did he insult you? I mean us, the race?"

"Not directly. Like most white racists, he was paternalistic. I would have preferred he slap me than that he talk down upon me. Then I could retaliate in kind."

I totally agreed. Some whites, in black company, beset by the contradiction between long-learned racism and the demands of courtesy, confusedly offend listening blacks. The stereotypical "Some of my best friends . . ." and other awkward attempts at what they think to be civility, elicit from black people an outburst of anger whites can neither comprehend nor avoid.

An inability to speak fluent Arabic and the difference in cultures made friendships with Egyptian women difficult. The secretaries in my office were neither brave enough (I understood that as a six-foot-tall black American female editor, I was somewhat of an oddity) nor had the time (many had taken jobs to help their needy parents and siblings) nor were interested enough (some were already betrothed and were working to pay for their trousseaus) to respond to my friendly overtures.

I had heard of Hanifa Fathy and noted the respect with which her name was spoken. Hanifa Fathy, the poet. Then, Hanifa, wife of a judge. It was unusual to hear an Egyptian woman's marital alliance not reported as her first accomplishment. When we finally met at a conference, I was surprised to find her pretty. I had never heard her looks described. She wore her light-brown hair long, in the manner of Lauren Bacall, and her strong feminine features reminded me of the bold American actress.

When we shook hands (her handshake was firm), she said she had been reading my work in the *Arab Observer* and was determined that we should meet. I accepted her invitation to meet some Egyptian female writers, scholars and teachers.

In Hanifa's modish living room, I met Egyptian women who had earned doctorates from European universities, and serious painters and talented actresses, but I found them too trained, too professionally fixed, to welcome the chummy contact of friendship. Hanifa, however, was warm and witty. We spent gossipy Saturday afternoons on the veranda of the Cairo country club.

My marriage had shape, responsibility and no romance, and although I was working ten hours a day at the *Arab Observer,* my salary slipped away like sand in an hourglass. There was never enough. Vus needed more clothes, more trips, more parties. Guy needed more clothes and more allowance. I needed more of everything, or at least I wanted an increase of the things I had and the possession of things I had never owned.

On the face of it, things looked bad, but I couldn't escape from a cheeriness which sat in my lap, lounged on my shoulders and ,spread itself in the palms of my hands. I was, after all, living in Cairo, Egypt, working, paying my own way. My son was well. Then there were David DuBois, Banti, Kebi and Hanifa.

I had the possibility of a brother and three sisters. It could have been much worse.

Banti gave a hilarious party, to which only women were invited. The occasion was a celebration of the birthday of a great Liberian female doctor. Elaborate food and a variety of drinks were served by uniformed attendants. The living room was decorated as if for a supreme Embassy function, and a trio of musicians played familiar melodies.

Wives and secretaries from the African embassies and a sprinkling of Egyptian women and I felt deliciously important. We ate, talked, drank and half the invitees finally danced, moving individually, across Banti's polished hardwood floor. Each woman observed the steps of her own country. Kebi, with her hands on her hips, slid her feet in tiny patterns, meanwhile raising first one shoulder, then the other, and rotating the shoulders in sensuous undulation. Banti and Mrs. Clelland from the Ghanian Embassy danced High Life, stepping lightly, with knees slightly bent, pushing their backsides a little to the left, a little to the right and directly behind themselves. I combined some Twist with the Swim and received approving laughter and applause from the nondancers who sat on the sidelines.

The party was nearing its end when a young woman took the floor. She wore West African national dress. The long printed skirt and matching blouse hugged a startling body. She had wide shoulders, large erect breasts, billowing hips and the waist of a child. All the dancers backed away and found seats, as the beautiful woman moved to the music. She swiveled and flourished, jostled and vibrated, accompanied by the audience's encouragement and laughter.

"Swing it, girl. Swing it."

"Show that thing, child. Show it."

"Whoo. Whoo."

She made her face sly, knowing, randy, and her large hips fluttered as if a bird, imprisoned in her pelvis was attempting flight.

The viewers' delight reminded me of the pleasure older black American women found in other women's sexiness. Years before when I had been a shake dancer, some ladies used to pat my hips and exclaim, "You've got it, baby. Shake it. Now, shake it." Their elation was pure, sensual and approving. If they were old they looked on female sensuality as an extension of their own, and were reminded of their youth. Younger women recollected the effects of their last love-making or were prompted by womanish sexuality into pleasant anticipation of their next satisfying encounter.

I was tickled that African women and black American women had the custom in common.

When the music and dancing were finished I joined the women who crowded around the dancer, patting, stroking her and laughing.

"I am from Northern Nigeria." Her voice was soft and she kept her eyes lowered, respecting the age and positions of the older women. "I am an unmarried girl with a good dowry. I'm here to stay with Egyptian friends and study Arabic."

Her name was Mendinah and she was obviously looking for a husband.

We complimented her on her beauty and welcomed her to Cairo, and I secretly wished her luck.

18

One week later Vus returned from Addis Ababa. He asked what had happened in his absence. I reported on my work and that David had found another way for me to supplement my salary. I had agreed to write commentary for Radio Egypt, and I would be paid four pounds for a review and an extra pound for each one I narrated.

Guy had earned acceptable grades on recent tests and had

generously spent more time at home while Vus was away. I also told Vus about the women's party and Mendinah. He accepted my news and told me drily of his trip. The once-exotic names no longer titillated me, and Vus had long since stopped trying to enchant me with tales of his perilous exploits. We returned to the sequence of our lives. Work occupied our days, and parsimonious love-making ended some stolid nights.

The news spread in the African diplomatic corps that Mendinah was a slut, a hussy, a whore, a home-breaking harlot. The rumor was hot oil poured into the ears of the African women who had admired her. She had sought appointments with four ambassadors. Three had reported to their wives that the pretty woman offered them her favors in return for money. In weeks she had cut a lascivious swath between members of the diplomatic corps and their wives. Her name became an alarm, forcing my female friends to assemble and close ranks against the dangerous intruder.

She would never be invited to another woman's home. She would be turned away from every door, and not addressed on the street. The husbands who had fallen for her charms would be dealt with in the privacy of their marriages, but her blatant disrespect of the African wives had to have public penalty.

Two months passed and for the African community Mendinah disappeared, lost her name, had no presence. Then one evening, an Egyptian woman, close acquaintance of the African women, gave a party. Vus and I arrived late. When we entered the first room, the informal lounge, Banti, Kebi and seven ladies already sat on the sofas, their multicolored dresses radiant against dark-brown skin. They greeted Vus, who responded and continued into the salon, where more guests stood talking. I stopped to exchange regards with my friends and the other ladies I had come to know and like.

Our small talk was suddenly pierced by "Good evening, Mrs. Make." The sound was disquietingly familiar. I looked up and saw Mendinah in the arched doorway leading to a hall passage. She

242

was standing by a record player. I nodded to her and she lifted the machine's arm, stopping the music. When she turned her fabulous body to face me, I saw again the cunning face, the small hint of cruelty.

"Mrs. Make, Mr. Make has been trying to reach me all day long. He called all over Cairo trying to get my number." Her words, voice and intent were pitiless and for seconds my heart opposed its natural function.

She poked her voice easily through my entire body. "When he finally reached me, he said he had to talk to me, to see me about something very important." As she glanced at the seated women, I gritted my teeth and held on to the sternness of my long-dead grandmother.

"I refused to let him come to my apartment." Her eyes hurriedly returned to fasten on me. "Then he said it had to do with you. That you needed someone to help you at the office. I have been looking for a job, you know." Again, her eyes rushed to the African women, and quickly back to me.

Nothing happened. No angel came to take me up to a deserved heaven. No one shook my shoulder to awaken me from the immobilizing nightmare. No one moved. I raked through my mind, gathering every shred of skill, art and craftiness and stepped toward her.

"Mendinah?" I kept my voice soft and haughty. She looked up into my face as I approached.

"I am Mendinah, Mrs. Make." The tone of her response was sassy.

"And were you willing to work for me? At a very high salary? With an allowance for rent and possibly your own car? Were you willing?"

Deceit left her face, and suddenly she became a young girl, who could have been my baby sister. Her defenses were down, she was vulnerable and I thrust at her with all my will.

"Unfortunately the job has been filled, but if it had not, dear Mendinah"—I was still speaking low—"you would never do. You are ignorant and you are a tramp." I gave her a filthy smile and walked past her into the salon.

Luckily a row of chairs was lined against a near wall. I went directly to a seat. Wind and pride had left my body. My stomach felt empty and my head light. I sat erect from habit and early training. Banti and Kebi rushed in and took seats beside me. Banti took my right hand and Kebi the other.

They both murmured consolation.

"You were wonderful, sister, wonderful." That was Banti.

"You made me proud of you, Maya." Kebi squeezed my hand.

"You looked like a queen mother."

"A princess."

"Don't cry. Not now. You have handled it. It is over."

Banti leaned toward me, forcing me to look in her serious face. "Sister, you will be avenged. Not to worry. You know what old man say in my country?" She had slipped from standard English into the melodic Liberian country accent. "Old man say, 'If you mess with Jesus Christ, God will make you shit.'"

She nodded her head, asserting her own affirmation.

The blasphemy and humor struck me at the same time. I was shocked and tickled. To arrange in the same sentence God, Jesus Christ, righteousness, revenge and the word "shit" was so incongruous I was startled away from the humiliation of Mendinah's announcement.

Both friends' faces were solemn with concern, both heads bobbed in agreement with Banti's old man's wisdom. At last I nodded, smiled and rose. Vus was standing alone near a distant window.

"Ah, my dear. Nice party, isn't it?"

"Vus, who is that girl playing records over there?"

He turned and looked straight at Mendinah, whose profile was distinct against the white walls.

Vus shook his head, "I don't know. No." Shaking his head, his eyes dark with puzzlement.

"Vus, you know her. Don't lie. At least don't lie."

244

He twisted toward me, sudden recognition smoothing the planes of his face. "Oh, say, is that that Mendinah you were telling me about?"

I wanted to slap him until he snapped and split open like popcorn.

I walked away. I wasn't sure what God would do if someone messed with His only Son, nor how I would fare when I dropped the obeisant attitude of an accepting wife and allowed my black American femaleness to emerge.

The silent ride home seemed endless. Vus drove slowly, letting the old rickety car choose its own speed.

When we were at last in the apartment, I checked Guy's room, and found him asleep. That part of my life was comfortably accounted for. Now all I had to do was face my lover and one-time love, whom I heard dragging furniture around in the living room. I went into our bedroom and stood in the dark, wondering how to begin.

"Maya. Maya, don't go to bed yet." I walked out and down the hall. The big man sat composed, and had arranged a chair to face him.

"Sit down here, Maya. I want to talk to you about Mendinah. Mendinah and all the others."

There was a moment's relief. At least I didn't have to start the conversation. That brief easement was pushed away with an abysmal fear. If he insisted that I accept his infidelity, I'd have to leave him. Condoning it would increase the misdeed. I had heard of men who brought other women into their homes, into the beds they shared with their wives. If Vus was planning such flagrancy, I would have to pick up my son and my heels, and get on the road, one more time.

I sat facing him, our knees touching.

"I am a man. An African man. I am neither primitive nor cruel. A nation of interlopers and most whites in the world would deny me on all counts, but let me deal with each of those stated conditions." It was going to be a long night.

"A man requires a certain amount of sexual gratification. Much more than a woman needs, wants or understands."

"That's a lie, Vus. You're not a woman, how do you know what I need?"

"I do not choose to argue a point which cannot be proved, but which is tacitly agreed upon. I will continue. As an African man, in my society, I have the right to marry more than one woman."

"But that is not true in my society and you knew that when we met."

"I met you in the U.S."—he smiled—"but now we are in Africa."

Was he implying that geography affected his gonads? I reminded him that he had been unfaithful in New York.

He looked shocked. "You have no evidence of that." He was almost correct. I had only the lingering scent of perfume, and the unforgotten cosmetics on his clothes.

When I said nothing, he relaxed and leaned back in his chair, spreading his vast thighs. "To an African man, the act of sex is only important as long as it lasts. It is not the factor which holds a family together. It pleases and relieves tension, so that one can get about the business of living."

I asked with sarcastic sweetness, "And what about African women? Don't they want pleasure and release?"

He frowned, offended. "Haven't I always satisfied you? Have I ever left you wanting? I have come home many nights, physically drained, and abstracted with my work, but I have done my duty to you. Deny that if you can."

The conversation was getting away from me. Onus and guilt were shifting into my lap, where they surely didn't belong.

"I don't love you anymore, Vus." It was the truth, but I used it not for declaration, so much as to startle him and take back a little advantage.

He stayed at ease. "I know that, my dear. I've known it for a long time. Nor am I, any longer, in romantic love with you. However, we respect and admire each other. We have the asset of mutual goals: the struggle for freedom, loyalty to Mother Africa." He paused for a second, then went on in a softer voice. "And Guy's future as an African man."

At that second, I hardened my heart. I didn't believe all the legitimizing drivel Vus concocted about African male infidelity and I would not allow him to teach such nonsense to my son.

"What about Mendinah? Tell me about her. Tell me why you put my name into your mouth, when all you wanted was to get her in bed?"

"I apologize to you for that. Sincerely." His quick mind served him quickly. "Although I did hear you say you wished there was another black woman in your office."

There have always been, for me, periods in arguments when my thoughts swirl around in semi-solid circles, leaving no protruding phrase for my mind to grab. I am rendered mute until the eddying jumble slows down and I am able to pick out enough words to form a first sentence. The moment had come. Ideas rushed around like crazed children in a mad tag game. Vus was African and his values were different from mine. Among the people I knew, my family and friends, promiscuity was the ultimate blow in a marriage. It struck down the pillars of trust which held the relationship aloft. It was also physically dangerous. Venereal diseases could easily be the result of indiscreet momentary gratification. It was disloyal and, finally, unfriendly. Nor was it a characteristic solely of African men. From the beginning of human history, all societies had tried to cope with the custom. The Judeo-Christian Bible forbade adultery, for both sexes. Usually, however, women paid the highest price, losing their hair to rough barbers, or their lives to an affronted community that stoned them to death.

In the United States white men, with the implements of slavery and racial oppression, had taken from black men their names, languages, power, wives, daughters, innate senses of self-value, their confidence. Because they had been unable, however, to kill the sexuality, white men began to envy it, extol it, adore and fear

247

it. A number of black men, finding that they had one thing left which was beyond the reach of their enemies' grasp commenced to identify themselves, to themselves, as sexual masters, possessors of the big dicks, the artful penises, the insatiable lust. White men greedily and enviously agreed. White women, in secret fantasies and rare public displays, yearned over the huge private parts. Some black women agreed that black men had rapacious appetites, and allowed their husbands and lovers the freedom of the fields. Some other women, with knives and guns, boiling water, poison and the divorce courts proved that they did not agree with the common attitude.

"Mendinah. It is said that she is a sexual glutton. Women like that are only good for one, at most two experiences." He had been talking for some time. I suddenly remembered the drone of his voice. "The men who have spoken about her consider her a pretty but temporary vessel."

I nodded, assured. I had finally found my words.

"I'm leaving you, Vus. I'm not sure when or where I'm going. But I'm leaving you."

His face didn't change from the placid sheet of control when I got up and went to bed.

Banti's telephone call at my office came unexpectedly. I had gone to her house early the morning following the Mendinah incident and told her of my plans to leave Vus. Her response had been that of a wife who had a faithful husband. "Sister, you have been a giant. Everyone admires your patience. Truly, you have proved yourself." With my decision made, the burden of tolerance lifted and the approval of my friend, I had gone to work buoyant.

"Sister," I heard her say on the telephone, "Joe and I want you to come to us, this evening. After dinner. Nine o'clock. Will you?"

I agreed. The day rushed along. Entire paragraphs leaped out of my typewriter, needing little, if any, revision.

Vus didn't appear for dinner, so Guy and I ate alone. He was reading, so was happy to hear that I had an appointment and he would have the house quiet and to himself.

The heavy door of the Liberian Residency was opened by a servant. I stepped into the foyer and heard a cloud of low voices. Banti hadn't advised me to dress for a party. But then, the tone wasn't party-like. I walked past the doorman two paces, and I was at the door of the salon, where a multitude of faces peered at me.

It was a surprise birthday party, months off schedule and lacking the gaiety of a fete.

About twenty people sat in a crescent of chairs. Kebi, Jarra and Banti were together. I hastily examined the familiar faces and felt that I had stumbled, unluckily, into a secret ritual or a dangerous kangaroo court.

No one smiled, not even my friends, and the awkward moment could have lasted forever. Joe Williamson's high melodic voice preceded his presence.

"Sister Maya. We are waiting for you. Come in. Come in. Abdul will bring you a drink. Come, you are to sit beside Brother Vus."

My eyes followed the general indication of his right hand. Vus sat, stiff and sober at the center of the row of chairs. I knew that I was befuddled, thrown and totally mystified, so I smiled and obeyed Joe's directive, finding an empty seat beside my husband. The low thrumming of voices did not stop. I leaned toward Vus and whispered, "What is this? What's happening?"

He gave me a calm look and said, "This is all for you." There was only weariness in his tone.

"Brothers and sisters." Joe walked in the center of the floor. "You know why you are here." I was handed a drink of Scotch. "Our sister from across the seas, and across the centuries, is planning to leave our brother from South Africa."

Damn. Vus knew it, I knew it, and I had told Banti a few hours earlier. I gazed at the African men and women, and found that the information was not news to them. No eyes widened, no jaws tightened at the announcement.

249

"Our sister and her son have returned to Africa. We all know that she has worked very hard and that she feels herself an African." A mumble of agreement followed his statement.

"Our South African brother wages a fight for all of us. No day passes but that he is on the battlefield. No night comes without Vusumzi Make at the gun, threatening the fortress of white oppression." Another rumble of accord lifted and floated in the room.

"Now, I, the brother to all of you, have called for palaver. Neither of these young people have family in Egypt, outside this small community. So I have asked you so that we can examine the points and weigh the matter." Panic was rising in my mind and paralyzing my legs.

Joe said, "I will ask this side of the room to argue for our sister, Maya, and this side for our brother, Vus."

I shook myself away from the numbing shock and stood up.

"Excuse me, Joe, but I'm not on trial. I'm going home." Joe spoke to me over the undertone of disapproval.

"Sister, you are going to stay in Africa. You have a son and a name. If you can sit through this palaver, the outcome will be news in Africa. You know, Maya, our people do not count on papers or magazines to tell us what we need to know. There are people here from Ghana, Mali, Guinea, Nigeria, Ethiopia and Liberia. Sister, try hard and sit down."

Years before I had understood that all I had to do, really had to do, was stay black and die. Nothing could be more interesting than the first, or more permanent than the latter. In truly critical moments I reminded myself of those discoveries. I walked back and sat down beside Vus, who had become a large, black stranger.

Joe Williamson placed a dining-room chair in the middle of the half-circle, talking all the while.

"The group from Maya, going right, will defend our brother. People left of Vus will support our sister. And please remember, folks, we are the only family they have in this strange land."

I looked to my right, and my heart raced. My friends, Banti,

250

Kebi, Margaret Young, a Nigerian close friend, and Jarra would be arguing for Vus. I turned and looked across to the other side and saw three infamous lechers, a few old indifferent men and three women whom I didn't know well. My team looked hopeless.

Joe took his seat and spoke to me.

"Sister, tell your complaint. Tell your side."

Black Americans had no custom of publicly baring the soul. In old-time churches, people used to rise and complain about the treatment they had received from fellow members, but those conferences had died out, leaving only the memory in ribald jokes.

Mrs. Jackson stood up in church and reported, "Reverend, brothers and sisters. I accuse Miss Taylor of going 'round town saying my husband has a wart on his private part." The congregation's "uh huh huhs" sounded like drumrolls. Miss Taylor got up and said, "I have to speak to clarify what I said. Brothers and sisters, I did not say that Mr. Jackson had a wart on his private part. I never did. 'Cause I never saw it. What I said, and this is all I said, was it felt like it was a wart."

There was no precedent in my life for airing private affairs. I held myself still and erect.

Joe repeated, "Sister, tell your part. Why do you find our brother impossible as a husband?"

I looked at Joe, then at my dear friends, lined up in Vus's defense. Banti, Kebi and Margaret know all my complaints, I had cried in their arms, and laid my head on their laps uncounted times. Now they sat with straight flat faces, as if we were strangers. I turned to look at the company gathered in my behalf. Their faces were also cold, unsupportive and strange. I was alone again, but then, since I was already black, all I had to do was die.

I said, "The man stuffs his thing in any opening he finds. I am faithful, he is not."

A few coughs fell from the mouths of my squad, and Vus's troop twitched and cleared their throats.

"I slave my ass off." (African women hardly ever used profanity in mixed company, but I wasn't strictly an African, and, after all, they had gathered to hear me speak and I was a black American. Mentioning slavery in present African company was a ploy. Their forefathers had been spared, or had negotiated for the sale of my ancestors. I knew it and they knew it. It gave me a little edge.)

"I put money into the house. At ten o'clock I go alone to the Broadcast Building to narrate an essay, and I'm paid one pound. Vus spends money as if we are rich. He expects me to be faithful and steady and he comes home smelling of cheap perfume and a whore's twat." They may not have heard the word before but everyone knew what it meant.

I reveled in the rustle of discomfort. They asked me and I told them.

Joe Williamson clapped his hands. "All right, Sister Maya has spoken. I call upon Vus's defense." In a snap, queries were directed at me.

"Have you kept yourself clean?"

"Do you refuse your husband his marital rights?"

"You are an American, after all; how well can you cook African food?"

"Do you curse and act unbecoming?"

"Do you try to dominate the man?"

"Do you press him to have sex when he is tired?"

"Do you obey him? listen to him carefully?"

I answered every question with openness and sass. The sooner they rejected me, the sooner this odd ritual would be over. I would be free or get whatever was coming to me.

When I finished responding, Joe turned to my squad. Their interrogation of Vus was weak and without heart.

"Do you love her?"

"Have you provided for her?"

"Do you satisfy her?"

"She had a child when she came to you. Have you tried to give her more children?"

"Do you want her?"

Vus answered honestly and quietly.

252

There was a hiatus when he finished while Joe called for drinks for the crowd. We remained seated, holding fresh icy glasses.

Joe began to prance in the clear plot of floor. Dainty, sure and masculine.

"It seems to me, brothers and sisters, that Maya is in the right. Her objection is stronger than our brother's reply. I suggest that in this palaver our brother is the loser."

He turned to Vus's supporters.

"Do you agree?" When the heads nodded, for the first time that night friendliness and smiles returned to the faces of my confidantes.

Joe went to stand in front of Vus, an arm's reach away.

"Bro Vus, it is decided that you are in the wrong, and Sister Maya is in the right. Do you agree?"

Vus lowered his large head in assent.

Joe bowed, taking the agreement, and continued.

"You must provide drink for everyone who has met here tonight. You must bring a lamb or goat for us all to chop." A rampage of laughter followed the pronouncement but was quelled with Joe's next words: "And our sister has the right to leave you."

Silence settled on the shoulders of the listeners. Falling from the air like particled smog.

Joe faced me. "Sister, you have done well. You have sat through African palaver and you have won. Now you may leave."

I was wrung dry by the ritual and only a little pleased by Joe's statement that now I had the right to leave. I never thought I needed anyone's approval but my own.

Joe stepped up to me, close enough for me to see clearly the whites of his eyes.

"Now, sister, now that the triumph is in your hands, now that people from six countries agree that you can leave your husband, and no guilt will fall on your head. Now. Now in your position of strength, we throw ourselves on your mercy." The group responded with jubilant laughter.

"We ask you, from your righteous pinnacle, would you please give the man one more chance?"

I looked at Banti, who instructed me with a nod. Kebi gave me a small smile. Margaret Young, my Nigerian friend, lifted her perfect eyebrows. I should say yes. I hadn't decided where to go, I had no date to leave, and if Joe was right, which I suspected, if I acted graciously, my name in Africa would be golden.

"Stay six months. Sister, give the man six months."

I looked at Vus. He was anxious. I knew immediately that his concern had less to do with me than it had to do with his repute. He had never knowingly or wittingly mistreated me. I could stay with him six months.

I said, "I will stay."

Chairs scraped the floor. Vus took me in his arms, and whispered. "You are a generous woman. My wife."

Joe Williamson shouted, "This time, we party. We wait for the fatted calf, but now we drink and celebrate the reunion of our brother and sister. We toast Mother Africa, who needs all her children."

19

Guy graduated from high school and then took a knapsack and joined Egyptian friends for a trek in the Sahara. My friendship with Kebi and Banti became stronger. More women were hired in my office and some found my presence incongruous and unacceptable. I spoke halting Arabic, smoked cigarettes openly, was not a Muslim, and was an American on top of that. On the day when President Kennedy and Khrushchev had their confrontation over the independence of Cuba, in the hours when the next world war hung like an unpaid debt over our heads, no one spoke to me. The male employees ignored me; as if by a time warp we were all returned to my first day at the *Arab Observer*. The

254

women were openly hostile. Papers which they needed to bring to my desk were handed over by the coffee server or the copy boy. Actions by people thousands of miles away, men who didn't know I was alive and whose sympathy I would never expect, influenced my peace, and rendered me odious. Kennedy was an American, and so was I. I didn't have the language to explain that being a black American was qualitatively different from being An American. I worried like everyone else, but made myself scarce in the office.

Vus was trying and so was I, but neither of us was able to infuse vitality into our wilting marriage. He steadily gained weight as I became thinner. Indifference became the mattress we lay on, so our sexual sharings disintegrated into unsatisfying periods of hasty and uncomfortable rubbings.

I had promised to stay for six months and we both felt the time was dragging.

Banti and Kebi found excuses to send their drivers to my house bearing food and crates of liquor. Accompanying notes stated that they had overordered or simply had no more storage room.

I became more dependent on our friendship. I spent nearly every evening in the company of one or the other or both of the sisterly women. When we talked, they told amusing tales of home, of their families, of the husbands they loved, of the children, of a merciful God and sometimes of their private fantasies. Vus was never mentioned.

After five months I began to think about my future and Guy's placement in an African school. Ghana's university was known to be the best institution of higher learning on the continent. I thought I'd be very lucky to enroll him there. I had no contacts in Ghana, but I did have Joe Williamson as a brother. I went to him.

"Joe, I'm leaving."

He showed no surprise.

"I want to go to West Africa. I want to place Guy in the University of Ghana and I need a job."

He nodded.

"And I need your help."

He nodded again and said he had been expecting my decision and had prepared for it. There was an offer of a job from the Liberian Department of Information, based on a white paper on Liberia which I had written for the United Arab Republic. He got up from his desk and hugged me.

"Sister, you will be an asset to Liberia."

Vus accepted my departure with undisguised relief. We had worn our marriage threadbare, and it was time to discard it. He would get tickets on United Arab Airlines. He had friends in Ghana we could stay with for a few days. If I got into trouble I could always count on him. I could have any of the furniture, which was now paid for, sent on to Liberia.

I thanked him for the plane arrangements and refused the furniture. I knew that other women would be in the house before the sheets lost my body's heat. He grinned and hugged me.

I had taken Guy into my confidence as far as was possible with a proud, distant seventeen-year-old boy. He knew that for the past year I had been unhappy. After the palaver, I had told him we would remain in Cairo for at least six more months, and he would have time to finish school.

He wanted to have a party. All his friends would come. Would Vus and I leave him the house for a few hours? Would Omanadia cook chicken and lamb and rice her special way? Maybe he could borrow records from the Williamsons and wouldn't it be all right if he served a little beer? His sudden jollity made me perceive how much he had been affected by our pleasureless home. I realized that it had been a long time since I had seen that wide innocent smile, or his fine dark eyes shine.

Banti and Joe gave us a farewell party. Kebi and Jarra prepared an authentic Ethiopian dinner for a merry crowd. David DuBois took us all out to an opulent restaurant near the pyramids. I had a goodbye lunch with Hanifa Fathy and her friends, and the day finally arrived to leave Cairo.

. . .

Guy held my hand on the plane. He leaned near and whispered, "It'll be O.K., Mom. Don't cry. I love you, Mom. Lots of people love you."

I made no attempt to explain that I was not crying because of a lack of love, or certainly not the loss of Vus's affection. I was mourning all my ancestors. I had never felt that Egypt was really Africa, but now that our route had taken us across the Sahara, I could look down from my window seat and see trees, and bushes, rivers and dense forest. It all began here. The jumble of poverty-stricken children sleeping in rat-infested tenements or abandoned cars. The terrifying moan of my grandmother, "Bread of Heaven, Bread of Heaven, feed me till I want no more." The drugged days and alcoholic nights of men for whom hope had not been born. The loneliness of women who would never know appreciation or a mite's share of honor. Here, there, along the banks of that river, someone was taken, tied with ropes, shackled with chains, forced to march for weeks carrying the double burden of neck irons and abysmal fear. In that large clump of trees, looking like wood moss from the plane's great height, boys and girls had been hunted like beasts, caught and tethered together. Sacrificial lambs on the altar of greed. America's period of orgiastic lynchings had begun on yonder broad savannah.

Every ill I knew at home, each hateful look on a white face, each odious rejection based on skin color, the mockery, the disenfranchisement, the lamentations and loud wailing for a lost world, irreclaimable security, all that long-onerous journey to misery, which had not ended yet, had begun just below our plane. I wept. Guy rose from time to time to bring fresh Kleenex, and I didn't dare speak to him of my thoughts. I would not make a sound. If I opened my mouth, I might not be able to close it again. Screams would pierce the air and I would race the aisles like a mad thing.

I cramped my lips together until the seam between them meshed, and allowed, as my only expression, the warm tears gliding like honey down my face.

· · ·

257

The airport at Accra sounded like an adult playground and looked like a festival. Single travelers, wearing Western suits or dresses which would be deemed fashionable in New York, were surrounded by hordes of well-wishers, swathed in floral prints or the rich plaid silk of Kente cloth. Languages turned the air into clouds of lusty sound. The sight of so many black people stirred my deepest emotions. I had been away from the colors too long. Guy and I grinned at each other and turned to see a sight which wiped our faces clean. Three black men walked past us wearing airline uniforms, visored caps, white pants and jackets whose shoulders bristled with epaulettes. Black pilots? Black captains? It was 1962. In our country, the cradle of democracy, whose anthem boasted "the land of the free, the home of the brave," the only black men in our airports fueled planes, cleaned cabins, loaded food or were skycaps, racing the pavement for tips. Guy nudged me and I turned to see another group of African officers walking unconcerned toward the gate which opened out on the tarmac.

Ghana was the place for my son to go to college. My toby (the Southern black word for a lucky talisman), had "hunched me right." Guy would be able to weigh his intelligence and test his skills without being influenced by racial discrimination.

We passed through customs, delighted to have our bags examined by black people. Our taxi driver was black. The dark night seemed friendly to me, and when the cab's lights illuminated a pedestrian, I saw a black face. By the time we reached the address Vus had given me, a knot in my stomach, which had bunched all my remembered life, had unfurled. I realized I hadn't seen a white face for over an hour. The feeling was light and extremely strange.

We stopped in front of a rambling white bungalow, which looked eerily fluorescent in the black night. A short reserved man answered Guy's knock. He welcomed us in and told us that he was Walter Nthia, and after embracing us both, showed us to rooms in the rear of the house. I joined him quickly in the living room to assure him that we didn't plan to stay long. I needed no more than a week to get my son's schooling arranged and get him a place to stay on campus, and I had to hurry on to Liberia, where I had a job waiting in the Department of Information.

Walter said Bro Vus was the pride of the PAC, and that my reputation had preceded me. We could stay as long as necessary. He was an economist, working for the Ghanaian government, was divorced and lived alone. He didn't entertain much, but he had asked a few South Africans and black Americans resident in Ghana to come that evening to greet us.

The visitors came together. There was a tall thin Yoruba man and his Canadian wife, who were introduced as Richard and Ellen, a South African man, whose name I could not decipher, and three black Americans. Frank, with his coppertone skin, smile of spaced teeth and merry eyes, hugged us as if we were cousins. Vickie Garvey was short, pretty. Her black hair lay in soft curls and she shook hands firmly, and spoke directly. Alice Windom took my heart the moment I saw her. She spoke in a Midwestern accent, and laughed as if she had a small cough. Her skin was dark-brown dusted black and her black eyes looked bluntly, unblinking. She had the prettiest legs I've ever seen.

We drank the brought gin, and I told them what I knew about Egypt. When I started talking I noticed that because of my friends and my husband, I knew more about Liberia, Ethiopia, South Africa and Tanzania than I knew of Cairo. They were all interested in politics and when they began speaking of Kwame Nkrumah, the President of Ghana, the Osagyefo, their eyes glistened and their speech was filled with glowing compliments.

"Why are you going to Liberia? It's backward. Stay in Ghana." Alice's question and invitation were seconded.

"Yes. Ghana is the place."

"Kwame Nkrumah is man pass man. Iron cut iron."

Guy caught on and explained, "He is a man who surpasses other men. An iron so strong that it cuts iron."

Frank clapped Guy on the shoulder. "You're smart, little brother. I'm glad you're going to stay, at least."

Vickie asked if I knew Julian Mayfield and if I knew that he and his wife lived in Accra. Julian, James Baldwin, Rosa Guy, John Killens and I had spent many nights until dawn, arguing, drinking, explaining and complaining in Paule Marshall's apartment.

Alice said I had been invited to Julian's house the next evening.

Richard and Ellen added little to the general conversation except to invite me and Guy to a picnic, two days later. They said everyone would be there. The man hadn't charmed me and his wife was dry as old bread. I declined their offer saying we were too tired. But Guy spoke up. "Mother has spoken for herself. I'll be happy to go."

Everyone in the room, including me, knew that I had been out of line. My son was bigger than anyone there, and nearly grown, and I had acted as if he were still a little boy. In the silence in which I left them, Richard, Ellen and Guy made their arrangements. They could come by early in the morning of the picnic. He didn't need to bring anything. All he had to do was be ready.

Frank promised to come and take me and Guy to Julian's house the next day. When they all left I was a little envious. They were in an exciting country at an exciting time. Kwame Nkrumah was the African hero. He had wedded Marxism to the innate African socialism, and was as loved by black people all over the world as he was hated and feared by whites in power. But Joe Williamson had called in debts to get me a job in Monrovia, and I had given my word that I would go there and make him proud. I couldn't change my fate.

Julian Mayfield had the looks to flutter a young girl's heart. He was tall, broad, black, witty, handsome and was married. Anna Livia Cordero Mayfield was a small dark-eyed beautiful Puerto Rican medical doctor, who was as opinionated as a runaway train on a downhill slope.

Our reunion was feverish with greetings and news. We retold old stories and exchanged new tales. Anna Livia gave me the names of people to see at the university. Julian promised to accompany me to the offices. We ended the evening howling at Julian's outguessing the American vigilantes, and making his circuitous way to African asylum. The crowd found Guy's importuning intelligence amusing, although I did not, and Julian said I could go to Liberia with a free mind. He would keep an eye on my son. He added, "Now, listen, boy, Ghanaian young folks call everybody six months older than themselves auntie or uncle. I'll look after you, but big and rusty as you are, don't you ever make the mistake of calling me 'Uncle Julian.' I'll be your big brother, and that's all." We all laughed and hugged and chose hours and dates to meet again.

Frank deposited us at Walter's. Guy and I said curt good nights. I had been less than pleased at his arrogant insistence into the adult conversation. He was displeased at my displeasure.

When I awakened the next morning, his bedroom was empty. Richard and Ellen had gathered him for their picnic, and Walter had left the house.

I spent the day examining Guy's clothes. Separating the things which could be mended, setting aside the jeans which were only good for dust cloths. I hung up his two good suits, in preparation for our trip to the university. I only unpacked two dresses and my underclothes. I would be leaving in such a short time, I would save the African three-piece outfits Banti had given me. She had vouched that by wearing them, I would travel through Liberian society as a Liberian.

I cooked, ate, folded clothes, read the titles in Walter's bookcase until dark.

At about six o'clock, I began to feel uncomfortable, edgy. I felt as if I had forgotten a commitment or stepped on and crushed some precious thing. I went into the kitchen and found Walter's bottle of gin. I was accustomed to drinking in company, but drinking alone had never appealed to me. I poured a small jelly glass to the rim with gin.

I was sipping the strong liquor when the doorbell rang. Alice Windom stood on the steps, with Frank standing behind her.

261

"Hey, Maya. I guess we're first. The rest will be here in a little while." I admitted them into the house and poured glasses of fruit juice, since neither of the two drank alcohol. I saw my gin glass was empty and refilled it.

We sat relaxed in the living room. Frank, unable to keep his eyes from Alice's face, or body or legs, talked about the picnic in episodes.

"Plenty food. Lots of good food. Right, Alice?"

She didn't quite smile, just adjusted her jaw muscles and showed a little teeth.

"Folk enjoyed themselves, had a good time. Right, Alice?"

She offered another friendly grimace to the room.

I asked, "What time do you think Guy will come home?"

Alice answered. "We passed them at Winneba. Richard got drunk at the picnic, so Guy was driving. They should be here in the next few minutes."

My mind adapted to her statement. If Guy was driving, everything was all right. His first driving lessons had been taken in a tired Citroën, along the crowded streets of Cairo. There was no question that he could handle a car.

Tires gusted on the driveway.

Alice said, "Here they are. They've arrived."

The old Arkansas toby, unimpressed by spanned oceans, quivered under my skin. I rose immediately and went to Guy's room and collected his passport. Across the tiny hall I found my passport and money and waited while Alice opened the door.

A short exchange of mumbles wavered down the passageway. Suddenly a voice cut through.

"Where is his mother? Isn't his mother here?"

I slid our passports and the English pounds I had collected into my bra and stepped out into the hall. Ellen was in the living room, tousled and covered with blood. When she saw me she screamed.

"Maya, it wasn't our fault. Nobody else was hurt, and anyway he's still alive." I understood every word and intent of her hysteric speech, and continued walking until I stood close to her red-spotted face. I came from a race used to violence and habituated to loss.

"Where is my son, Ellen? I need to go there now." I used the control I remembered in my grandmother's voice when she heard of a lynching.

Ellen was sobbing on Alice's shoulder. "He's in Korle Bu Hospital. But I swear, he was still breathing."

When we got into the car I asked Ellen to stop whimpering. It was neither her life nor her son. We rode to the hospital quickly, and in a quiet broken only by Ellen's intermittent snuffles and snorts.

Korle Bu's emergency ward was painfully bright. I started down the corridor and found myself in a white tunnel, interrupted by a single loaded gurney, resting against a distant wall. I walked up to the movable table and saw my son, stretched his full length under white sheets. His rich golden skin paled to ash-grey. His eyes closed and his head at an unusual angle.

I took my arm away from Alice's grasp and told Katie to stop her stupid snuffling. When they backed away, I looked at my son, my real life. He was born to me when I was seventeen. I had taken him away from my mother's house when he was two months old, and except for a year I spent in Europe without him, and a month when he was stolen by a deranged woman, we had spent our lives together. My grown life lay stretched before me, stiff as a pine board, in a strange country, blood caked on his face and clotted on his clothes.

Richard came up behind me and grabbed my shoulders. I turned and nearly suffocated in the breath of old whiskey and rotten teeth.

"Maya, it was not my fault."

He slurred the words out of wet dripping lips. My control fled. I reached for him, for his throat, his eyes, his nose, but before I could get my hands on him, I felt hands stroking my back, holding my waist.

"Sister, please. Please. Exercise patience."

I turned to see a strange couple, old and sweet-faced with wisdom.

They continued. "This is your son?" I nodded. "Sister, we found him on the side of the road. We brought him to Korle Bu."

Their kindness cracked my armor. I screamed and they gathered me in their arms. "Sister, look at him. He's still breathing."

They forced me to face the long body and I saw the chest rising and falling in calm rhythm.

"Sister, please say thanks to God." The woman still held my waist and the man held my hands.

"He was hit by a truck. His car was stopped, the motor was off. If he had been moving, your son would be dead."

"We arrived and the folks in the car had pulled him out and laid him beside the road."

"We saw the wreck and picked him up and brought him to Korle Bu."

"Now thank God that he's alive."

I looked over at my unconscious son and said, "I thank God. And I thank you."

The couple embraced me, and walked over to my baby. A nurse appeared. "Who is responsible here?"

I said, "I am responsible. I am his mother."

She was efficient and without tenderness. "You both are black American?" I nodded, wondering if our place of birth would have as negative an impact in Ghana as our color had in our homeland. She rattled her spiel, "He must have X-rays. One of our X-ray technicians is also a black American. I will call him, but you must register down the hall and make payments at the cashier's desk."

I didn't want to leave Guy unattended in the hall. I looked for the Ghanaian couple but they had disappeared.

"I'll stay with him, Maya." Alice put her hand on my arm. Her face was just solemn enough to let me know she was serious, but not so gloomy as to add to my building hysteria.

I finished the registration and hastened after a line of people who paraded behind my son's gurney. The X-ray technician and

I exchanged names. He pointed the cart on which Guy lay toward a door.

We entered. The drunken Richard, his apologetic mousy wife, Alice and a few whose faces I didn't know, lounged against the wall. The technician dismissed all the visitors except Alice and me.

"I'll need someone to hold him and to position him. He's unconscious, but I've got to X-ray his whole body."

Alice and I slid Guy's heavy body onto a new table. We shifted him, turned him, placed his arms neatly at his sides, arranged his legs, positioned his head until every inch of his body had been exposed to the baleful eye of the X-ray machine. We pushed him back onto the rolling tray, and I asked the technician to step aside.

"How long will he be unconscious?"

"I can't tell you. I think he's in shock. But he may be in a coma. The picture will be back tomorrow. Come back in the morning. Maybe there'll be some news." Two nurses met us at the door and wheeled Guy quickly down the hall. I started to follow, but Alice touched my arm.

"Let them have him. They'll make him comfortable. That's their business."

I watched the gurney disappear, carrying away the closest person in the world to me.

I went back to Walter's house and made a pot of coffee. I drank cup after cup, cooling the boiling liquid with gin. Alice went home, Walter went to bed, but at dawn I found a phone directory and called a taxi.

In the clear day, the hospital looked like a normal hospital. I was shown to Guy's room, he recognized me and my spirits soared.

"Hi, Mom, what happened?"

His voice was faint and his skin the color of a hot-house lemon.

I told him about the accident, but before I could finish the story, he had drifted back into unconsciousness. I sat for an hour, willing him to awareness, wiping his face with the edge of his

265

pillow case. Worrying if he was going to die, and wondering how I could go on, where I could go, what I would have to live for if he died.

A doctor met me outside the room.

"You are Mrs. Angelou?" (I had written my old name on the admission form.)

"Yes, Doctor, how is he? Will he live?"

"He has a broken arm, broken leg and possible internal injuries. But he is young. I think he will come through."

I spent the day in Guy's room, watching him slide in and out of consciousness. When I took a taxi to Julian's house, it was because the nurses had pointedly asked me to leave. Visiting hours were posted and everyone had to observe them.

Anna Livia opened the door, and I collapsed in her arms. She had heard about the accident and when the hysteria dissipated, she said that although she was not assigned to Korle Bu Hospital, she would make a visit to Guy that evening. I should go get a night's sleep. She dropped me at Walter's house. The door leading to Guy's room looked ominous, still I knocked, hoping to hear him say, "Yes, Mom. I'm busy. I'll be out in a minute."

I turned and sat down on my borrowed bed. The next thing I knew, Walter was shaking my shoulder. "Sister Maya. Sister. Dr. Codero is on the telephone."

I followed him, fumbling my way down the hall. I didn't know any Dr. Codero, nor did I recognize the man who awakened me or even the house I was reeling through.

"Hello. Maya Angelou here." That was the way Vus answered the phone, with his full name.

"Maya, it's Anna Livia. I had some new X-rays done. They've been developed. I'm at Korle Bu now. The accident was more serious than the other doctors thought. Guy's neck is broken."

The crash, my pale son, his awful clammy skin, my love for him, all rushed into my brain at once.

"In three places. I have ordered him moved. He is going to be put in a body, arm and leg cast. Are you there, Maya?"

266

I was nowhere. Certainly nowhere I had ever been before. I said, "Yes, of course."

She explained that she had contacts at a military hospital and when the plaster hardened he would be taken there. He was quite tense, so it was better that I held off my visit until he calmed down.

I said, "I'm on my way."

She meant well, but she didn't know my son. She didn't know the cocky boy who had to live daily with his father's rejection, or the young man who had lived with the certainty of white insolence and the unsureness of moving from school to school, coast to coast, and was made to find his way through another continent and new cultures. A person whose only certitude lay in the knowledge that Mom, effective or not, was never too far away.

"I'm on my way."

I waited in the halls and yard and canteen of the hospital while the plaster hardened, then joined my son in the ambulance for his transfer. The still-damp cast emitted a sour odor, but my sedated son looked like a pale-yellow angel in a long white gown.

20

Accra became a wondrous city as Guy's health improved. The sprawling Makola market drew me into its heaving perfumed bosom, and held me there for hours. Black women, sitting before stalls, offered for sale peanuts, peanut butter, wax-printed cloth, cutlery, Pond's face cream, tinned milk, sandals, men's pants, hot pepper, pepper sauce, tomatoes, plates, palm oil, palm butter and palm wine.

The open-air shopping center, alive with shouted language and blaring music, its odors and running children, its haggling customers and adamant saleswomen, made America's great department stores seem colorless and vacant by contrast.

I walked around and around Flagstaff House and the Parliament, where black people sat debating the future plans for their own country. I felt heady just being near their power. When Guy was out of danger, I wrote to Mother. I told her of the accident and explained that I had held off writing because there was nothing she could have done except help me to worry.

She sent me a large sum of money and said if I wanted her to come, she'd be in Africa before I knew it.

Guy would be in the hospital for one month, then he'd have to recover at home for three months. I moved into the YWCA, and wrote to Joe and Banti Williamson. Going to Liberia had to be canceled. I would find a job and stay in Ghana. Anna Livia allowed me to use her kitchen to cook daily meals for Guy. I hitch-hiked, found rides, or took the mammy lorry (a jitney service) to the hospital. My money was leaking away and I had to find work. Guy would be released, and I had to have a home for him to come to.

Julian suggested that I meet Efuah Sutherland, poet, playwright and head of Ghana's theater. She received me cordially. We sat under a fixed awning at her house, drinking coffee and looking out on the grassy slope of her inner compound.

Yes, she had heard of me. And she knew of my son's accident. This was Africa. News traveled.

Efuah was black and her slim body was draped in fine white linen. In respose, her face had the cool beauty found in the bust of Nefertiti, but when she smiled, she looked like a mischievous girl who kept a delicious secret.

I explained my need for work, and listed my credentials. She arranged for me to meet Professor J. H. Nketia, ethnomusicologist and head of the Institute of African Studies. Dr. Nketia called his staff together: Joseph de Graaf, professor of drama, Bertie Okpoku, dance professor, and Grace Nuamah, dance mistress. He introduced me, and said they would talk together and let me know very soon.

Efuah phoned before the week was out. I had a job at the University of Ghana as administrative assistant. Since I had no academic degrees, I couldn't be processed through the usual channels. Which meant that I could not expect to receive the salary other foreigners were paid. I would be paid as a Ghanaian, which was a little more than half the foreign wage. (I was later informed that non-Ghanaians received more money because they had to pay twice as much as nationals for everything.)

I tried to speak, but Efuah continued. "An instructor we know is on leave for six months. We have arranged for you to have his house."

I cried out gratefully and Efuah's cool voice brushed my ear. "Sister, I am a mother, too." She hung up.

I collected the trunk which I had left at Walter's, the suitcases I had stowed in the YWCA's storeroom and the bag I had been living out of, and moved into a nicely furnished house on campus.

When I picked up Guy from the hospital, he reminded me of a big tree about to fall. He had grown another inch and put on a few pounds from inactivity. The cast, which covered his head and spread out over his shoulders like a monk's cowl, was grey with dirt, but he had to wear it another three months.

We celebrated his homecoming with roast chicken and dressing, our favorite food. He was in high spirits. He had lived. Anna Livia said he was mending well. He'd made a few friends in the hospital and soon he'd be enrolled in the university. The next day I took his diploma and report cards to the Registrar's office and was told bluntly that my son could not enter the university. He was not qualified. The University of Ghana had been modeled on the British system. Students had to have completed the sixth form —or as Americans call it, junior college. I was dismissed peremptorily.

That was unacceptable. Guy had been through as much as I could handle.

Conor Cruise O'Brien was vice-chancellor of the University, and Nana Kobina Nketsia IV, a paramount chief, was former vice-chancellor. I made an appointment to see Dr. O'Brien, and Efuah introduced me to the Nana.

I pleaded and talked, moaned **and** whined, said I wasn't asking for a scholarship or any financial aid. I would pay tuition and for his books. After weeks of haunting the offices, collaring the men in halls, catching up with them on the campus paths, I was finally told that they had decided it was not fair to penalize students coming from American schools.

They had arranged a three-part test. Guy would be expected to take the examination on Monday at nine o'clock.

I took Guy the news, and since I hadn't told him of the trouble, he took it casually. "O.K., Mom. I'll be ready."

Monday morning my desk felt like sponge and the papers on it were unintelligible. I looked at my watch every five minutes. Efuah passed and stopped to chat, but I was too distracted to keep up my end of the conversation.

At last, Guy came loping across the campus, his cast helmet looking almost white under the noonday sun. I forced myself to remain seated. He entered my tiny office, taking up its spare room.

"Finished." His complexion looked healthy, and his eyes were free of worry.

"How did you do?"

"Great. I won't get the results for a couple of days. But I did great. Mom, do you know that Conor Cruise O'Brien is the same man who headed the U.N. Congo project?"

I knew.

"Well, one of my questions was 'What role has the European in African development?' " He chuckled with pleasure. "Well, I'll tell you. I ate Dr. O'Brien up in little pieces. I read his book *To Katanga and Back* in Cairo."

He leaned over and kissed my cheek. "I'm going to meet some guys in the Junior Common Room."

Speechless, I watched him bound away. I had tommed, mewled and begged to get him registered, and in an attempt to show how manly he was, the smartass had bungled everything. I allowed myself to relish the fury.

After an hour, when I could walk without my knees wobbling

270

and speak without yelling, I crossed the campus and found Dr. O'Brien in the Senior Common Room. I grinned for him and was prepared to shuffle and scratch. My people had written the book on dealing with white men.

I spoke out of a mealy mouth. "Dr. O'Brien, Guy told me how he answered one of those questions. You haven't had a chance to see his exam yet . . ."

"Oh, but I have, Miss Angelou. His answers are fine. His registration papers will be sent to your office. We want minds like that in the university."

I grinned again and backed away.

Sooner or later, I was going to have to admit that I didn't understand black men or black boys and certainly not all white men.

Guy was moving into Mensa Sarba Hall. I had seen his room in the dormitory and it looked too small and too dark, but he loved it. For the first time in his life, he was going to live alone, away from my persistent commands. Responsible to himself and for himself. My reaction was in direct contrast with his excitement. I was going to be alone, also, for the first time. I was in my mother's house at his birth, and we had been together ever since. Sometimes we lived with others or they lived with us, but he had always been the powerful axle of my life.

He dragged the old trunk toward the door, but I stopped him. "Don't lift heavy things like that. You could hurt yourself. I want you to be careful. Remember your neck."

He put the trunk down and turned. "Mom, I know I'm your only child and you love me." His face was quiet and his voice calm. "But there's something for you to remember. It is my neck and my life. I will live it whole or not at all."

He pulled me to him and wrapped his arms around me. "I love you, Mom. Maybe now you'll have a chance to grow up."

A car horn honked outside. Guy opened the door and called. "Come on in. I'm ready." Two Ghanaian young men leaped on the porch, shouting, and blustered into the room. When they saw me, they composed themselves.

I offered them a drink, a beer, some food. I wanted to delay the departure. All refused. They had to return the car to their uncle, and Guy had to begin his new life.

They shared Guy's possessions, trundling the boxes, grips and trunk into a new Mercedes Benz. Guy gave me one more squeeze, then they piled into the car and drove away.

I closed the door and held my breath. Waiting for the wave of emotion to surge over me, knock me down, take my breath away. Nothing happened. I didn't feel bereft or desolate. I didn't feel lonely or abandoned.

I sat down, still waiting. The first thought that came to me, perfectly formed and promising, was "At last, I'll be able to eat the whole breast of a roast chicken by myself."

Also by Maya Angelou

I KNOW WHY THE CAGED BIRD SINGS

'Once again the reader must marvel at this gifted woman's spirit and resistance and applaud the gusto with which she recaptures a past that has been plagued by indignities as often as it has been blessed by love' – Paul Bailey, *Observer*

'Its humour, even in the face of appalling discrimination, is robust. Autobiographical writing at its very best'
– Philip Oakes

In this first volume of her extraordinary autobiography, Maya Angelou beautifully evokes her childhood in the American South of the 1930s. She and her brother live with their grandmother in Stamps, Arkansas, where Maya learns the power of the 'whitefolks' at the other end of town. A visit to her adored mother ends in tragedy when Maya is raped by her mother's lover. But her extraordinary sense of wholeness emerges; she discovers the pleasures of dance and drama and gives birth to a treasured son.

GATHER TOGETHER IN MY NAME

'She has warmth and humour and a sense of wholeness and content that glows through' – Polly Toynbee, *Guardian*

'Remarkable, devoid of bitterness; pungent; funny . . . with that rare gift for hope in adversity'
– Fiona Maddocks, *New Statesman*

In this moving sequel to her bestselling *I Know Why The Caged Bird Sings*, the war is over and Maya has given birth to a son. Unemployed, isolated, she embarks on a series of brief lonely affairs and transient jobs – in shops, restaurants and nighclubs. Finally she turns to prostitution and the world of narcotics. But even in great adversity, Maya Angelou invests life with the remarkable sense of richness that has won her such an enormous following.

SINGIN' AND SWINGIN' AND GETTIN' MERRY LIKE CHRISTMAS

'She sees everything with an eye full of relish'
– Hilary Bailey, *Guardian*

'I know that not since the days of my childhood, when people in books were more real than the people one saw every day, have I found myself so moved' – James Baldwin

At twenty–one Maya Angelou's life has a double focus – music and her son. Working in a record store to support both, she is on the edge of new worlds: marriage, show business and, in 1954, a triumphant tour of Europe and North Africa as feature dancer with *Porgy and Bess*. There are setbacks and disappointments, but energy and a profound confidence in her ability to survive keep Maya buoyant. A joyful celebration of music and dance, travel and friendship, this is the third volume of Maya Angelou's marvellous autobiography.

ALL GOD'S CHILDREN NEED TRAVELLING SHOES

'She continues with all the freshness and warmth of her earlier books' – *Evening Standard*

'Maya Angelou has an amazing ability to take readers into her personal maze and lead them out again feeling refreshed and even jubilant' – Clancy Sigal, *Guardian*

In the fifth volume of her brilliant autobiography Maya Angelou emigrates to Ghana, only to discover that 'you can't go home again'. Initially she experiences the joy of being Black in a Black country, certain that Africa must be her Promised Land. But Ghana leads its own paradoxical life: she finds official sexism but loving female friendships; Black solidarity but distrust of Black Americans. Through the circumstances of her new life – an affair with a seductive Malian, her son's near-tragic accident, politics, partying – her myth of 'Mother Africa' is dismantled. Encountering the country on its own terms, she comes to a new awareness of herself, of slavery and Black betrayal, of civil rights and mothering.

Also of interest

ORDER OUT OF CHAOS
The Autobiographical Works of Maya Angelou

Dolly A. McPherson

'Admirers of Maya Angelou's fascinating volumes have a real treat in store . . . a fresh and unusual insight, into the author and her method' – Jessica Mitford

'I know of no other autobiographer in American letters who celebrates and sings her life with as much verve and display of vulnerability': with this acknowledgement of Maya Angelou's unique achievement, Dolly McPherson richly reveals her place within the Black autobiographical tradition, delineating her 'special stance' in relation to the self, the family and community, a stance far more personal than other Black writers. With fascinating insights into Maya Angelou's life and creativity, and a shrewd examination of her recurring themes and techniques, Dolly McPherson provides us with a picture of this extraordinary woman's life and a reading of these rich autobiographical writings that is accessible, yet persuasive and informative. She remarks, too, on Maya Angelou's exceptional ear, her recording of the precise, vivid word and phrase, and on the warmth, wit and humour in her writing. The book closes with a remarkable interview between these two friends – a wonderful epilogue to this picture of a greatly admired woman.

EVEN THE STARS LOOK LONESOME

Maya Angelou

There is no one quite like Maya Angelou. Poet to the president, champion of the people, best-selling autobiographer, her experiences as dancer, singer, waitress, activist, director, teacher, wife and mother, have made her one of the few people truly qualified to share her lessons of a lifetime. With her customary courage and humour – and always with style and grace – she reflects on the people and places she has known. She talks about Africa and ageing, she gives us a profile on her great friend and 'daughter' Oprah Winfrey, she sings the praises of sensuality. But here too are her thoughts on the end of a much-wanted marriage, confessions of rage and the importance of solitude.

Poetry by Maya Angelou

'Maya Angelou liberates and exhilarates through her magical, lyrical, mystical medium – poetry' – Mary Bryce, *Tribune*

On the Pulse of Morning
Maya Angelou's remarkable, historic poem written for the Inauguration of President Clinton of America, 1993.

And Still I Rise
Maya Angelou's poetry – lyrical and dramatic, exuberant and playful – speaks of love, longing, partings; or freedom and of shattered dreams.

Just Give Me a Cool Drink of Water 'Fore I Diiie
Tender poems of longing, wry glances at betrayal and isolation combine with a fierce insight into 'hate and hateful wrath' in an unforgettable picture of the hopes and concerns of one of America's finest contemporary Black writers.

I Shall Not Be Moved
In her newest collection of verse, Maya Angelou winds skeins of desire and longing; throws punches – some tough, some tender; flaunts and beguiles – and pokes fun. With a new bittersweet mellowness, she sings the pleasures and pains of ageing.

Now you can order superb titles directly from Virago

☐	I Know Why the Caged Bird Sings	Maya Angelou	£7.99
☐	Gather Together In My Name	Maya Angelou	£6.99
☐	Singin' and Swingin' and Gettin' Merry Like Christmas	Maya Angelou	£6.99
☐	All God's Children Need Travelling Shoes	Maya Angelou	£7.99
☐	The Complete Collected Poetry	Maya Angelou	£9.99
☐	Even the Stars Look Lonesome	Maya Angelou	£5.99

Please allow for postage and packing: **Free UK delivery.**
Europe; add 25% of retail price; Rest of World; 45% of retail price.

To order any of the above or any other Virago titles, please call our credit card orderline or fill in this coupon and send/fax it to:

Virago, P.O. Box 121, Kettering, Northants NN14 4ZQ
Tel: 01832 737526   Fax: 01832 733076
Email: aspenhouse@FSBDial.co.uk

☐ I enclose a UK bank cheque made payable to Virago for £ ....

☐ Please charge £.............. to my Access, Visa, Delta, Switch Card No.

☐☐☐☐ ☐☐☐☐ ☐☐☐☐ ☐☐☐☐ ☐☐☐☐ ☐☐

Expiry Date ☐☐☐☐   Switch Issue No. ☐☐

NAME (Block letters please) ....

ADDRESS ....

....

....

Postcode ....Telephone ....

Signature ....

Please allow 28 days for delivery within the UK. Offer subject to price and availability.

Please do not send any further mailings from companies carefully selected by Virago ☐